DEC 1 4 2015

9-16(b)

GETTING GAMERS

GETTING GAMERS

The Psychology of Video Games and Their Impact on the People Who Play Them

Jamie Madigan

ROWMAN & LITTLEFIELD
Lanham • Boulder • New York • London

Published by Rowman & Littlefield
A wholly owned subsidiary of The Rowman & Littlefield Publishing Group, Inc.
4501 Forbes Boulevard, Suite 200, Lanham, Maryland 20706
www.rowman.com

Unit A, Whitacre Mews, 26-34 Stannary Street, London SE11 4AB

British Library Cataloguing in Publication Information Available

Library of Congress Cataloging-in-Publication Data

Madigan, Jamie.
Getting gamers : the psychology of video games and their impact on the people who play them / Jamie Madigan.
pages cm
Includes bibliographical references and index.
ISBN 978-1-4422-3999-9 (cloth : alk. paper) -- ISBN 978-1-4422-4000-1 (electronic)
1. Video games--Psychological aspects. I. Title.
GV1469.34.P79M33 2015
794.8--dc23
2015014719

Printed in the United States of America

For my GameSpy peeps. For showing me how to be passionate about video games.

CONTENTS

PART 4: THE GAMES THEMSELVES

ACKNOWLEDGMENTS

I am grateful for many people who encouraged and helped me while I worked on this book. Thanks to my wife, Geralyn, for cheering me on. Even though she doesn't completely understand my obsession with video games, she knows they are important to me. And to my daughters, Sammy and Mandy, for playing games with me and talking to me about them. Thanks to my agent, Courtney Miller-Callahan, and my editor, Suzanne Staszak-Silva, who both believed me when I was trying to convince everyone that this book was a good idea. A big thank-you also to people who took time to talk to me on the phone or via e-mail to help, including Jeffrey Lin, David McRaney, Andrew Przybylski, Scott Rigby, Nick Yee, Ron Faber, Dmitri Williams, Nir Eyal, Nicholas Davidson, Jeremy Blackburn, Morris Hollbrook, Robert Schindler, Nicholas Bowman, Mike Ambinder, Max Loh, Wai Yen Tang, Dave Mark, and Steve Gaynor. Thank you to Samantha Naumann for saving me a few trips to the library. And the biggest thank-you of all to everyone who visited www.psychologyofgames.com, especially those of you who wrote to me or introduced themselves at conferences. Ultimately, you're the ones who convinced me to write this book. Good job.

INTRODUCTION

The history of video games started in a small Norwegian village during the 1680s, when a precocious young fisherman named Billy "SadPanda42" Jackson created *Call of Duty 3* out of sticks and moxie. Strictly speaking, parts of that sentence are not true, but I'm told that every book about video games has to have a section up front on the history of the medium. Something about how some inventive nerd at MIT made *Spacewar!* in 1962 and about how *Pong* was originally found only in bars. So I thought I'd just get that out of the way as quickly as possible and with as little research as possible so that we could get to the good stuff that everybody cares about: the video games of today.

They're huge! Here, have some impressive numbers: a 2015 report by the Entertainment Software Association (ESA) shows that 51 percent of the households in the United States own at least one console dedicated to gaming (e.g., a Nintendo Wii U, a PlayStation, or an Xbox). Furthermore, the ESA reported that 155 million Americans play games regularly and that they spent $22.4 billion on their hobby. Those numbers are much higher when you consider other gaming devices, such as phones, tablets, and personal computers. The Google Play store and the Apple App store have more than 800,000 apps each, and Apple recently reported in a January 2015 press release that in 2014 customers spent more than $10 billion on downloads (many of them games) in their app store alone.[1] Highly anticipated games in big franchises are events unto themselves and can get gamers to stampede to the store to get in on the excitement of a new release. The open world game *Grand Theft Auto V*, for example, made $800 million in sales on just the first day of its availability. Then, as if that weren't impressive enough, it went on to gobble up $200 million more over the next 48 hours.[2] We live in a world where a video game can make over $1 billion in less time than it takes most of us to get caught up on laundry.

Gaming is also becoming more social and more of a shared experience. More than 70,000 gamers traveled to Seattle to attend the 2013 Penny Arcade Expo (PAX), where they spent three straight days sharing their passion for games, seeing new titles, and listening to their idols talk about the process of making games. The event sold out within six hours, with tickets between $40 and $95, depending on how many days one wanted to attend. The coveted 4-day passes sold out in just 23 minutes. In reaction to its growing popularity, the PAX organizers have added expos of similar size in Boston, San Antonio, and even Sydney, Australia. They all still sell out in hours to people who will travel from all over the world to attend. Other consumer-oriented annual events like Blizzcon and Quakecon also draw in many tens of thousands of attendees each, and video games have a growing presence at even more massive events like San Diego Comic-Con and South by Southwest. These events can each have hundreds of thousands of attendees.

Even if you don't play the big console releases or drive to Seattle and sleep in your car for three days so you can attend an expo, games are still all around you. Smart phones, Facebook, and the Web are stuffed with video games of all different kinds. Phones and tablets are the fastest growing area for video games, according to some market analysts and every bored commuter in the last few years.[3] If you've ever had a few minutes to kill waiting in line or sitting on a dull conference call at work, you've probably played some *Game of War*, *Dragon City*, *Clash of Clans*, or one of the many games like them. And so has the person on the other end of that conference call. King, the developers of the colorful puzzle game *Candy Crush Saga*, announced in a November 2013 press release that in just its first year the game was downloaded and installed on Facebook and mobile devices more than half a billion times.[4] That sounds ridiculous, but while King is leading the pack with its game, others aren't far behind. Mobile and social games are stretching the definition of "video game" to fill in all the corners of popular culture.

What, for example, could be more traditional than the Boy Scouts of America and soft drinks? Along with merit badges for starting fires and finding their way out of the woods (which are now on fire), Boy Scouts can now earn a "Game Design" merit badge by scrutinizing four video games they have played and thinking about them critically in terms of their design and themes. They might do this while sipping on a specially packaged "Spartan Fuel" bottle of Mountain Dew featuring Master Chief, the hero from the *Halo* series of first-person shooter games. In 2013, the Smithsonian American Art Museum even started accessioning games like That Game Company's *Flower* into its permanent collection in order to better preserve the modern relics of art and culture.[5] And, of course, I don't have to tell you how easy it is to find characters in television shows like *Big Bang Theory* that play games, or product placements like when Walt Jr. played the appropriately named *Rage* during an episode of *Breaking Bad*.

And to their credit, these television shows are more and more often showing gamers as they are in real life: normal. It's worth noting that I use the term "gamer" very generally throughout this book. Some people don't like the label, thinking that it's too restrictive, too awkward, or invokes too many unpleasant stereotypes. I get all that, but let's be honest: I'm not going to write "people who play video games" every time a pithier and equally descriptive single word will do. And just as the definition of video games is evolving, the idea of what qualifies as a "gamer" is also changing. For one, they're not just for kids; many adults who grew up playing games with Mario, Link, or the *Doom* Space Marine still love now what they loved then. The ESA report that I mentioned above also found that 74 percent of video game players were older than 18, with an average age of 35. Fifty percent of all gamers are female, either girls or grown women. Both of my daughters love playing games, for example, as do many of their friends. Gamers are also not a monolithic group in terms of how they play games. Marketers love to talk about different segments of gamers: core gamers, serious gamers, casual gamers, mobile gamers. Which you fall into isn't really the point, just like figuring out what category of "snack food consumer" Frito Lay thinks you fall into isn't particularly worthwhile. The point is that you're probably one type of gamer or another, and so are most of the people you know. Old stereotypes of gamers as kids, social misfits, or base-ment-dwelling recluses just don't hold up. In a 2014 article bombastically titled "Unpopular, Overweight, and Socially Inept: Reconsidering the Stereotype of Online Gamers," Rachel Kowert, Ruth Festl, and Thorsten Quandt randomly surveyed 4,500 video game players using an ancient technology referred to as "the telephone."[6] After grilling the hapless subjects about their popularity, their attractiveness, their idleness, and their sociability, the researchers found no differences between those who play games and those who do not. There are just too many opportunities out there in the world to play games for the hobby to remain limited to one group.

And even if you're somehow still confident that you've never played a video game, a smartphone game, or a browser game in your life, they are still affecting you in ways that you may not even be aware of. The lessons of how to make an activity engaging, satisfying, fun, and social are finding their way from video games to all aspects of life. This is thanks to a movement often called "serious gaming" that applies game designs to nonentertainment purposes. Membership and reward programs for shoppers or website users, for example, draw on many of the same design principles. Whenever a website like LinkedIn shows a progress bar for completing your profile and building a social network, it's acting like a game. So are more serious enterprises the Block by Block project used the building game *Minecraft* to form a partnership between young gamers and the United Nations Human Settlements Programme to prototype new plans for public spaces affected by natural disasters and poverty. Kids can use the sandbox mode of *Minecraft* to map out designs for parks and soccer fields in the Les Cayes waterfront in Haiti. I never got to do anything half as awesome as a kid with my Lincoln Logs and blocks.

Video games are also being used in classrooms to teach kids and adults in new ways. And I'm not just talking about *Buster the Bored Bunny Teaches Typing or Whatever*. Schools are using games like *Portal* and *Civilization*, originally conceived as entertainment products, to teach coding, physics, architecture, political science, and history with great success. Games are even making their way into the workplace through applications of "gamification" that treat work activities as games in order to make employees more satisfied, productive, and happy. All of these serious games applications work because of the same psychology and quirks of human nature that are in play in the video games that are played as entertainment. We should understand that psychology will also help you not only when you play but also when you shop, learn, work, and engage in the political process. It will also help you understand why you engage with product and services that rely on the same psychological tricks, such as Twitter, Pinterest, e-mail, message boards, Facebook, and any other social media platform. Applying the psychology of games to other software products is more of an inferential hop than a leap.

This is one of the reasons why academic interest in video games has risen alongside sales records. Like those who play them just for fun, many of today's brightest scholars grew up with video games, and they want to study what interests them and what they see as the most important medium of their age. As a result, many of these academics are donning their lab jackets, grabbing a clipboard, and advancing the fields of sociology, economics, and communications through research involving video games and virtual worlds. Psychology, the study of mental processes and behavior, has been a particularly productive field for understanding video games and the people who play them. Not too many years ago it would have seemed absurd to see scientific, peer-reviewed publications like the *Journal for Virtual Worlds Research*, *Games and Culture*, *Computers in Human Behavior*, *International Journal of Human-Computer Psychology*, and *Cyberpsychology, Behavior, and Social Networking*. And yet here they are: real, physical publications that you can hold, read, and smack people around with. Even august, well-established journals like the *Journal of Applied Psychology*, *Journal of Personality and Social Psychology*, and *Psychological Bulletin* frequently publish research on virtual worlds and video games. And though many of these scientists happily do their work at universities, more than a few have also been scooped up by video game development companies to do research from inside the industry and use their insights on the psychology of video games. As we will see later in this book, if you've played a game developed by Valve, UbiSoft, Electronic Arts, Riot Games, Microsoft, or many others, you've benefited from this research and enjoyed something that a psychologist has helped make better.

Everyone can get something out of this book. If you play games, there's plenty here for you. Are you curious about why people play games, why they sometimes cheat at them, and what makes some of them rage and trash-talk so harshly online? Those of us who play games can use the contents of this book to better understand and control our own behavior—to be better teammates, to enjoy our victories more, to moderate and regulate our play, to get more enjoyment out of our purchases, and to choose more appropriate games for ourselves or our children. What's more, we can also use it to do all that for other players, given how our behavior affects their perceptions and thoughts.

Video game developers and those studying to be developers will also find a lot of value in this book. One thing I've noticed while writing about the topic of video game psychology is that those who design games and manage the communities around them are smart. They pay attention to what works, and they iterate it. Much of their success is built on an understanding of psychology, even if it's not expressly labeled as such. But having a common vocabulary to talk about what's going on in players' minds will benefit everyone trying to have discussions about it. Fully understanding the minds, thought processes, decision-making, and emotions of players will help game developers craft better games by just about any metric that matters. Psychology is the key to making games that are more fun, that get played for longer before being shelved or traded in, and that get talked about more. Those things don't happen by accident, and in this book I will clearly label and describe many buttons that developers can push to make their players feel proud, exhilarated, motivated, and joyous. The same goes for those who manage communities of players and customers, even if they never write a line of code or playtest a single prototype. Social psychology is full of findings that can help groups of players get along better, share, and cooperate—or compete, antagonize, and dabble in zealotry if that's what you're aiming for. I'm not here to judge.

And of course we shouldn't leave the sales folks out of the picture. Understanding the psychology behind gamers' motivations to play games and their perceptions of how they spend money will help sell more product, be they physical or digital. Games are no longer sold in just $50 or $60 boxes at the store. Mobile games try to squeeze revenue out of their players 99 cents at a time, digital distribution and in-game storefronts have created new opportunities for impulse purchases if timed right, and getting players to share their gaming activities on social networking services is sometimes as important as getting a sale. Psychology will help those in sales and marketing understand why some tactics work better than others, and under what circumstances they'll work even better. (And don't tell the marketing folks this, but players armed with this information will be better able to protect themselves against the occasional predatory sales tactic.)

This book is organized into four parts: (1) why gamers do what they do, (2) why game developers do what they do, (3) why those who market and sell games do what they do, and (4) how video games affect us. I shall certainly review research done specifically in the context of video games and virtual worlds, but I won't limit myself to that burgeoning space. If a classic study in psychology has something to offer today's gamers through its examination of universal truths about the human mind, I'll apply it to the topic at hand. Unlike many other books, this one takes a wide view and hits on many different aspects of video game psychology instead of focusing on just one. Looking at the popular press, and even the academic journals, it's easy to get bogged down in the same few controversial issues, such as video game violence and addiction, or tightly focused topics such as gamification and educational games. I'll address those topics, but psychology has much more to offer the players and makers of video games than many news headlines would suggest.

In part 1, "Those Who Play," I will examine some of the most important questions psychology can answer about common player behaviors and attitudes. Some of these topics will look at vexing aspects of gaming culture, such as why people cheat at video games, why we get so competitive, and why trash-talking and verbal abuse can get out of hand. But I will also explore what psychology has to say about how to curb these behaviors in yourself and in others. You will learn how the right context or the correct mental nudge can make people more cooperative, more inclusive, and more satisfied with their accomplishments. This part of the book will also examine the psychological roots of nostalgia for old games and why we love revisiting classics.

Part 2, "Those Who Make," examines questions of interest to both gamers and game developers about why certain design tropes are so widespread. Mostly it's because they work, and the reason they work often has to do with psychology. We will explore the motivating nature of game quests and achievements, and how they can be better designed to play off what a healthy human mind wants out of a video game. We will also look at how loot (think "treasure") and reward systems in video games can be best designed to click with the human mind, and how to create an immersive game world that will absorb players for hours at a time.

In part 3, "Those Who Sell," I will shed light on some of the marketing and sales tricks that companies use to get money and publicity out of players and why some of these are unique to video games. This part will draw from decision-making and consumer psychology research to see how digital distribution affects the psychology of the sales event, when players are likely to sign up for subscription services, and when players are more likely to spend a little money (or even a lot of money) on in-game purchases. We will also explore how games get players to willingly do the job of marketing a game to their friends and why so many people stick with subscription services without ever canceling.

Finally in part 4, "The Games Themselves," I'll close the loop by looking at what effects video games have on us, the players. We will look at not only how our choice of an in-game avatar says things about us, but also how it can actually affect our behavior both inside and outside the game. The question of whether video game violence affects us will be examined, and why virtual violence is often so appealing. I'll warn you, though—it may not be what you expect. Finally, I'll flip over the assumption that games make us dull-witted and shorten our attention span by looking at some research saying that the right kind of game may actually improve your mental abilities.

That's a broad array of topics, I know, and it's going to be a fun and interesting trip. I may drop some gaming lingo on you from time to time, but I'll do my best to explain things and assume no specialized or in-depth knowledge about video games. But if you do know all about games, that's cool too. We should hang out. The great thing about the psychology of video games is that it's so widely applicable. The principles, theories, and research findings I'll be discussing are applicable to a wide variety of video games. If you're not intimately familiar with *Dota 2* or the "Match Three" genre of puzzle games, don't sweat it; this stuff will apply just as well to games that you do know or that you come across in the future.

It's also worth mentioning that I've created a website, www.psychologyofgames.com, to serve as a companion for this book. You can go there to get more information, updated studies, and interesting stories or research findings that didn't manage to make their way into this book. But since you're here with the book now, let's get started.

Part I

Those Who Play

I

WHY DO PERFECTLY NORMAL PEOPLE BECOME RAVING LUNATICS ONLINE?

"Gamers aren't innately toxic. It's all about context. It's about context inside the game and outside the game and how they can twist behaviors. How they can create toxic behaviors even in good people."
—Jeffrey Lin, lead social systems designer for *League of Legends*[1]

The online game *League of Legends* is ridiculously popular. A hulking, 800-pound member in the "Multiplayer Online Battle Arena" (MOBA) genre, the game pits two teams of five players against each other for control of a map. To play really well requires cooperation, quick decision-making, and an incredibly deep knowledge of more than 100 different character classes that each player can choose from. Known by players as "champions," each of these character classes has its own strengths, weaknesses, and lists of other champions that it's strong or weak against. By 2013, *League of Legends* had been played by about 70 million people, about 32 million of whom were playing it regularly.[2] The competitive championship scene in the game is so popular that in October 2013 its grand championship competition was held at the Staples Center sports arena where the Los Angeles Clippers play basketball. People from all over the world came to sit in the stands and watch professional matches played live on giant screens. Just one year later, the 2014 championships outgrew even that venue and had to move to various enormous stages in Asia. The grand finals were so well attended that they were held at Sangam Stadium in Seoul, South Korea. That's the same massive stadium where Seoul hosted the 2002 World Cup, and 27 million additional people watched the finals online and on television.[3] That's more viewers than the final game of the 2014 World Series (23.5 million) and more than the NBA finals of the same year (15.5 million per game, on average).[4]

Despite this popularity, soon after the game's 2009 release, Riot Games founders Brandon Beck (a former business consultant) and Mark Merrill (a former marketing specialist) knew that *League of Legends* was going to have an image problem to go with its success. The game was an offshoot of a community modification for another game, *Warcraft III*, and the same players were migrating to *League of Legends*. Some of these people could be just awful. I mean, the worst. Dipping your toe into certain parts of the *League of Legends* community might get it smeared with all the insults, sexism, homophobia, racism, and general nastiness that the Internet has to offer. Let's be clear: There also were perfectly fine, friendly people playing; I know some of them. But the sheer number of players in *League of Legends* combined with competition, anonymity, and freedom from consequence to create enough toxic behavior to be a problem. It was a problem Beck and Merrill wanted solved.

For help, they turned to a young psychology Ph.D. named Jeffrey Lin. A lifelong gamer, Lin had become fascinated by cognitive neuroscience. He was particularly interested in how the environment affects our visual systems and can trick them into doing things we don't expect but that teach us a lot about how the mind works. Lin pursued a doctoral degree in the subject from the University of Washington, scoring several awards and scholarships. He eventually merged that love for scientific research with his passion for video games, landing a job working at the Seattle-area Valve Corporation—makers of fine game franchises such as *Half-Life*, *Portal*, and *Left 4 Dead*. He had received offers to do more traditional scientific work elsewhere, but Lin knew he wanted a career in the gaming industry. While working for Valve, Lin continued to occasionally indulge in massively multiplayer online games, like *Everquest*, where many players connect to the same online world to play and socialize. During one gaming convention in 2011, Lin and some of his *Everquest* friends decided to take the opportunity to meet in person. To his surprise, some of these people, who rarely talked about their personal lives while online, were also working in the gaming industry. One, Christina Norman, had been a lead designer on Bioware's popular *Mass Effect* series. She and another in-game friend from *Everquest* were currently working at Riot Games on *League of Legends*, and they invited Lin there for a visit.[5]

Meetings continued throughout the visit. "A common theme rang throughout the day," Lin told me during an e-mail conversation. "Most game developers treated player behavior as an unsolvable problem."[6] But Lin thought otherwise. At the end of the day when he met with Riot's founders Beck and Merrill, they were eager to talk to someone about the psychology behind toxic behavior in online games. More importantly, they wanted to know how someone with Lin's credentials and toolset could help solve the problem. Lin had an answer. "I wanted to build games with the psychology of players in mind," he recalled. "I wanted to shape player behaviors through the features of a game." It would be a hard task, and might even turn out to be impossible. But what an opportunity!

A short time later, Lin was at Riot working with a cross-discipline "Player Behavior Team" whose ranks have included social scientists, statisticians, human factors engineers, sociologists, anthropologists, and one guy who nobody knows what he does but he seems all right, I guess. The team's goal? Get people to stop being such awful, awful jerks and get them to exhibit more sportsmanship. They got right to work.

The challenge faced by Riot's Player Behavior Team was hardly unique. All online games suffer from toxic player behavior to some extent, and the blame is often laid at the feet of player anonymity and freedom to act without consequences when online. Massively multiplayer online games like *World of Warcraft* and *Eve Online* are full of friends and pleasantries, but they also have many people who will verbally assault or harass other players in ways that would be unthinkable in the real world. The culture of communities like Xbox Live has received such a bad rap for so long that they've become the punch line for jokes about "dudebros" and socially stunted teenage boys. Websites like The Bigot Gamer (www.thebigotgamer.com) have built large audiences simply by recording the antics of such awful people and posting them on the Internet as a form of shaming. And visitors to Fat, Ugly or Slutty (www.fatuglyorslutty.com), a similar website that catalogs abuse toward female gamers, know that things are worse if the target happens to be a woman. One 2013 study in the journal *New Media and Society* backed this up, finding that in-game chatter using a female voice earned Xbox Live players three times as much verbal abuse as using a male voice.[7]

Why does toxic behavior happen online? What compels someone to transform from "Ted in Accounting" or "that one guy in your social studies class" once he dons a headset and plops down in front of his TV to play some *Halo*? Why did the founders of Riot Games have to hire a whole slew of experts like Lin to rehabilitate the abusive types plaguing their games? One word: "deindividuation."

Deindividuation is a mental state where people's identity fades into the background of their thoughts so much that they become much more susceptible to cues from the environment and people around them as to how to behave.[8] This is caused by both reduced social accountability ("you can't see me") and reduced self-monitoring of their own impulses ("I can't see me"). Psychologists have been developing deindividuation theories for decades to explain what goes on in people's heads when you make them feel anonymous, unaccountable for their actions, and like a faceless part of a crowd. As far as research programs go, the one on deindividuation is pretty awesome. It involves painful electric shocks, turning children against each another, and reviling the Ku Klux Klan— but let's not get ahead of ourselves. To fully understand how awful people can be when given half a chance, let us first consider a failed community-management policy by a multibillion dollar company and adorable children on the hunt for Halloween candy.

REDUCED SOCIAL ACCOUNTABILITY: "YOU CAN'T SEE ME"

In early July 2010, Blizzard Entertainment, makers of the aforementioned online game *World of Warcraft*, announced that in order to play games and use its message boards players would have to share their real names instead of made-up screen handles. With this one big move, the company tried to yank the veil of anonymity away from millions of gamers like an amateur magician pulling a tablecloth out from under a rather surly set of china. Unfortunately it turned out to be less of a "ta-da!" moment and more "OH GOD, WHAT HAVE WE DONE? WE'RE SORRY! WE'RE SORRY!"

Like Riot Games, Blizzard wanted to make its multiplayer games and message boards a bit friendlier and a bit less horrifyingly awful. Trolls, out-of-control arguments, and vitriol in 48 flavors were a big problem in Blizzard's virtual gathering places, and the game developer thought it could rob the crowds of some heat by making people use their real names. "The official forums have always been a great place to discuss the latest info on our games, offer ideas and suggestions, and share experiences with other players," Blizzard CEO Mike Morhaime began in a July 7, 2006, post on their official forums before raising another +5 Shoe of Righteousness and letting it drop. "However, the forums have also earned a reputation as a place where flame wars, trolling, and other unpleasantness run wild. Removing the veil of anonymity typical to online dialogue will contribute to a more positive forum environment, promote constructive conversations, and connect the Blizzard community in ways they haven't been connected before." So even though "xxXZombiePope420Xxx" would be willing to hide behind his anonymity and scream terrible things at someone for no reason, Blizzard figured "Eugene Miller" would not. It was all about anonymity, the company reasoned. Strip payers of that and they will behave themselves better.

Unfortunately, we never really got to find out if the plan would have worked as intended. Seconds after the announcement, tens of thousands of players promptly flipped out and lost their collective mind, flooding message boards with screeds and petitions to undo the new policy. Blizzard recanted after just three days and said that maybe they were wrong and being anonymous is actually super awesome and stuff.[9]

But was it that simple? Was Blizzard originally on the right track? Would eliminating anonymity have changed people's behaviors? No. At least, the answer isn't as simple as anonymity, because there are additional aspects to the psychology of deindividuation. Back in 1976, Edward Diener and his colleagues published a study about one of these factors. It had an intriguing title: "Effects of Deindividuation Variables on Stealing among Halloween Trick-or-Treaters."[10] They didn't know it, but these psychologists laid the foundation for understanding the problems that Blizzard and Riot Games would have decades later with their virtual playgrounds. And they did it by giving delicious, 1970s candy to kids wearing Spider-Man or Bionic Woman masks.

Diener and his buddies were interested in what situational factors lead children to engage in antisocial behavior, such as stealing and breaking rules. So in a clever little quasi-experimental study, they had researchers in Seattle, Washington, turn 1,352 Halloween trick-or-treaters into unwitting study participants. The researchers set up the entryways of several houses with two bowls—one with fun-sized candies and another with money. When children came up to the door, the experimenter would greet them and tell them to take only one candy per kid from the bowl. The experimenter would then say she had to attend to something out of sight in another room, but would actually go behind a fake wall and spy on the children through a peep hole.

That was the general setup, but experimenters at different households also introduced what a Research Methods 101 textbook would call "manipulations" because of how they manipulated or changed one of the factors of interest. For the *anonymity* manipulation, kids were asked their names and address, much like Blizzard asked people to reveal the name behind their screen handle. The researchers also took note of which kids came up to the door by themselves and which came as part of a group.

The results were stark. The kids who stole the least were those who came to the door alone (that is, not part of a group) and who were robbed of their anonymity by being asked their name and address. They only engaged in antisocial behavior 7.5 percent of the time. In contrast, simply being in a group—even when everyone provided identifying information—almost tripled the transgression rate to 20.8 percent. But behavior was even worse for those costumed kids who believed the researcher didn't know who they were. Even when alone, 21.4 percent of those anonymous kids raked extra goodies into their trick-or-treat bags, and when in a group that figure more than doubled to 57.7 percent. So much stolen candy.

This study encapsulates what happens in many online video games—and on many message boards, chat clients, and website comment sections, for that matter. We feel reduced accountability from those around us because we're in a group, because we're anonymous, and because there are unlikely to be repercussions for our misdeeds. Like the trick-or-treaters approaching houses in groups, we see our abusive text and voice chat blend into the babble of the crowd. There's safety to our identity in numbers, and the bigger the group the less likely it is that our behavior will be singled out or remembered. Like Halloween costumes, screen names mask our real-life identities. The people in the game and the people working the keyboard may as well be different individuals entirely. And like the candy thieves who are left without adult supervision, nothing really bad comes to us after treating other players poorly. Nobody is going to show up at your door or complain to your friends, family, or co-workers if you act like a total degenerate. Well, probably.

And though the Diener Halloween experiment is a nice illustration of how reduced social accountability can lead to deindividuation, it's not even the whole picture in the context of video games and other online interactions. Transient connections with other players, for example, can also bring about this effect. Most players form relationships with others that only last for the duration of their match, quest, or session. And though we may play games with friends or regular groups, we are still anonymous to the people outside our group. Research on deindividuation has shown that this is the most important distinction.[11] Other research has shown that merely having our behavior pass through the conduit of a computer, gaming console, or other device is enough for us to feel like less of an individual and part of a crowd or a part of a system. Not physically being there matters.[12]

So even though a player in a competitive online game like *League of Legends* or *Call of Duty* may know exactly what he's doing when he screams obscenities at opponents, he also knows that his social identity isn't on the line. It isn't even really in play, because they're thinking, "You can't see me." But hiding our identity from others isn't the only way we get to a state of deindividuation. We can also get there by hiding it from ourselves.

REDUCED SELF-MONITORING: "I CAN'T SEE ME"

Let's consider another famous psychology experiment on deindividuation. Legendary psychologist and amateur electrician Phillip Zimbardo describes in his book *The Lucifer Effect* an experiment where he had female college students hide their identities under hoods, bulky lab coats, and ID tags with only numbers on them.[13] He then sat them down in front of a big button that would supposedly administer a painful electric shock to someone the participant could see, but who couldn't see her. During a study supposedly testing the effects of stress (via shocking) on creativity, these anonymous ladies doled out longer electric shocks compared to counterparts with no such obstruction of their identities. And it didn't matter if the target acted pleasant or surly—participants shocked her equally long. In reality, of course, the supposed recipients of the 75 volts were actors pretending to be electrocuted. In psychological parlance, this is called "lying," and it is a very important tool when designing experiments.

This experiment offers additional illustrations of several of the "you can't see me" triggers present in the trick-or-treat scenario described above. Participants wore clothing that masked their identity. They didn't use their real names. They were addressed by the experimenter as a group, without any one-on-one interaction. They had limited interactions with their victims/partners before and after the experiment. There were no consequences for giving the shocks. This all meant that they were already well on their way to deindividuation by way of reduced social accountability. But Zimbardo's experiment also included a few factors that also helped participants get there by reducing how much the study participants monitored their own motivations and inhibited their own impulsive behavior.

One of the best ways to reduce self-monitoring is to assign the blame for your actions to someone else. In Zimbardo's experiment, many participants later reported that they did what they did because the experimenter had told them that it was their job. They were also able to notice when fellow students doing the experiment jammed on the "shock the bajeezus out of them" button, since everyone in the group was working with the same target at the same time. This outward focus on instructions from an authority figure, the actions of their peers, and the surreal situation in general reduced the participants' natural inclination to think, "Wait, what am I doing?" The stronger the group's identity, the more powerful the authority figure, and the more ambiguous the situation, the more powerful this dampening of self-monitoring will be.

In fact, Diener and his colleagues also found this kind of scapegoat effect on self-monitoring with the trick-or-treat study. One additional manipulation in that study I haven't mentioned yet is that for some groups, the researcher would single out one kid and charge that tyke with responsibility if anyone took too much candy or stole any of the money. No doubt this child was often baffled and more than a little distressed. But his companions seemed to think it was a wonderful idea because the most terrible offenders were those groups of kids that were anonymous and for which the experimenter had singled out one kid and said, "I will hold you responsible if any extra candies are missing." Of those groups, 80 percent had kids who stole candy or money—EIGHTY PERCENT! So having a scapegoat, an authority figure, or lots of peers who are behaving badly matters quite a bit in determining how much effort we put into curbing our own behavior.

We see often see these same factors interfering with our better judgment in video games. Highly competitive games foster greater feelings of belonging and dislike for those not on our team, which leads us to snowballing effects when we view the bad behavior of teammates as indications of how we are behaving. Competitive games featuring voice or text chat in themselves can also be seen as a scapegoat for our actions, given the line that "if the developers didn't want us to use them, they wouldn't have put them in there." This is also true of mechanics or rules that don't preclude murdering teammates with friendly fire, scooping up in-game resources that others need, or leaving teammates to be outnumbered by dropping out of a match when things don't go your way.

Emotional and physical arousal also play a part in the "I can't see me" effect. The more worked up we get about a hard-fought match, the more our emotions have a monopoly on our mental resources. This means there's less mental energy available for things like monitoring our own intentions and controlling rash impulses. I remember one LAN party years ago when I and a bunch of other people in the same room were playing *Battlefield 1942*, a team-based first-person shooter with a World War II theme. During one particularly demanding match, my team drove the opposition back into their bunkers while contesting the final capture point needed to win. The other team would come swarming out of their spawn points like ants, but we had the benefit of position and artillery, so we were able to just barely keep them down. It was so exhilarating that at some point I started yelling something I'd rather not repeat, only to realize with substantial embarrassment, once the match ended and I took off my headphones, that I had been the only one letting loose with such ill-mannered taunts. And yet I'm not alone, ironically. Zimbardo noted in his own study that his subjects engaged in an upward spiral of emotional arousal as they became more worked up over administering painful shocks, which led them to engage in less inhibition, which led them to administer longer shocks. Those people were just lucky they weren't wired up to my mouse and keyboard.

So these are the two things that often work in concert to lead us into a state of deindividuation: reduced social accountability and reduced self-monitoring. Once our individual identity fades into the background, bad things can come out of our mouths and off the tips of our fingers. But is "antisocial lunatic" our default setting once we feel like we're anonymous, unaccountable for our actions, and failing to inhibit our own impulses?

Nope. Turns out it isn't.

DEINDIVIDUATION AND SOCIAL CUES

New research has recognized that people experiencing deindividuation can behave a number of different ways—some of them even noble and helpful. When people become deindividualized they may indeed feel free of restrictions and less self-aware. But instead of automatically dipping into some deep, internal well of venom, what people actually do is look to the environment and the group that they're in for guidance on how to behave. If there's a strong, external directive about what's expected or what's normal, people will be more affected by it if they're experiencing deindividuation.

Because it's so much fun, let's turn back to those experiments where subjects thought they were shocking the daylights out of other people in the name of science. In a subsequent iteration of Zimbardo's experiment, researchers Robert Johnson and Leslie Downing had subjects dress up as Ku Klux Klan members.[14] No, seriously! Then they had another group dress up as nurses. Once deindividuation kicked in, those dressed up as members of the hate group tried to administer enough electricity to light their target up like a fuse box that's not quite up to code, but those who were also made anonymous but dressed as nurses—a profession known for compassion—shocked significantly less.

Why is this? Even though these people were dressed up and made to feel like part of an anonymous crowd and even though the mental controls that monitor the motivations for their own behavior were redirected, they didn't quite know how to behave. Like in most online games, they could have done many things given that there would be no repercussions and their real identity wasn't on the line. Yet because the human mind hates uncertainty, people in those situations will often give much more weight to environmental cues to determine their behavior. They tend to look at what role they're supposed to be playing, what others around them are doing, and what might be expected of them by the rest of the group. Environmental and social clues matter greatly when you feel like an anonymous part of a crowd.

Think about what this means for different kinds of video games. Those with strong military or war themes and that put a lot of emphasis on domination will cause people to behave more in line with those expectations. Other experiences, such as the cooperative game modes in the *Left 4 Dead*, emphasize helping, coordination, and teamwork. With different social cues, different roles, and different expectations come more prosocial behavior, even when you are anonymous, acting without the burden of consequences, and feel caught up in the situation. All it takes is someone to set the tone for the group, and deindividuation can actually be a force for good.

DEINDIVIDUATION GAMEPLAY AND GAME DESIGN

With all this information about how deindividuation is caused and what effects it can have on behavior—both good and bad—let's turn back to the task that Jeff Lin and the other people on his Player Behavior Team were tackling at Riot Games. They knew that *League of Legends* players were infamous for their toxic behavior, but they also knew that a small, nimble company like Riot Games could give them data and experimental opportunities that psychologists in traditional academic institutions could only dream of. And they could see and act on results from their experiments almost immediately. During a series of presentations at the 2013 and 2014 Game Developer Conference (GDC) meetings in San Francisco, Lin presented some of the experiments they had been conducting with *League of Legends* and what effects they had on toxic player behavior.[15, 16] Lin never calls out anonymity or deindividuation as specific topics in his talks, but the interventions Riot Games has put in place clearly address many of the psychological mechanisms discussed above. "Players are inherently good," says Lin in the introduction for his 2014 presentation, "but bad context can create bad behaviors."

One of the first things that the Player Behavior Team tried was simply to give options to mute obnoxious players on the other team. If team members didn't hear trash-talking voice or text chat from the other team, they would not be tempted to reciprocate, and not having that content out there would lower the likelihood of creating signals to deindividualized players that this kind of behavior was expected. Players on your own team are more likely to chat in a more friendly way and talk about cooperation and teamwork. Using software and trained raters to do a language analysis of matches where this feature was used, the researchers found a 32.7 percent decrease in what they called "negative chat" and a 35.5 percent increase in "positive chat." Those are huge numbers for such a simple feature. They later saw similar results from another experiment with "restricted chat," which lets players know that they are unable to chat for a certain number of days on account of complaints from other players. It's worth noting that other game developers are experimenting with similar truncations of chat abilities. Blizzard, who seems to be exploring more subtle avenues of influence after their attempted exposure of real names failed, implemented only very simple message macros in its online card game, *Hearthstone: Heroes of Warcraft*. Somehow using a menu of chat commands to select "That was a mistake!" from a short list of statements is less awful than a lot of things people can come up with when given complete freedom.

Another way that the Player Behavior Team preempted the effects of deindividuation in an already competitive environment was through a simple priming manipulation. In psychology, "priming" means exposing someone to one stimulus—perhaps even at an unconscious level—to affect their behavior in some way without the person realizing it. The idea is that a concept is made more salient and more easily retrieved in the mind by making someone think of related concepts. Activation or priming of those concepts causes a cascade of thoughts, which can even affect behaviors. Having a screen saver featuring dollar bills in the background of a scene, for example, can make people think about saving money and behave more selfishly.[17] At Riot Games, the researchers tried priming players with different messages shown at the game's loading screen. One such message read, "Teammates perform worse if you harass them after a mistake." Another read something along the lines of,

"Players who cooperate with their teammates win more games." In one experimental condition, the former message resulted in an 8.34 percent reduction in verbal abuse, a 6.22 percent decrease in offensive language, and an 11 percent decrease in overall reports of bad behavior by other players. Interestingly, Riot had one message seemingly backfire on them. When they put up text asking, "Who will be the most sportsmanlike player in this match?," they got a huge swell in complaints against other players. Lin noted in hindsight that this was probably caused by what's known as the "spotlighting effect." Because they were made to think about who was the most sportsmanlike, players were also on the lookout for unsportsmanlike behavior and were more likely to act on it. But the key thing to understand is that it was the number of reports for poor sportsmanship that increased, not necessarily the number of acts.

Those may not seem like large numbers at first glance, but in a game with tens of millions of monthly players, they're huge on a galactic scale—all from putting a simple text message in front of players while they wait for their game to start. The nudge worked because it primed many players to think about teamwork, cooperation, and sportsmanship when under the effects of deindividuation and trying to figure out what behavior was expected by their situation and their teammates. In terms of the experiment described earlier, Riot had supplied them with nurse uniforms instead of Klan robes.

But muting the other team only takes care of about half the sources of toxic behavior cues for a deindividualized player. Priming is worthwhile and easy to do, but it doesn't address the effects other players can have on each other. As a final attack on this linchpin of churlish conduct, Riot looked at team composition. Playing online games only with your friends is the ultimate solution to this whole problem of toxic behavior. We treat our friends better, or if we do verbally abuse them it's understood that it's all in jest. Plus, friends are more likely to communicate, help, and exhibit the teamwork that's critical to winning in *League of Legends*. In what Lin characterized as an "experiment in social chemistry," the Player Behavior Team looked at how different combinations of friends and strangers on the five-person teams in *League of Legends* would affect toxic behavior. Would two friends and three strangers yield better results than five strangers? What about two friends, two different friends, and one stranger? What they found was that though five friends was clearly optimal, even just having one pair of friends thrown in with three strangers who were each there on their own had a big impact on reports of toxic behavior.[18] Those teams yielded 26 percent fewer complaints against players and 18 percent more kudos for good behavior. Why? "By having one core group of friends forming the core identity of a team," Lin tells me, "it was much more likely that solo players followed the lead of the group."[19] Deindividualized players frequently pick up on this core identity and run with that attitude instead of a more toxic one.

Riot Games has also attacked toxic behaviors by creating real, meaningful repercussions for players found guilty of them. Nobody from the Player Behavior Team will be showing up at your door to slap you upside the head or show your mom what kind of language you've been using, but they did implement a system where players can nominate each other for "honor points," which are not only supposed to be prestigious, but which can also be used in the game to unlock rewards. On the flipside, Riot instituted what it calls a "Tribunal system" where players accused of toxic behavior can be reported, have their case reviewed by a jury of select players, and then maybe be locked out of their game account for anywhere from a day to forever. The restricted chat system mentioned earlier works the same way: Abusers are severely limited in the number of chat messages they can make, forcing them to carefully choose what they want to say. They get three chat messages per match to start, then are awarded more and more if their behavior stays acceptable. Lin said in the 2013 GDC presentation that the results are immediate and dramatic: 71 percent of players subjected to this silent purgatory never required a return visit to learn their lesson, and as a group they received 20 percent fewer complaints from other players.

The team at Riot Games has even tried to address the links between and among stress, deindividuation, and bad behavior by making the pregame lobby less stressful. A group of 5 players originally had just 90 seconds to choose which of the more than 100 champions they wished to play, what positions each person would play on the map, and an overall strategy for the team. A team of just five players leaves no room for duplication of efforts or unoccupied roles. Thus these harried, pregame negotiations could be stressful, especially when conflicts arose over who should be allowed to do what. To counter this, Riot Games experimented with a system where players would express these prefer-ences before they were grouped up with others. The game would then match them according to their desired roles. This eliminated many opportunities for interactions to start off with conflict and made things less stressful. Once again, the Player Behavior Team found huge reduc-tions in the number of complaints and brighter results from language analyses performed on chat logs.

So there are things that can be done to change the amount of toxic behavior brought on by anonymity and deindividuation. But there are other forms of bad behavior to consider. What happens when being rude isn't enough? What happens when someone outright cheats? Do the same lessons apply? Let's consider that in the next chapter.

THINGS TO REMEMBER FROM THIS CHAPTER

- Anonymity may lead to toxic behavior in games, but it's not the root cause.
- "Deindividuation" is a state where one's personal identity fades into the background, usually into a crowd.
- Reduced social accountability helps create deindividuation—the "you can't see me" effect.
- Reduced self-monitoring also helps—the "I can't see me" effect.
- When experiencing deindividuation, we pay more attention than usu-al to the environment and people around us for cues as to how to behave. This can result in either prosocial or antisocial behavior, depending.
- Games, systems, and community-management tools can help prevent or shape the effects of deindividuation by controlling social account-ability, self-monitoring, and assumptions about group norms.

2

WHY DO PEOPLE CHEAT, HACK, AND PEEK AT STRATEGY GUIDES?

"Drug-free sport in general is Utopia . . . There are 400 million people practicing sport on this globe; there are not 400 million saints on earth. Cheating is embedded in human nature."

— Jacques Rogge,
president of the International Olympic Committee[1]

Max Loh currently makes a living as a composer for films and video games, but back when he was an undergraduate at the University of California, Berkley, he found himself low on cash. Instead of taking a work-study assignment or a part-time job delivering pizzas, Loh decided to try a little experiment involving the scripting language AutoIt and his *World of Warcraft* account. A friend of his had recently bragged that he was making $40 a day just by using a computer program to generate gold in the massively multiplayer online game, then selling it on the open market. Sure, this was against the game's terms of service and widely considered to be a blight on the game's economy as it is in other games,[2] but, hey, forty bucks a day just to leave a computer running is good money. Loh started out simple, writing a script that would cause his in-game avatar to almost literally fish for money. He could position his character at one of the game's many fishing holes and leave the script running to repeatedly cast, reel, and discard anything that was junk. This left his inventory bursting with only the fish that were most coveted as ingredients for in-game power-ups. The fish were converted to virtual gold at the game's (legitimate) auction house, and then the gold was converted to real U.S. dollars by selling it to (illegitimate) Chinese brokers, known colloquially as "gold farmers."

Loh's initial antics at Azeroth's fishing holes were crude enough to get him caught by the game's developer and the account was locked before he earned much more than $100. But this was only a temporary setback. Loh gained access to a second account from a friend and then applied the lessons learned from the first experience to write a more sophisticated script. This one would have his avatar roam the game's world looking for areas to mine valuable metals. After finding that the bot (that is, an avatar controlled by a computer program instead of a person) kept getting stuck in ruts or environmental outcrops, Loh started having it create logs of its activity so he could analyze the problems and fix them. Soon the bot was smart enough to pause its rule-violating behavior to get itself unstuck and even defend itself if attacked. This allowed Loh to leave it running for long periods while he attended classes, ran errands, or even went to bed. This time, though, he took care to trade his illicit gold under the radar of Blizzard, the game's developer. He wasn't getting rich, but minus about 30 minutes a day to manually list stacks of ore on the auction house it was essentially free money.

Unfortunately for Loh, about the time he really got rolling he was hoisted on his own petard. A website that he had previously approached about buying his gold wrote him back, but it did so posing as Blizzard. The scammers then said they had detected illegal activity on Loh's account and that he should click the provided link to get further details. This seems like the kind of painfully obvious phishing attempt that only a true novice would be taken in by, but Loh, being something less than a seasoned criminal and constantly expecting to be caught, took the bait. "I fell for it due to a combination of stupidity and my fear of getting caught," he told me in an e-mail, where he also shared this whole story. The scammers stole Loh's account and cleaned it out. He thought that was a good point to call it quits, and so he did.

Statistically speaking, misbehavior like what Max Loh did is rare. But there are many kinds of cheating out there that don't involve running scripts, bots, or hacked software. Back in 2009, players of the new *Call of Duty: Modern Warfare 2* game faced a problem much uglier than some bot camping at a prime fishing spot. Soon after *Modern Warfare 2*'s release, players started getting hit by what became known as "the javelin glitch." Somehow, someone had figured out that through a bizarre sequence of button presses and goat sacrifices, you could glitch the game so that when you died in a multiplayer match you would self-destruct and murder everyone within 30 feet. This often resulted in a net gain in points, so the technique for recreating this glitch spread virally via YouTube videos and message boards until servers everywhere were filled with exploding nincompoops screaming "LOL!" into their microphones. The situation got so bad so quickly that developer Infinity Ward had to rush out a patch to fix it.

Developers can only do so much so quickly, though. There are websites like FPScheats.com and Project-7.net that cater to cheaters by selling them software that lets them gain unfair advantage in online games, such as those in the *Battlefield* and *Call of Duty* franchises. And these aren't scummy-looking sites that seem like they'd install viruses on your computer before you were even finished typing in the URL. They're slick and professional-looking. FPScheats.com even claims to have given away an all-expenses-paid "Big Ass Cruise" to one of their VIP customers. All you need is a credit card and a desire to bend the rules of online gaming until they snap in half. You want to see through walls? Cool, you can do that. You want instantly accurate aiming? That's a very popular choice. Hey, you want to kill everybody on the server with just the press of one button? You're a man of rare taste, and you're going want the "Massmurder" package. Step into my office and let's talk financing.

And financing is actually pretty simple. Many of these sites have adopted the "software as a service" model wholeheartedly, selling monthly subscriptions to constantly updated hacking tools, just as Netflix sells access to streaming movies and TV shows. As I write this, buying a hack pack for the latest *Call of Duty* game will cost you $25 a month on one such site, or you can save almost 50 percent by buying six months at just $65. What's kind of hilarious about all this is that some game developers have, on occasion, decided that joining them is better than beating them. During *Battlefield 3*'s heyday, developer DICE would sell you a watered-down version of these advantages by letting you buy "shortcuts" to instantly unlock gear and perks that would have taken many of hours of play to acquire otherwise. *Forza 5* does something similar for the car-racing genre, letting you role-play as that one kid from my high school whose dad owned a car dealership and always let him just take whatever he wanted off the lot instead of earning it. Sure, it's not cheating in the same way that wall hacks or Max Loh's hacking code to automate gold collection in *World of Warcraft* was cheating, but it's still an exchange of money for advantage.

And that's where the topic of cheating in video games starts to get squishy and vague. Most players—and I hope this includes you, because I like you—will never purchase cheats or exploit a glitch, but many of us engage in smaller acts of cheating that seem close enough to harmless. I admit: I once tabbed over to Dictionary.com to score points in an online game of the *Scrabble* knockoff *Words with Friends*. I have a friend who paid real money to have someone—a sweatshop worker in China, as far as he knows—level up his *Everquest* character and stuff its purse with valuables. I had another friend who admitted to using glitches to create copies of rare weapons and other items in the online game *Borderlands 2*, and many *Starcraft* players have groaned in frustration when an opponent drops out of a losing battle in order to preserve his win/loss ratio.

Why do people cheat in these ways? Do people buy grossly unfair hacks for the same reasons that others peek at online dictionaries and others pay for high-level gear? Fortunately, the psychology of cheating has been a popular topic in other domains, so there are many theories to draw on. And it turns out that we cheat in games for the same reasons and under the same influences that drive us to cheat in academics, business, and personal life. The bad news is that we tend to cheat as much as we can without admitting to ourselves that we're cheating. The good news is that we can mitigate it both in ourselves and often in others if we know what to do.

CHEATING IS A SOCIAL DISEASE

Cheaters breed. Well, not literally, though I suppose some number of them must hook up. What I mean is that people are more likely to try cheating when they see others around them cheat first. Some researchers think that this is especially true in ambiguous situations where we think the chances of getting caught are low and the morality of the action is in a grey zone. And like it or not, that grey zone probably covers cheating in something generally as inconsequential as video games.

To test this idea, behavioral economist Dan Ariely and his colleagues set up an experiment at Carnegie Mellon University where people were given an opportunity to solve puzzles in exchange for cash.[3] Study participants sat in a group and were given sheets of paper, each containing 20 matrices of 9 numbers. The numbers were not nice and round like 2 and 8; they were jagged and exact like 1.57 and 8.43. The subjects' task was to find and circle the two numbers in each matrix that added up to 10. Not difficult, but not so trivial that people would be likely to find all 20 pairs of numbers within the five-minute time limit they were given. In addition to the papers, each subject was also given an envelope with cash inside, from which they were told they would extract their earnings at the end of the experiment. Each correctly solved matrix was worth 50 cents. The more matrix puzzles they solved, the more money they got—up to the whole $10 in the envelope.

Ariely and his colleagues ran several versions of this experiment with different conditions, but in one of them they were interested in whether people would cheat if given the chance to do so with absolutely no chance of getting caught. To create this opportunity, the researchers not only let subjects self-report the number of problems they solved after time was up, but they also had them feed their papers into a shredder without ever showing them to anyone. The person supposedly running the experiments blatantly affected a "look at all the cares I don't give" attitude toward the whole task and buried her nose in a book. So people had both incentive to cheat (they were paid for each solution) and freedom to do it (they were required to destroy the evidence of their actual performance and self-report).

Many of them took the opportunity. How do we know this given that everyone shredded their work? Ariely had determined an average for how many of the puzzles people could do in five minutes by giving it to people and then actually scoring their performance. The subjects who were given incentive and opportunity to cheat claimed to have solved, on average, 12 matrices versus this control group's 7. Given the way that the experimenters had controlled for everything else, cheating was the only explanation.

So some people cheated. But what would happen if participants knew for sure that they weren't the only ones cheating? What if someone got that money ball rolling for them? To answer that question, the researchers redid the experiment, but this time had a confederate—an actor pretending to be just another subject taking part in the study—do just that. A few seconds into the five-minute session, this person stood up and was like, "DONE! What now?" This was obviously impossible, since the time-consuming nature of the matrix problems meant nobody should have been able to do them all that fast. Yet the person running the experiment, who was also in on the act, just waved her hand toward the shredder and told the confederate to destroy his sheets before paying himself from the envelope on his desk. The confederate did so, then made a big show of dumping all the money into his greedy palm before marching out the door with what I have to imagine was a "see ya, suckers!" kind of backward glance at the remaining subjects. The charade ended, the subjects were left with a clear impression: That dude had totally cheated and gotten away with it.

Did this make them more likely to misrepresent their own performance? Yep. As a group they cheated even more, reporting 15 problems solved. That's more than twice the baseline number that the researchers had found by actually scoring the sheets of the control group, and significantly more than when they were given the chance to cheat but provided no role model.

Results like this have also been found in other groups. Agata Blachnio and Malgorzata Weremko, for example, gave Polish students a similar opportunity to get away with cheating.[4] Students taking a spelling test thought they were left unattended with a conspicuous stack of books in the middle of the room. Experimenters were, however, using the old trick of watching them through a one-way mirror. The stack of books in the room included dictionaries, and there was a sign saying something along the lines of, "Hey, don't use these to cheat on that spelling test, okay?" Similar to Ariely's study, these experimenters rigged the situation by having a confederate pretending to be just another student go over to the books and use a dictionary during the test. Relative to those who were in a session without a cheating confederate, these people cheated more often.

The same thing can happen with video games. Simply seeing other players cheat or admit to cheating could be enough to tip the scales in favor of thinking that it's an acceptable behavior, especially if the context is vague. When situations are uncertain, such as in a new game or playing online with a bunch of strangers, we tend to look to those around us for guidance as to what to do. Hey, we talked about this in chapter 1 on anonymity and deindividuation, remember? Similarly, our behaviors online and in-game are particularly dependent on who is in our group and who is on our friends list.

To take a closer look at social networking among cheaters, University of South Florida's Jeremy Blackburn and his colleagues decided to scrape a ton of data on such villains and their friends from Valve's Steam platform.[5] The computer program Steam not only acts as a digital storefront, but it also has a number of features that facilitate social interaction and buddying up. Chief among these is its friends list, which lets you keep track of your pals, send them messages, and invite them to play games with you. Valve also runs what it calls the Valve Anti-Cheat System, or "VAC" for short. This is a tool that's in use by more than 60 games, at the time of this writing, to curb cheating and hacking by detecting such antics and placing a big red "CHEATER" flag on the offending user's Steam account. Those who run multiplayer game servers usually configure them to kick such cheaters square in the crotch and off the server, so getting such a VAC ban has serious consequences. This is especially true considering that all the games you buy with a given Steam account are indelibly attached to that account, so getting around the ban usually requires repurchasing games under a new identity. On top of that, a big "Bans on Record" is displayed in red text on the cheater's public profile—a mark that Blackburn wittily calls the "Scarlet C" in reference to another scarlet letter made famous by novelist Nathaniel Hawthorne. Valve likes to keep the details of how VAC works a secret, for obvious reasons, but the website VACBanned.com estimates that it has resulted in more than 2 million such bans since its release in 2002.[6]

Blackburn and his colleagues pulled Steam profile information for more than 12 million members of the Steam community through its website, including 700,000 or so marked with the scarlet C of a VAC ban. After running the data through complex social-graphing methods, the researchers found several results that support the idea that people tend to cheat in video games more often when their friends cheat. "Cheating appears to spread through a social mechanism," the researchers write of their analysis of known cheaters' friends lists.[7] "The presence and the number of cheater friends of a [noncheating] player is

correlated with the likelihood of her becoming a cheater in the future."
A full 15 percent of cheaters have mostly other cheaters on their friends
list, and 70 percent of cheaters have friends lists that are at least 10
percent cheaters. This is far different than the population of noncheaters, Blackburn and his co-authors note. Although their analysis doesn't
preclude the contribution of other factors to this outcome (e.g., maybe
cheaters find and befriend each other through their common interest in
such knavery), it does show that having someone on your friends list
who gets branded with the scarlet C increases the probability that you
will join them.

What's more, Blackburn and his colleagues found that cheaters tend
to try to hide when caught and lose people from their friends list over
time, probably thanks to being unable to play with them on VAC-se-
cured servers. They are also more than twice as likely relative to noncheaters to make their Steam profiles private, presumably to hide their
villainy. After comparing their original sample to a new one taken six
months later, the researchers saw that relative to noncheaters, newly
flagged cheaters were almost five times more likely to set their profile
to private. About 44 percent of cheaters lost friends in that six months,
compared to only 25 percent of noncheaters. I've seen data that also
bear this out.[8] A few years ago when some colleagues from IGN.com
and I examined a data set describing the connections among friends for
the *Mario Kart Wii* racing game, we found that people who cheated by
using glitches to send spoof superior race times were much more likely
to have fewer online friends overall.[9]

Blackburn's findings about the importance of social networks in
cheating also aligns with another iteration of the matrix-solving experiments, described above, conducted by Francesca Gino, Shahar Ayal,
and Dan Ariely.[10] The setup was similar to the other experiments I
discussed: Subjects set out to solve puzzles, they were given incentive
and means to get away with dishonesty, and one confederate working
for the experimenter made a show of cheating. In this study, though,
the experimenters manipulated how likely the Carnegie Mellon University student subjects were to perceive the flagrant cheater as a member
of their in-group and social network. In one condition, he wore a Carnegie Mellon University T-shirt, suggesting that he was a fellow student
there. In another condition, he wore a University of Pittsburgh shirt,
suggesting a much looser connection to the subjects' social network.

When the cheater seemed to share a social group, subjects cheated 24.3 percent of the time. When he didn't, they only cheated 3.6 percent of the time.[11]

So, just as those experiencing deindividuation pick up on social cues as to how to behave, cheaters also flock together. Sometimes, though, it doesn't matter what we see other people do. Sometimes the decision to cheat or not depends on what's at stake for us.

CHEATING TO KEEP FROM LOSING

People hate to lose something more than they like gaining something of equal value—about two to three times as much, depending on the circumstances.[12] This near-universal truth about the human psyche has become known as "loss aversion," and it can explain much irrational behavior. Framing options in terms of losses or gains, for example, can influence people's choices. Circumventing a $5 surcharge (avoiding a loss) is more attractive than getting a $5 refund (receiving a gain), even though the results are the same.

Given loss aversion, it may not be surprising that many acts of dishonesty and cheating in the real world are born from fear of losing something we value. Pressure to avoid getting an "F" in a class leads many students to smuggle cheat sheets into exams more so than does the possibility of getting an "A." Pressure to avoid losing market share leads those in business to break laws more often than does setting new sales records. Not owing the government additional money is a bigger motivator for cheating on taxes than is getting a bigger refund. Sure, in all these cases gains like the bigger sales figure or the bigger refund may motivate people to cheat, but the point is that they'll never be as motivating as avoiding a loss of equal magnitude. If you're listing out the advantages cheating, avoiding a loss will be in 18-point font, compared to a modest 12-point font used to list a plain gain. It's just how we're wired.

A 2011 study by researchers in the Netherlands, for example, found that people were more likely to cheat on a task when given what are called "performance-related goals" rather than "mastery goals."[13] That is, if they were concerned about doing better than other people, they were more likely to cheat than if they were just trying to improve their own performance. This makes sense, because though there would be no point to lying to yourself if trying to beat your own best time in a 500-meter dash, you might take whatever advantage you could get if you were running an important race against someone else. Furthermore, the researchers found that intentions to cheat and actual cheating were more likely in what they called "performance-avoidance" situations where you were trying to avoid doing worse than someone else. We will talk more about this specific idea in chapter 5 on scores and competition.

Loss aversion is an important concept for video games because modern game design leans on these kinds of performance-avoidance situations pretty heavily, not to motivate you to cheat, but for other reasons: getting you to play more, motivating you to compete with friends, and enticing you to buy stuff. The temptation to cheat is just an unwanted side effect. Games—especially multiplayer games but increasingly even single-player ones—track a lot of information these days. Rankings and ratings are everywhere, and most built-in leaderboard systems make comparing your achievements to others quite easy. *Trials Fusion*, for example, is an entry in the side-scrolling, motorcycle-driving game series with a heavy emphasis on making it through each track as quickly as you can. One of the things that the game's developer, RedLynx, gets right is the leaderboard system. Not only do you get to see how your quickest time stacks up against other players, but you can also generate a "ghost" of another player's best time, against which you can race. You're always aware of where you stand, and, more importantly, you're aware of how much you're falling behind as other players get better at the game and keep throwing themselves against their (and your) best times. Similarly, the Xbox Arcade game *Geometry Wars* flat out lists the next highest score of a person on your friends list, showing you whom you need to beat. The result is usually two friends tugging back and forth in their own little contest. Loss of standing—or the threat of it—is constant, and, as we'll see in a later chapter, it hurts more when the game goes out of its way to compare you to a small group of your friends.

Other games rely on leaderboards for more than just bragging rights. The highly competitive online game *Starcraft II* uses them to place you in a league ranging from dusty Bronze to austere Grandmaster. Winning enough games to break into a higher-level league is a moment of great joy for any serious *Starcraft* player, but you don't get to kick back and rest once you're there. If you don't keep winning games, you risk dropping back down. That's why people in *Starcraft* and other games with rankings, such as *League of Legends*, are motivated to cheat the system by dropping out of matches when things start to go poorly on them. Loss aversion is strongly motivating them to preserve their number of wins and minimize their losses. But so is what other people think about them if they get caught.

YOU CAN CHEAT, BUT DON'T BE A CHEATER

My wife was once highly offended by a cartoon mole. One of the few games I've ever been able to get her into was *Animal Crossing* on the Nintendo GameCube. The *Animal Crossing* games are cute and easy titles where you control an adorable little newcomer to a town populated by friendly animals. You walk around talking to your new neighbors and collecting objects to trade for money or decorate your house. Very little of it involves machine guns or punching people in half, so I thought the game would be a good gateway through which to lead my wife into the hobby. But one day she just up and announced that she was done with the game.

"That stupid mole called me a cheater," she said, and I immediately understood. Though he was ostensibly there to remind players about the importance of saving their game, Mr. Resetti the mole was also *Animal Crossing*'s reaction to people who tried to cheat by turning the game off without saving. Why do this? Because the town's general store was stocked with random items each day. You could turn the Game-Cube off and back on without saving to trick the game into restocking the store and thus maybe giving you a better selection. But Mr. Resetti would know if you did, and he'd be super pissed.

My wife wasn't trying to cheat in this way, but she had assumed the game autosaved and thus just hit the power button when she was done playing. The result was an unavoidable, unskippable, and lengthy lecture from "the stupid mole" that stood in stark contrast to the saccharin tone of the rest of the game. During one of his diatribes, he actually berates the player by saying, "You oughta be ashamed. Huh? What's that? Speak up, you reset-happy CHEATER."

That stings, even if you were purposely resetting the game, because "cheater"—the scarlet C—is a powerful label. As I mentioned, Jeremy Blackburn and his colleagues found in their examination of cheaters' social networks that these miscreants would often create new Steam profiles or set their existing profiles to "Private" just to ditch or hide the "Bans on Record" label. But breaking rules in video games can cover a wide range of activities. There are flagrant acts of cheating, such as using hacked files or glitches to gain unfair advantage over opponents. Then there are smaller acts of cheating that many of us may be guilty of: using utilities to restore archived saved-game files after a boss fight goes poorly, editing saved files in *Dungeon Defenders* to get impossibly awesome equipment, or dropping out of online games like *League of Legends* in order to avoid getting a loss on our records. These happen much more frequently.

And there are small acts of cheating that most of us may even defend as not really cheating at all. Is consulting a walkthrough cheating? Letting your little brother beat a boss you're having trouble with? Excessive quicksaving? Making sanctioned in-game purchases for experience boosters? These questions are outside the scope of this chapter, and their answers don't really change the larger message that even though there are hardcore cheaters out there, most of us cheat. But we only cheat a little and only in ways that let us continue feeling okay about ourselves. Recent studies have shown that the threat of having to update our own self-image as a "cheater" or "a dishonest person" can be a surprisingly strong deterrent.

Researchers Christopher Bryan, Benoit Monin, and Gabrielle Adams tested this idea directly on the campus of Stanford University.[14] They contacted students and asked them to participate in what must have sounded like some pretty stupid experiments. One of the studies boiled down to a script along the lines of, "Think of a number. I'll give you cash money if it was an even number. Was it an even number? It was? You win five dollars! HIGH FIVE!" Another task in their series of experiments was flipping a coin 10 times and trying to use the "power of your mind" to make it land on heads as much as possible. The researchers set subjects up to be able to cheat on this last one by recruiting them online and asking them to perform the task in the privacy of their dorm room. To motivate them to consider cheating, the experimenters offered $1 for every heads the subjects supposedly produced. In other words, they had every opportunity to cheat and get away with it.

Here's the thing, though: Half the subjects were given instructions that said, "PLEASE DON'T CHEAT," at the top of their self-report form, and the other half were told, "PLEASE DON'T BE A CHEAT-ER." It's a subtle but important distinction. The researchers guessed that the latter would be a more effective deterrent, since it more direct-ly attacked people's self-concept. And indeed, such a simple nudge caused those in the "Don't be a cheater" condition to report significant-ly fewer heads. The difference wasn't huge, but it was there: an average of 4.88 heads for the "Don't be a cheater" group and an average of 5.49 heads for the "Don't cheat" group.

But other researchers have found similar and much bigger effects through other, equally simple invocations of self-image. Nina Mazar, On Amir, and Dan Ariely did another great series of experiments based on the matrix exercise I described earlier in the chapter.[15] Mazar and her colleagues ran several versions of this experiment, but once again the general setup was that some subjects were given a chance to cheat. They were told to destroy their papers in a shredder, then self-report how many matrices they had solved. A control group did the same task but knew that their answers were actually going to be scored before payment was determined and thus had no chance to cheat. [16]

The researchers wanted to know if they could manipulate how often people cheated by either protecting or endangering subjects' self-im-age. Specifically, they wanted to draw attention to each participant's image of him- or herself as an honest person. In one iteration of the experiment, they highlighted moral standards by having subjects write down as many of the Ten Commandments as they could. (Amusingly, most subjects at the American university where this research was done could only think of about 4 of the 10 commandments.) The result? People who had the opportunity to cheat without getting caught didn't cheat. At all. Similar results happened when the researchers had sub-jects indicate that they understood that their conduct fell under the purview of the university's (fictitious) honor code. Another study by researchers at Harvard University used Ariely's matrix-solving problem, but they modified the sheet to make it look and feel like subjects were completing a tax form.[17] They gave participants a chance to get up to 24 more dollars in the form of reimbursements for self-reported travel expenses. Participants also added their signature to the form next to a "This is all totally true" statement, but half of them had this signature at the top (before they completed the form) and half at the bottom (after they had completed the form). Those who started the process with an agreement that they were going to be honest at the top of the form lied and cheated on this mock tax form much less.

This is one reason why I think games would benefit from having players include anticheating messages on loading screens or even agree to an occasional "I agree not to cheat/drop out/grief/whatever" statement before joining a multiplayer match. We saw in chapter 1 how this kind of priming worked for curbing toxic behavior in *League of Legends*, and there's no reason why it should not work for cheating. Many games and services have these kinds of anticheating messages buried in their end-user licensing agreements, but nobody reads those.

It also turns out that people can be nudged into cheating more through a different manipulation that relies on the same principle. In one experiment, Mazar and her colleagues wanted to make it easier for people to label their behavior as something other than cheating. To do this, they simply paid people in tokens. This was kind of silly since subjects immediately turned around and exchanged the tokens for cash, but it worked. In fact, it worked really well. Subjects who cheated to get more tokens reported solving, on average, almost three times as many problems as those in the control group. Just by letting them think, "I'm claiming tokens," instead of, "I'm stealing money."[18]

This may sound absurd, but it matches up with the real world quite well. Stealing cash from the register? No way. Taking an extra-long lunch break or going home a little early without reporting it? Well, yeah. Or what about rounding up on an expense report or fudging the number of billable hours for a client? That happens a lot more than stealing cash of equal value. Video games even facilitate this kind of cheating by their nature. Nothing in video games is physical or represented in a way that makes you think of it as real money. It's often abstracted. In fact, as we will see in the chapter about in-app and in-game purchases, game designers go to great lengths to decouple thoughts of real money and in-game resources, even when you can trade one for the other. Selling gold in *World of Warcraft*? Using glitches to create copies of items in *Diablo III* and then dumping them in the real-money auction house? If you're saying, "That's different," or

"That's not cheating," then you're doing exactly what Mazar describes: protecting your self-concept as a noncheater by categorizing your behavior as something other than cheating.

But here's the positive spin on all this: Even when given chances to do otherwise, people in these experiments only cheated a little. Only a few more heads-side-up coin tosses were reported and only a few extra matrices were reported as solved. The main way that people seem to protect their self-image is by putting a throttle on their cheating impulses. Reminders of or attacks on our self-image can often lower them even more. Irate cartoon moles are optional, but apparently they are also effective.

Yes, there are those who embrace the role of "Cheater!" by running hacks or abusing glitches. Many of us have encountered them, and we hate them. But the answer to "Why do they do it?" is probably mundane. They find it entertaining to cause grief, they enjoy the technical challenge, or they like feeling special because they can do something that few others know how to do.[19] But most of us have an internal governor on our cheating impulses. And it's not cheating if you're not a cheater; otherwise it's cheating and you are a cheater. Keep that in mind.

THINGS TO REMEMBER FROM THIS CHAPTER

- Cheating in video games covers many different kinds of behaviors. Many of the systems in modern games (scores, rankings, losing in-game rewards) incentivize cheating thanks to psychological phenomena such as loss aversion, overvaluing sunk costs, and a desire to win out during social comparisons.
- Cheating is like a social disease. It spreads when people observe others doing it—especially if they get away with it.
- If someone has cheaters in his social network (e.g., on a friends list) it increases the chances that he will become a cheater, too.
- Inserting a level of abstraction between a cheating behavior and outcomes can lead to more cheating (e.g., stealing tokens or in-game items versus real money).
- Appeals to and attacks on one's identity as a cheater or noncheater can curb impulses to cheat, even if you can totally get away with it.

- Fortunately, research shows that most people only cheat a little bit—enough to gain some advantage but not enough to damage their reputation or image they have of themselves.

3

WHY ARE FANBOYS AND FANGIRLS SO READY FOR A FIGHT?

"I don't think of [my fans] as fanatical, so much as extraordinarily tasteful. They have great taste, they've very smart, and they're better than other people."

— Joss Whedon, writer and director[1]

Police in Norwich, England, once had to break up a fist fight between Imperial Stormtroopers and Time Lords. The *Star Wars* versus *Doctor Who* feud was the result of a long-standing schism between factions within the Norwich Sci Fi Club, several members of which had shown up at a *Star Wars* convention dressed as members of their respective science fiction franchise. This came after figurative shots had previously been fired from one group to the other in the form of angry Facebook comments and warnings to stay away from this particular event. Those warnings were ignored, but fortunately nobody was hurt. Indeed, according to Norwich police, it was less of an "assault" and more of a "very minor altercation."[2]

But they don't always feel minor. These kinds of clashes between fans of differing camps are a staple of geek and video game culture that can result in real conflict. One can hardly go onto a video game message board or comment section without seeing fans of one game, platform, or publisher trying to build themselves up while simultaneously tearing down the competition. These gaming "fanboys" and "fangirls" are kind of like mascots for sports teams, except they disrupt events with flying tackles against opposing players during free throws instead of just goofing around at halftime. They can wreck civil discourse, sour the culture of gathering places, and only participate in conversations by dumping onto the wrong side of the signal/noise ratio.

They can, as it turns out, also turn the tide of wars.

Well, not real wars. Let's not go that far. But in 2013, superfans definitely steered the course of one marketplace battle that decided what features and restrictions Sony's and Microsoft's newest generation of video game consoles would have. It started early in the year when the two companies were getting ready to launch their respective entries into the next generation of gaming hardware: PlayStation 4 and Xbox One. Nintendo's lackluster entry into the new generation with its Wii U console aside, this was the first time that consumers had seen powerful new consoles in almost seven years. Everyone who followed the video game scene was excited, especially when Microsoft and Sony announced that they would be launching the machines within a couple of weeks of each other.

This was about as head-to-head as you could get in what many gaming journalists and fans declared a new console war.[3] In the weeks and days leading up to 2013 Electronic Entertainment Expo (E[3]), new announcements and rumors about the capabilities and limitations of each machine began to flitter around the Internet, dorms, and break rooms. Would Microsoft's console require its voice-control and motion-tracking Kinect hardware to be active all the time? Would Sony's machine lock you out of borrowing or buying used games? Which games were going to be available at launch, and which were going to be exclusives for one platform or another? It was delicious drama for those of us into such things. In the spirit of getting carried away with the hype, many fans began declaring who was winning before the final specifications and features of the machines had even been announced.

The console war's biggest battle culminated in a series of press events around E[3], where Microsoft and Sony traded shots like cannon broadsides from two ships of the line. In a press event about a month before the main expo, Microsoft officially revealed the Xbox One hardware. Executives gave a presentation that ended up being roundly criticized for leaning heavily on the machine's ability to do video conferencing and manage television programming instead of playing awesome games.[4] Sony fans got a good chortle out of this and started calling it the "Xbone."[5]

But that was only the beginning for the Xbox One. Later, when Sony had its press conferences, they gleefully rubbed Microsoft's face in fans' early reactions to the television integration, privacy concerns, and restrictions on used games. The PlayStation 4, Sony said during the E^3 press conference, would have none of these shortcomings, and it would be an easier platform for independent game developers to work with and get published on.[6] Oh, and it would be $100 cheaper—EAT IT, MICROSOFT! Seconds after Sony's executives were done with their stage presentation, the company even released a YouTube video to mock Microsoft's used-game restrictions. Entitled "Official PlayStation 4 Used Game Instructional Video: How to Share PlayStation 4 Games," the majority of the video consisted of a title card reading, "Step 1: Sharing the Game." This was followed by a four-second scene where one Sony executive handed a game disk to another, who replied with, "Thanks!," before the video abruptly ended.

Faced with outrage from their own camp and snide laughter from Sony fans, Microsoft backpedaled on key features of the Xbox One, including the requirement that it always be connected to the Internet and digital rights management policies that restricted the use of second-hand games. "After a one-time system set-up with a new Xbox One, you can play any disc based game without ever connecting online again," said Microsoft's Don Mattrick in an official announcement.[7] Then, a couple of lines later, Mattrick put the issue of of used games to rest: "There will be no limitations to using and sharing games." Microsoft even removed the requirement that the motion- and voice-detection Kinect hardware be plugged in at all times,[8] possibly in order to appease those who claimed that the corporate giant would ogle players lounging in their underpants. About a year later, Microsoft would go even further by announcing a Kinect-free version of the console for sale.[9] Microsoft did all this despite the fact that the Kinect was a core feature Microsoft was leaning on to differentiate itself from the competition. Looking back, we can see how fanboys and fangirls clearly helped direct the conversation and shape the decisions of Sony and Microsoft, right up to the eleventh hour, before the machines were rolled off assembly lines and into the marketplace.

But as far as displays of fandom go, this console war actually wasn't the most extreme or caustic that the gaming scene has had to offer. Gaming's traditionally male, hardcore base has had some problems dealing with the entry of casual gamers and women into its realm. To put it mildly, some video game fans can be downright hostile toward anyone different from them or who makes creative decisions they don't like. Jennifer Hepler, who was the senior writer on the *Dragon Age* series of role-playing games, threw her hands up and quit after abusive phone calls and death threats were leveled against her and her children based on some decisions she made with the game's story and characters.[10] As we'll see later in this chapter, she's not the only woman to deal with such treatment as a result of perceived intrusion on fans' sacred ground. Some devoted gamers have a similar chip on their shoulder for "casual gamers" and "*Madden* dudebros," who are increasingly coming to enjoy mobile games like *Candy Crush Saga* or annual sports games. The perception that these people aren't "real" gamers is pervasive in some places.

Why do we do this? Why do fanboys and fangirls so often attack others while building up their favorite games, hardware, and franchises? What kinks in human psychology trip us up and cause us to fall ass over elbows into such extreme positions? Well, it's often about protecting our identity and our ego. Understanding how will require road trips to the horse races, a summer camp in rural Oklahoma, and the nearest supermarket. Get in the car. I'll explain on the way.

CHOICE-SUPPORTIVE BIAS AND THE BATTLE AGAINST BUYER'S REMORSE

Psychologists Robert Knox and James Inkster once decided to visit the Exhibition Park Race Track in Vancouver, British Columbia, so they could spend the day at the horse races. The park was near the University of British Columbia, where the pair worked, but they weren't into horses or gambling. At least I don't think so. Instead they were interested in certain people: the track's resident gamblers themselves. Knox and Inkster employed the help of more than 140 racetrack patrons to test a theory they had about how placing a bet on a horse affected one's judgments. The researchers approached about half of the patrons just before they reached the front of the line for the betting window. The other patrons were approached just after they had made their bets.[11]

Some of the gamblers didn't speak English or told the nosey little men to get lost. But most of them happily responded to a simple question: "What chance do you think the horse you are going to bet on, or have just bet on, has of winning this race?" The bemused racetrack patrons were to answer the question with a scale, including anchors for 1 ("Slight") to 3 ("Fair") to 5 ("Good") to 7 ("Excellent").

Knox and Inkster found that something in the few seconds between heading for the betting window and walking away from it had a big impact on the gamblers' perceptions of how awesome a horse is. It didn't represent a gigantic change, but just the act of putting down $2 on a bet was enough to change people's opinion of a horse from "fair" to "good." What had happened in those few seconds, of course, was that the gamblers had committed themselves to a horse by placing a bet.

The researchers concluded that cognitive dissonance, the hot new psychology topic of the day, was to blame for this inflation of confidence. The idea is that whenever we have a mismatch between our actions and our beliefs, a kind of cognitive tension is created, and we are motivated to relieve it by changing either our belief or our behavior. The racetrack gamblers, for example, didn't want to think that they had bet on a horse that had poor chances of winning, so they changed their attitudes to be in line with the bet they had just made. This reduced or avoided cognitive dissonance, which might have been particularly important to do given the scrutiny by the funny little men with the clipboards and seven-point rating scales. Similarly, none of the people who buy one gaming console want to think they bet on the wrong horse, so to speak. If Knox and Inkster asked shoppers, "How likely do you think it is that this system is going to have the better library of games two years from now?," these gamers would be more optimistic right after plunking down $400 to $500 than they would be right before—even though their purchasing intentions didn't change in those few seconds.

Cognitive dissonance is a popular topic in consumer psychology because it creates a whole constellation of biases and mental hiccups that lead shoppers into irrational and weird behavior. Something called "choice-supportive bias" is the biggest of these. Like the people betting on horses, gamers often have to make wagers about what games will be better than others, since they don't have the time or money to play them all. This is even truer of video game systems and hardware upgrades. Choosing among a Sony, Microsoft, or Nintendo console requires a big bet. So does choosing between different Apple and Android smartphones, or tablet computers, for that matter.

This choice-supportive bias gets to work by leading us to selectively perceive and attribute more importance to information that confirms the idea that we've made the right choice, and to do the opposite for information to the contrary. And it's not as simple as paying attention to some information and ignoring other information. A 1981 study where participants listened to the story of an unsolved murder found it much easier to recall from memory clues that implicated the person they had fingered for the crime, even though the clues for the other guy were just as numerous and suggestive.[12] Unfortunately for the eyewitness testimonies of the world, our ego is pretty important to us, and this selective nature of perception and memory runs an effective interference pattern.

In fact, it's often the pros of our beloved choices that we remember more than the cons. To test this bias in a slightly different context, researchers Mara Mather, Eldar Shafir (whom we will talk about more in a moment), and Marcia Johnson had subjects choose between multiple candidates for co-workers, roommates, and even blind dates.[13] Each candidate was described with both positive traits and negative traits before subjects were asked to make a choice. One potential roommate, for example, may be described as both "rarely in a bad mood" and as someone who "leaves dirty laundry piled around the room." When quizzed later about this list of pros and cons, subjects in all situations were much more likely to remember that their chosen roommate was cheerful than they were to remember that she left dirty clothes lying about. But when asked about the people they didn't choose, subjects could readily confirm that they remembered reading that the person "snored at night." This was despite the fact that such a defect of character was nowhere to be found on the original list they were trying to remember—the researchers were pulling a fast one on their biased memory. Subjects just saw the negative trait on a list and said, "Yep, that sounds like something that fits with the decision I made, so it's probably true."

Gamers commit this kind of mental fabrication all the time. Xbox One fans may misremember how the "it always needs to be connected to the Internet" debacle of the 2013 console wars went down, or forget that it even happened at all, given their ultimate purchase. On top of that, they may actually claim to remember that the PlayStation 4 had gone back on a promise of backward compatibility with PlayStation 3 games, when in reality backward compatibility was never promised. PC gaming superfans also get caught up in choice-supportive bias when they talk about how great a game looks on a computer, even though they probably couldn't tell the difference between the same game running at the same resolution on a high-end PC and a new-generation console. Or if they did pick one in a blind taste test, they'd insist they could see the superiority if they picked the PC version, or decry some kind of trickery if they had chosen the console version.

I even caught myself falling prey to this selective memory when a friend recently asked me how often I made use of the ability to control much of the Xbox One's functionality through voice commands. I told them, "Oh, lots! I use it to go between apps, pause video playback, send messages, and other stuff." But sitting here looking at the paragraphs I've written above, I have to confide that "Xbox, on" and "Xbox, turn off" make up 99 percent of the voice commands I've given it in the last few months. Which is still pretty cool, but if I'm being honest, I'm not sure it qualifies as "I use it all the time."

It's natural to want to think we made the right choices when we buy something. We don't need the kind of stress and mental taxation that comes from second-guessing every decision. We'd never make it out of our bedroom in the morning if we did that. These mental shortcuts and biases are adaptive. But the situations created by superfans aren't just about any one decision maker in isolation. A fan club rarely has just one member on its roster, because we want to band together with people who are like us. To explore this more, let's leave the racetrack and take a new look at one of the most famous experiments on social dynamics in all of psychology.

BUILDING A BETTER FANBOY THROUGH SOCIAL IDENTITY THEORY AND KIDNAPPING

In the summer of 1953, psychologist Muzafer Sherif went shopping for children. He and some of his fellow researchers went around to different middle schools in Oklahoma City and stood at the periphery of playgrounds during recess. After watching the children at a given school play for a while, Sherif would call out and targeted certain fifth-grade boys that he wanted to get more information on. What's more, this request was fulfilled by school principals, who helpfully told Sherif everything he wanted to know. Sherif even gained access to academic and disciplinary records to further narrow down their search for the most average specimens they could find.[14]

Based on his spying and perusal of school records, Sherif compiled a list of 50 boys that were all 11 years old and complete strangers to one another. They had average IQ scores, they were all healthy, they all were from middle-class homes, and none had a history of delinquency. But instead of the straight-up kidnapping you might be expecting at this point, one of Sherif's colleagues presented himself at the doorsteps of each child's parents—accompanied, I like to think, by an ominous thunderclap, regardless of weather conditions. This person told the parents that their child had won a very special prize: He was eligible to attend a camping trip sponsored the nearby state university. For just $25, their child could spend a hunk of the summer in the wilds of Robbers Cave State Park, several miles outside the small town of Wilburton, Oklahoma. Oh, and while he was there he would be experimented upon. Visitation or communication of any kind would be strictly prohibited.

Let me break that down for you: A man visited playgrounds to spy on prepubescent boys, made a list of the 50 he liked best, and then asked their parents if he could steal them away for three weeks to the woods of central Oklahoma to conduct experiments on them. Furthermore, the parents would have to pay $25 for the privilege. And they say psychology is underrepresented among mad scientists! Amazingly, about half the parents decided that this was a heck of a good deal and had their kids packed and ready to go when Sherif's bus rolled around to pick them up a few weeks later.

Sherif didn't actually have anything particularly evil in mind, and he was up front with parents about everything that was going to happen. He went through this elaborate process of selecting a homogenous group of boys because he wanted them to be as similar as possible so that he could make careful, controlled changes to their social structures and see what happened. If some boys were older, or of another religion, or of another race, that would be much more difficult to do. Sherif and his colleagues wanted to study how social relationships and hierarchies spontaneously developed among strangers, even when there were none of the typical differences between them. He and his fellow researchers went into Robbers Cave with lots of hypotheses about how the status of group members would shake out and how this would affect group solidarity and perceptions of how cool each boy thought the other was. This was just one big experiment, but they did implement certain safeguards and protocols to keep bloodshed and actual danger to a minimum.

The researchers didn't have to wait long for things to start popping. The first busload of boys arrived to the camping site on June 19, 1954, and was kept separate from the second group, which arrived shortly thereafter. In a display of typical proto-macho attitude, this first group of boys dubbed themselves the "Rattlers" and went about yelling and establishing what was and what wasn't acceptable behavior. No crying. Baseball is super awesome. Kids from Texas are the worst. That kind of thing. About six days into the trip, the Rattlers were allowed to come into contact with the "Eagles," the second busload of boys that had arrived.

This was the moment of truth for the researchers, since they wanted to know how these two groups would react to the realization that there were other people like them present. An "us vs. them" attitude sprouted up immediately and dramatically. Upon learning that the Eagles existed, the Rattlers declared that they should claim the baseball diamond and other parts of camp as their exclusive property. Why? Because screw those guys, that's why. Various kinds of smack talk was also formed, often including the delightfully 1950s phrase "dem dirty bums." Seriously, Sherif quotes the kids' trash talk at length in his book, *Intergroup Conflict and Cooperation: The Robbers Cave Experiment.* Some of it is pretty funny.

Seeing a spark, the researchers did the sensible thing and lobbed a gallon of gasoline onto it. They followed through on their plans to see what would happen if they pitted the two groups against each other in contests like baseball and tug-of-war. This figurative fire gave way to literal flames as the Eagles set the Rattler's hand-made flag ablaze and draped the charred remains near the baseball diamond as a warning. I'm not sure what they were trying to warn the Rattlers about, and I suspect the Eagles were similarly fuzzy on the details. Didn't matter. The adults, continuing to show themselves to be paragons of good judgment and responsibility, responded by organizing a formal tournament where the victors would win a set of knives. Let me repeat that: The adult researchers had two groups of children that hated each other and had already expressed many intentions of bodily harm—and decided to arm half of them. As Sherif dryly notes in his book, "The prizes had great appeal to the boys."[15] No doubt.

The thing to remember is that all of these boys were very similar: All were from the same kinds of families, all were the same religion, all were Caucasian, all were the same age, all had similar interests, and all were there for the same camping trip. They weren't set up as rivals at first, and they weren't in competition for limited camp resources. Yet animosity and antagonism toward another group came naturally just because their group had ridden in together on the same bus and were given an excuse to think of themselves as a group. The Robbers Cave experiment has many methodological shortcomings and deals with a very specific group of people in a very specific set of circumstances, but research done in its wake has confirmed that we need very little provocation to think of one group as our in-group and another as the out-group. We're tribal. It's in our nature.

This is something that social psychologists ascribe to "self-categorization theory." People are inclined to construct social identities based on membership in and identification with different groups. You may have any number of these identities. Some of mine include gamer, man, American, parent, and coffee drinker. Each of these identities carries assumptions about what it means to be a member of that class: what people in that group think, what qualities they have, what they value, and so on. This has the function of reducing uncertainty about how to behave when acting as a member of that group, which is usually a good thing.[16] We are also biased toward thinking highly of the groups we are in, which is a related phenomenon called "self-enhancement." Understanding what it means to be a student, for example, helps us do well in school. It also helps us differentiate our identities from those of other people. Given how useful all this is to navigating our social environments, it's understandable that we have developed a bias toward looking out for information about social groups and where we fit into them. But in certain situations, those assumptions and that tendency to avoid uncertainty mean sticking to ascribed behaviors and attitudes can steer us wrong. This is especially true if we are facing uncertainty, anxiety, or even just a really weird situation.

For example, British social psychologist Henri Tajfel once took a group of kids and showed them paintings by Swiss artist Paul Klee and Russian artist Wassily Kandinsky.[17] If you want to go Google examples of paintings by those artists, I can wait for you here. No? Well, just know that though the paintings were different, a preference one way or the other shouldn't have been remarkable, and on the surface didn't say much about the viewer. After they shrugged their shoulders and picked which artist they liked more, the kids were labeled according to their choice. I mean that literally: They had labels about their artist preference attached to their shirts. All of them then played a game where they were allowed to distribute points that could be exchanged for real money. This allocation was done privately so that not even the recipients knew who gave them the money. Also keep in mind that none of the kids expected to ever interact with each another again. None had any reason to split the money one way or another beyond giving everyone an equal share out of a sense of fairness. I bet you can imagine what happened, though. Klee fans tended to give more money to other Klee fans and to hold back from those stinking Kandinsky fans. With very little effort, Tajfel had manufactured art fanboys on the spot. Just imagine if they had been asked whether they preferred PlayStations or Xboxes.

Valve Software created their own "Rattlers versus Eagles" and "Klee versus Kandinsky" scenario during their "Demoman versus Soldier" event for the game *Team Fortress 2*. Harnessing their flabbergasting ability to track player statistics through the game, Valve promised a new in-game weapon as a reward for the character class (Demoman or Soldier) that scored the most overall kills against his opponent during the competition. This rivalry was completely fabricated, but players seized on it and got into the event, creating renewed buzz for the game. I think the Soldier explained it best as part of the event's promotional materials on the official *Team Fortress* website: "Gentlemen, I have no idea what this weapon is. I don't even know if I'll want it. But by God, I know what's important, and it's that WE get it and the Demoman does not." In case you were wondering, Soldier won the shootout, but just barely—6,372,979 Soldiers gibbed vs. 6,406,065 Demomen.

This kind of infighting isn't rare, and it doesn't only take place in the game. Blizzard Entertainment puts on the annual Blizzcon convention where you can come and revel in the shared experience of being a fanboy or fangirl when it comes to Blizzard's games and properties. The developers of the *Call of Duty* games did the same thing in 2011 with their Call of Duty XP event. These conventions create rivalries between similar games, such as *League of Legends* (Riot Games) vs. *DOTA 2* (Blizzard), or *Call of Duty* (Activision) vs. *Battlefield* (Electronic Arts). And don't forget about how Sony and Microsoft all but put out enlistment posters for the 2013 console war described at the top of this chapter. Your fandom can be determined by the simplest thing, even if simply owning the game isn't enough.

Now let's look at where the concepts of group membership and choice-supportive bias come together, because that intersection can help us understand something far more controversial than taking children away from their parents to perform experiments on them. It can help understand why women who play video games are often given such a hard time for it.

STUFF VS. IDENTITY VS. TROPES VS. VIDEO GAMES VS. AMBIVALENCE

Every year, women are playing more and more video games. A 2014 study by the Entertainment Software Association showed that about 48 percent of people playing games are women or girls.[18] But as one might guess from the discussion of social identity theory above, many of those women are relegated to out-groups and often regarded as "fake geek girls" for their interest in traditionally male corners of the entertainment world. This kind of reaction has many of the same psychological roots as fanboyism, as we can see by looking at the case of one person who decided to tackle the topic of how women are depicted in video games.

Anita Sarkeesian is a media critic who has built a large following by examining the portrayal of women in comic books, movies, television, and other vessels of popular culture. Her website, Feministfrequency.com, is the main clearinghouse for her work, along with her YouTube channel. In 2012, Sarkeesian used the crowdfunding website Kickstarter to gather enough donations from her fans to finance a series of "Tropes vs. Women in Gaming" videos. The goal of these videos was to criticize the use of various gender-oriented tropes in video games.

Among the videos she went on to produce are ones critiquing game designers' overreliance on a damsel in distress as a plot device, the limitations that come with "Ms. Male" character trope (think putting a bow on Pac-Man to make Ms. Pac-Man), and the misuse of the women as background decorations in a scene. Sarkeesian's videos are the products of lengthy research and generally argue that the use of these game designs and narrative devices is objectively harmful for gamers in general and women in particular. This is where the controversy comes in.

Well, a lot of controversy and more than a little hate. Each new entry in the Tropes vs. Women in Video Games project elicited waves of dismissal, anger, hate, and even actual threats of violence against its creator. People told Sarkeesian to shut up, die in a house fire, and keep her gender politics out of their games.[19] And those were just the milder rebukes. Many more used language too vulgar to reprint here—or anywhere, really. One detractor even went so far as to use photographs of Sarkeesian to create a Web game where you could simulate beating her to a bloody pulp. In August 2014, Sarkeesian actually felt compelled to leave her house after specific, credible death threats were made against her. "Some very scary threats have just been made against me and my family. Contacting authorities now," she wrote on Twitter at the time.[20] In October 2014, Sarkeesian canceled a lecture she was to give at Utah State University because someone had sent organizers a letter threatening to bomb the event and shoot it up with a semi-automatic weapon. "One way or another, I'm going to make sure they die," the letter writer threatened. The Utah State University organizers said they were unable to screen attendees for weapons, citing the state's open carry laws, so Sarkeesian ultimately canceled.[21]

This doesn't seem normal to most people like you and me, but it's actually a more extreme version of the treatment that many women working in the gaming industry receive—and it happens to girls and women who just want to play games. In fact, in 2014, Sarkeesian's ordeals were part of a larger campaign of loosely organized attacks against women in technology (video games in particular) that resulted in several women fleeing their homes or leaving the industry in disgust.[22] Those who remained had to face abuse or a perpetual threat of the same. Why do some people react this way? Well, not to be too blasé about the harassment, but at least part of the reason can be explained by research into why people love Coca-Cola and iPhones so much.

In 2004, Baylor University researcher Read Montague and his team had people from around campus take the "Pepsi Challenge" while monitoring their brain activity and blood flow on an fMRI machine.[23] When tasting unknown sodas from unmarked cups, about half of the participants preferred Pepsi. But when Montague then revealed which samples contained Coke and which contained Pepsi, something weird happened. Some people, habitual Coke drinkers, said that the Coke samples tasted better. Activity increased in their medial prefrontal cortex, a bit of grey matter that controls higher thinking and reasoning. Subjects' loyalty to the Coke brand and their concept of themselves as "Coke drinkers" overrode their senses of taste.

Those in marketing and the field of consumer psychology have known for quite some time that people construct much of their identity out of their belongings and use those belongings to communicate that identity to onlookers. The stereotype of a man coping with a midlife identity crisis by buying a new sports car is trite, but it does sometimes happen. In his article "Possessions and the Extended Self," Russell Belk quotes the new owner of an expensive Porsche 928 sports car:

> Nothing else in my life compares—except driving along Sunset at night in the 928, with sodium-vapor lamps reflecting off the wine-red finish, with the air inside reeking of tan glove-leather upholstery and the Blaupunkt playing the Shirelles so loud it makes my hair vibrate. And with the girls I will never see again pulling up next to me, giving the car a once-over, and looking at me as if I were a cool guy, not a worried, overextended 40-year-old schnook writer. [24]

It's not just balding car enthusiasts, either. You can easily argue that Apple has made a fortune in marketing an identity to go with their products. Most of their recent advertising campaigns don't even mention hardware specifications. They just talk about what kind of person you can be if you own their little doo-dad. Apple's famous "Think Different" ad from 1997 lauded the crazy "square pegs in round holes" characters like Albert Einstein, Bob Dylan, Martin Luther King Jr., and Pablo Picasso. To see for yourself, just go to YouTube.com and search for "Apple 1997 Think Different Ad." There's not an actual product in sight but the message is clear: Buy our stuff and you will be a misunderstood genius, too. I'm reminded of how successful this tactic is every time I see someone sporting an iPhone case with a conspicuous hole in it that serves no other purpose than letting the Apple logo on the back of the phone show through.

Consumer psychologists consider Apple and Porsche fanatics like this to have "high self-brand connection" and note that marketers like to exploit this kind of connection by creating situations and experiences that make certain parts of our identity more salient. It works on the best of us, unfortunately. People tend to have high self-brand connections with products that are high-cost and require a great deal of effort. Gaming consoles and even individual games fit that bill because they require an abundance of thought, money, and time. Five hundred dollars for a console and $60 per game is serious money for most of us, not to mention the time we invest in playing games. Once they make a decision on a gaming console or choose to get really good at *Battlefield* over *Call of Duty*, most people are locked in for a while. That product becomes a carrier for their identity and a tool by which they communicate it. We are gamers because we spend so much time and money on games.

So what happens, then, when someone like Anita Sarkeesian comes along and criticizes the product we have used to craft our identity? Even if her target is just one example drawn from one game among hundreds of games? It hurts, because an attack on that gaming platform or that franchise feels like a criticism of our own concept of who we are. It can actually lower our self-esteem if we let it. But we usually don't allow it to get us down because of, you know, human nature.

Researchers Rohini Ahluwalia, Robert Burnkrant, and Rao Unnava were interested in how people would handle this kind of criticism and negative publicity about brands of athletic shoes that they loved.[25] Under the conceit of participating in a marketing survey, subjects were shown press clippings (e.g., *Consumer Reports* reviews and advertisements) that were unfavorable toward shoe brands that they had previously said they liked. They also saw some similar clippings that were favorable. When asked to write down their reactions to the clippings, those who were fans of the athletic shoes argued most strongly against the negative information and rated it as being less useful for a hypothetical shopper wanting information on the shoes. They were also less likely to be ambivalent about the brand. That is, they didn't hold multiple, conflicting opinions about it. Others who didn't care about the shoes, on the other hand, tended to argue less. They also changed their opinions of the shoes in light of new information and were able to hold multiple opinions about them (e.g., they're good in this way, but bad in others).

It's worth pausing here for a quick vocabulary refresher. The word "ambivalent" is often misused to mean "not having an opinion either way." What it actually means is to have multiple opinions, especially some that are positive and some that are negative. The term originated in the psychology literature to describe the mental tax that comes from holding multiple and contradictory impulses, emotions, or thoughts about something. It turns out that humans don't do ambivalence very well when our identities or sense of self-worth are on the line. It's threatening and it takes cognitive effort, which is a tough combination to handle. So we generally try to resolve ambivalence instead of coping with it.

This double whammy of threatening and difficult is what happened in the wake of Sarkeesian's videos. She provided negative information about a brand—that of being a gamer in general, or at least being a fan of the specific games discussed in the video. This is a brand that many of us use to create and communicate our identity, and that's especially true of hardcore gamers who grew up with social stigmas on account of their hobby. As a response, it's possible that we could reevaluate our attitude toward and connection to these products in light of this new information and perspectives. Or we could invest the resources needed to become ambivalent about them so that we could acknowledge the parts of our beloved hobby that are flawed.

But some people obviously don't do these things because they're difficult and more mentally demanding. Attacking or ignoring the information and its source is much easier. This is not to say that there aren't legitimate criticisms of Sarkeesian's work, or that any disagreement with her positions amounts to intellectual laziness. But legitimate critics aren't the ones we're talking about in this chapter. We're talking about knee-jerk, hostile reactions unalloyed by any kind of effortful thought or analysis. Thus we see reactions along the lines of, "She's not a real gamer," or "She's got an agenda," or even "I can provide one counterexample, so her entire argument is invalid." Indeed, these mirror the arguments made by high self-brand connection subjects in the sports shoe study mentioned above.

A group of German researchers found evidence for this kind of behavior among gamers in a 2014 study that addressed a similarly touchy topic: the effects of video game violence on real-life violence.[26] The researchers wondered if scientific findings about harm from video game violence would be devalued and criticized more if the recipient was a gamer. Indeed, they found that the degree to which someone considered himself a gamer predicted very well how dismissive they would be to research that called acceptability of that identity into question. Furthermore, one of their experiments found that when subjects were told that they were participating in a study on video game violence, those who considered themselves gamers were more likely to try to sabotage the results of a word-completion task by omitting responses that suggested aggressive thoughts.[27] Those participants who did not consider themselves gamers exhibited no such impression management, nor did gamers when the purpose of the experiment was cloaked in terms unrelated to the effects of video game violence.

So we tend to not react well to criticisms of a high-involvement product that we have used to build an identity. There's a solution to this problem, though, and to rampant fanboyism in general. Some researchers have reasoned that if we react this way to threats to high self-brand connections in order to protect our identity, taking additional steps to protect that sense of self might help us deal with negative information better. A 2011 study published in the *Journal of Consumer Psychology* showed that even just having subjects do some self-affirmation by writing a few sentences about their best qualities let them avoid this habit.[28] Another study had Canadian subjects read an essay by some jerk being critical of Canada, and the understandable dislike of the author was lesser when subjects were first made to think positively about their country.[29] This is related to one of the reasons why the charity Child's Play, which was started by the geek celebrities behind the *Penny Arcade* webcomic, is so popular among gamers. Going through Child's Play to donate money and toys to children's hospitals not only lets us do a good deed, but it also lets us affirm something good about our subculture and our identity in the face of criticisms about video games and the scene surrounding them.

So a dogged link between our purchases and our identity shouldn't take ambivalence off the table for this or for any other issue. As Sarkeesian herself got into the habit of noting near the top of each new video in the Tropes vs. Women in Video Games series, "It's important to keep in mind that it's entirely possible to be critical of some aspects of a piece of media while still finding other parts valuable or enjoyable." So here are some things anyone can try to remember or remind people of when fanboyism starts to get out of control: Games have benefits. They are fun. They can teach. They can give you a sense of accomplishment and competence. Games are often gateways to new skills, interests, and accomplishments, such as learning how to code, how to write, and how to create art. Video games often foster friendships and other important social ties that make lives better. Building yourself up doesn't mean that you have to tear another person down. The people around you can be different and they can even be from clearly different groups. But your identity should not be a complete slave to what's printed on a sales receipt.

However, thinking back about your history with video games and how much they mattered to you can have many psychological benefits. We will explore that more in the next chapter.

THINGS TO REMEMBER FROM THIS CHAPTER

- Commitment to a product or choice increases your evaluation of it, relative to those who have made no such commitment. This is known as "choice-supportive bias." It also leads us to selectively perceive and weight information to support our choice.
- This happens because of our bias to avoid cognitive dissonance between what we do and think.
- This crazy psychologist once bused a bunch of 11-year-old boys into the Oklahoma wilderness and made them turn on each other.
- Self-categorization theory and social identity theory hold that we form multiple identities based on group membership in order to reduce uncertainty about how to behave or what to think. This requires very little prompting.
- Possessions also help define our identity, especially high-commitment ones like gaming that require a great deal of time and/or money.
- When someone devalues a product we base one of our identities on, we react poorly to that source of information.

- Humans don't handle ambivalence well. That is, we find it hard to maintain multiple opinions about different aspects of the same thing. This leads us to pick a side. The backlash against feminist critiques of games and attitudes toward studies of video game violence are two prominent examples of this.

4

WHY DO WE GET NOSTALGIC ABOUT GOOD OLD GAMES?

"There is no greater sorrow / Than to recall a happy time / When miserable."

—Dante Alighieri, *The Inferno*

Remember Odysseus, the hero from the 2,800-year-old epic poem *The Odyssey*? You were supposed to read it for class that one time, and you totally should have. The story of that old Greek hero is more relevant than you think to all those reboots of old gaming franchises like *Duck-Tales: Remastered*, *Killer Instinct*, or the otherwise inexplicable *Typing of the Dead: Overkill*. As University of Southampton researcher Tim Wildschut notes in an article about the triggers and function of the emotion, Odysseus's ordeal is a good illustration of nostalgia as it was originally conceived.[1] The word itself derives from the Greek words *nostos* ("returning") and *algos* ("suffering"). For 10 years after the fall of Troy, Odysseus suffered a massive bout of nostalgia as he longed to return to the way things were. It's been a while since I read the story myself, but from what I recall he wanted so badly to return to his wife, Penelope, and all his favorite games from the 16-bit generation that he turned down all kinds of offers from sexy sorceresses and a not very sexy cyclops to do so. Eventually he made it home and got a much needed mental pick-me-up by reconnecting with his home and by appreciating the way things were before he had to go off to war. Also he murdered everyone in sight for eating all his snacks and hitting on his wife, so that was probably therapeutic.

Much later, in the 1600s, Swiss physicians and fans of neologisms coined the term "nostalgia" in reference to just this kind of homesickness, minus the bit at the end about killing everyone. They saw the condition as a literal mental illness caused by yearnings for past lives on the part of Swiss mercenaries who were off fighting for foreign kings. It was an idea that stuck, since even years later nostalgia was called "immigrant psychosis." But although the Swiss physicians correctly put their finger on nostalgia as a mental state, these proto-psychologists of the day weren't very good at figuring out the causes. For years they thought nostalgia was caused by things such as little demons living in one's head, changes in atmospheric pressure, or the incessant clamor of cow bells. This was, in fact, hardly ever the case.

Fortunately we've come a long way since then. Today, nostalgia is generally defined as a sentimental longing for the past, especially in reference to how things used to be better. It exists across every culture and country where it has been examined, including Australia, Cameroon, China, Ireland, Japan, Romania, and more.[2] And it's not just the province of old men sitting on porches and yelling at clouds. Nostalgia has been measured in children as young as seven when they think back on family vacations or particularly awesome birthday parties.[3]

And don't think that those operating the marketing machines of the world haven't noticed. Appeals to nostalgia are everywhere and remain of interest to both psychologists and advertising executives. Darth Vader was used to sell the 2012 Volkswagen Passat, and a while back Nikon released a new, high-tech DSLR camera that looked like something you'd find sitting around in your parents' basement. Then there are revivals of beloved (or at least fondly remembered) properties like My Little Pony, Transformers, the Muppets, and Teenage Mutant Ninja Turtles. Many of them have even been updated to older audiences, retaining just enough of the old concepts to induce nostalgia (they're turtle-like, they fight like ninjas) but made sufficiently gritty, dark, and action-packed so as to appeal to adults.

Video games are no exception to this trend, and nostalgia is frequently the active ingredient in the recipe for their success. At this point the medium has been around long enough that it's not uncommon to encounter people thinking back wistfully about the days of blowing the dust off cartridge contacts, fiddling with HIMEM.SYS files, and covering their 28.8K modem with a pillow so their parents didn't hear them calling a friend to play some *DOOM* deathmatch. Games like 2014's *Shovel Knight* appeal to a retro look, and for every new gaming franchise that comes along, it seems there are two others that are just relaunches of old properties. The 2013 game *The Legend of Zelda: A Link between Worlds* is a prime example of this. It was released as a direct sequel to a 22-year-old game that's universally considered a classic. Many parents today who are buying the game for their kids remember playing and loving what came before it. Like many other games in the *Zelda* series, *Link between Worlds* repeats the basic plot structure, items, protagonists, antagonists, and gameplay that we've been familiar with for decades. Some even call the game crass in its blatant appeal to *Zelda* nostalgia.

This begs a few questions, though. For example, just why do we get so nostalgic about video games and other media from our childhood? The good old days are certainly old at this point, but are they really still good or are we looking at them through a rose-colored heads-up display? And even if we do tend to get all nostalgic, is that necessarily a bad thing? Is it a valid reason to love a remake of a game or the revival of an old franchise? Researchers in psychology and consumer behavior have studied these questions, and what they've found suggests that video games may have the potential to elicit more nostalgia than any other medium.

THE BENEFITS OF NOSTALGIA

First, let's consider the nature of the emotion in question. Nostalgia is often experienced as bittersweet remembrance tinged with regret about things lost to the passage of time. But immersing ourselves in nostalgic experiences can have many benefits. The things we remember while wallowing in nostalgia are generally positive: hanging out with friends, fun or exciting vacations, important experiences that defined our character. The positive and social nature of these experiences means they fulfill important psychological roles.

Coping with stress and melancholy may be one of these roles. For example, when researchers from the University of Southampton had study participants think about meaningful memories and write what kinds of experiences or states made them feel nostalgic, they found that sadness was far and away the most frequently reported trigger.[4] In fact, simply putting someone in a bad mood makes him more sensitive to nostalgia-inducing stimuli and makes it easier to dredge up cherished memories about how things used to be. Nostalgia seems to act as an antidote to sadness and feelings of loss. It elevates our mood, and other research has found that people who tend to get nostalgic tend to have higher self-esteem, find it easier to trust others, and suffer less from depression. After diving into nostalgic memories, people typically report being in a better mood, feeling better about themselves, and report having more self-esteem. And games like *Link between Worlds* grab our hand and lead us right through these memories, since the game takes pains to make sure we're constantly noticing what's there, what's not there, and how things are different.

So why does hearing the classic *Zelda* theme or catching a whiff of something that smells like an old arcade bring us out of a funk and lift our spirits when we have no way to recapture the original experience? It's not just about the place or the thing. On a basic level, thinking about positive things elevates our mood. Recalling that you had fun sitting on the couch with friends and playing a fighting game like *Soul Calibur* will make you happy, just like thinking about warm puppy noses will. But on a more complex level, the *Soul Calibur* experience is different from the puppy noses one because recalling it makes us feel stronger social connections. Tim Wildschut and Constantine Sedikides published some research in the *Journal of Personality and Social Psychology* where they asked people to describe their nostalgic memories. They found that the memories almost always involved stories of interacting and bonding with friends, family, or lovers.[5] We tend to star in our nostalgic memories, it seems, but we usually have a supporting cast and go through some kind of redemptive arc where things start bad but turn out good in the end.

Psychologists, being the manipulative types that we are, have found that it's easy to use this as a trigger to make people nostalgic. For example, researcher Katherine Loveland and her colleagues published a study in the *Journal of Consumer Research* that directly tested the idea that nostalgia is related to social connections and that it can relieve loneliness.[6] Working on the hypothesis that consumption of old, nostalgia-inducing products restores feelings of belongingness, the researchers manipulated participants' need to belong to a social group by presenting them with words related to belonging (e.g., "belong" or "together") as part of a supposedly nonconscious language-association task. As I've noted before, this is a common technique used in psychological studies called "priming" that is surprisingly effective, and the researchers verified that it worked through a subtly worded survey given right after the word task. The researchers then measured subjects' preference for contemporary versus vintage cookies, soup, crackers, cars, movies, television, and soap. Loveland and her colleagues found that making people feel lonely made them prefer the vintage versions and letting subjects tear open a package of cookies that were popular in their youth and eat them actually decreased their feelings of loneliness.

This intertwining of social relationships and nostalgia has huge implications for video games. You may reminisce about playing the original *Starcraft*, but chances are you're most nostalgic thinking about throwing down with friends in multiplayer games or bonding with them over the shared experience of how you each managed the single-player campaign. For us gamers, our most nostalgic memories probably revolve around sharing the hobby with others, making new friends through gaming, and enjoying a good couch co-op experience.

Social connections aren't the only important facet of nostalgia, though. Much of its psychological weight results from how nostalgia relates to our identity and maintains congruity between current and past concept of ourselves. This is especially true when we think about our role in cultural traditions and experiences during our formative years. Morris Holbrook, a professor at Columbia University, and his colleague Robert Schindler have studied this aspect of nostalgia extensively. Holbrook believes that we have a critical period during which we tend to form a strong liking for whatever things we encounter over and over again. Not just media, but celebrities, clothing styles, automobile designs, and food. It varies from person to person, but the peak time for forming strong preferences is usually around 20 years old.[7]

It is experiences during these periods when we are crafting our identities and finding out who we are that come to mind later in life when we need a quick emotional boost or a reminder of what we have to be proud of. This can be achieved by thinking back on holiday dinners or school functions, but for many of us we create continuity between our current and ideal selves by remembering the special landmarks in the history of gaming that we were part of. Maybe you were hardcore into *Ultima Online* or *Everquest* and thus can see yourself as part of the birth of massively multiplayer games. Maybe you used to read trailblazing gaming news sites like PlanetQuake or Stomped and can feel like you helped support the burgeoning field of games journalism. Maybe you're terrible at the latest *Battlefield* game, but how many of those kids at the top of that game can say that they remember getting the original Desert Combat mod for *Battlefield 1942* to work? How many of these kids even know what a mod is? In all cases, we enjoy a mental pick-me-up by connecting our current selves to the big picture through our accomplishments in the past. Some of Tim Wildschut's other research has shown that getting all nostalgic about our past selves results in significant optimism for our future, for these exact reasons.[8]

THE PSYCHOLOGICAL WEIGHT OF HISTORY

Given that we like to feel good and celebrate our past choices, it's not surprising that nostalgia is so common. But there are other cognitive quirks that make us love old stuff. Our history with a brand or object has a heavy psychological weight such that we tend to value something more once we own it. This is called the "endowment effect" and it's surprisingly easy to trigger.

Behavioral economist Dan Ariely provides a great demonstration of the endowment effect through an experiment involving Duke University students and highly coveted tickets to basketball games.[9] When Duke's fervor over its basketball team outstrips the supply of stadium seating, opportunities to buy tickets are given out according to a random lottery. One season, Ariely contacted those who had won the right to tickets from the lottery and asked how much it would cost to buy them. Similarly, he contacted those students who had entered but lost the lottery and asked them how much they'd be willing to pay for tickets if he could find a seller. Same ticket, same game, the only difference was that the person already owned the ticket or was seeking it out. On average, those who had won the lottery demanded an amazing price of $1,400, and those who did not have tickets offered to pay only an average of $170 to get them. It was a huge disparity, yet both sides probably thought that they were being totally reasonable and that the other person was crazy. This was the endowment effect in action. Other experiments have found similar results when researchers gave people low-value items, such as pens and coffee mugs.[10]

There's more to this phenomenon, though, because other research has shown that the endowment effect is rooted in something deeper that relates to nostalgia: that the object has significance. A few years ago I got into photography and tried to come up with some cash to buy a fancy new camera. After rooting around in my closet a bit, selling off my old game video collection on eBay seemed like a good way to come up with the cash. I listed a lot of games with minimum bids that had to be met before I'd sell, but I priced a lot of other stuff cheap. That copy of *Freedom Force* I never got around to playing went for $5. A spare copy of *Age of Empires II* sold for just over $7. An unopened copy of *Black & White* was the big winner, fetching almost $25 for some reason I don't understand, since I had skipped playing it.

But some games I found myself unable to list with a rock-bottom, minimum bid and thus didn't get any interested buyers. One was 1999's *Command and Conquer: Tiberian Sun*. I priced it too high and got absolutely no interested buyers. Just like the people who wanted $1,400 for a ticket to one college basketball game, I wanted no less than $30 for my copy of this mostly unremarkable strategy game from the previous century. I now realize that this title had special meaning to me: It was the first game that I was paid to review for the gaming news site GameSpy.com. More than that, that game review eventually led to my moving out to California in early 2000 to work full-time for GameSpy and start one of the best times I've had in my life to date. That beat-up copy of a *Command and Conquer* game with bits of FedEx label still on it evoked enormous nostalgia for me. It reminded me of a time in my life when I was able to take a huge risk that resulted in meeting people with whom I'm still friends today and feeling like an integral part of the historic dot-com boom of the early 2000s. It was valuable to me as a vessel of nostalgia, but not to anybody else.

This is because the endowment effect and our sense of nostalgia really get ramped up the more personally significant an item is to someone. This shouldn't be shocking, because we're all familiar with the concept of "sentimental value." What's really amazing is that not only can that meaning be invoked by simple ownership, but it can also be elicited simply by knowing that an item has a history—any history. You don't even have to be a part of its story. This is the principle upon which the philanthropic project SignificantObjects.com is founded.

The team at Significant Objects buys junk from the flea markets, thrift shops, and garage sales of the world and then has professional writers make up elaborate and interesting faux histories for those objects. These fake histories are then incorporated into eBay auctions. But here's the catch, or rather the lack of a catch: The eBay bidders are in on the act because the Significant Objects team makes it perfectly clear that the stories paired with these objects are fictional and in no way true. Still, the results are amazing. A fork bought at a thrift store for 50 cents sells for $26.01 because the seller featured it in a story about someone's dead wife. A snow globe containing a miniature Utah landscape cost 99 cents but sells for $59.00 just because the seller wrote about how he stole it from his grandfather's hidden stash of treasures. A felt monkey puppet that cost $2.99 new sells used for $47.20 because the author claimed that it had not only been owned by novelist Franz Kafka but had been the inspiration for a never-released novel, *Metamorphosis II: Monkey Puppet*. Framing an object in terms of its elaborate, personal, and sometimes ludicrous history makes the buyers perceive it as having more significance and meaning. And lest you become too indignant about such manipulation, know that the Significant Objects project donates some of its earnings to charity.

This idea of objects having an essence or nature that makes them unique has been studied by other researchers. Yale University's Paul Bloom and his fellow researcher from the University of Bristol, Bruce Hood, wanted to see if invoking an item's history could make it more valuable.[11] Capitalizing on a recent visit by the Queen of England, the researchers showed a bunch of six-year-old children spoons and cups that had supposedly belonged to the queen. They then placed the items in a mock "duplicating machine" that would supposedly make copies of the items. The machine consisted of a pair of boxes with hidden doors in the back through which one could slip an item's twin in order to trick the kids into thinking that the original item had been duplicated. You may think that this is selling the average six-year-old's intelligence a bit short, but Bloom makes a good point:

> When we showed this machine to children, none thought it was a trick. This fits with other research that finds that children are perfectly credulous about unusual machines. There is no reason why they should be skeptical. They live in a world with giant flying canisters, metal-cutting laser beams, talking computers, and so on. And we already have a rudimentary two-dimensional duplicating machines—you can take a piece of paper with Michael Jordon's autograph on it, put it in a photocopy machine, press the button, and end up with something indistinguishable from the original. What is so strange about a three-dimensional version of this?[12]

Indeed, one could actually imagine doing this study using scanners and 3D printers without resorting to trickery. We live in the future, people. Let's start acting like it and use our technology to more thoroughly deceive our children in the name of science.

The supposed copying complete, the researchers then had children assign values to both the original and to the duplicate items. Not surprisingly, the children prized the original items much more highly because they had a history with the queen. It was a history seen as nontransferable to copies. To see if the same effect would happen when it was one's own history that went with the object, Bloom and Hood conducted a follow-up study where they offered to duplicate kids' security objects, such as blankets or stuffed animals that some kids will never sleep without. Most of the children exhibited a strong (and in all likelihood appropriate) distrust of the researchers and did not allow their special objects to be subjected to such shenanigans. But for those that did, the researchers offered to let them take home either the original or the copy. Almost all of them chose to keep the original.

This sense of history endows our video games with great value, both personal and monetary. Sometimes it's the original object that we get attached to, as in my refusal to sell that copy of *Tiberian Sun* and other games that were personally important to me. But to the extent that marketers and game developers can evoke the history of those special objects when trying to get us to make purchases, the association will work in their favor. A newcomer to the *Legend of Zelda* series may think that the latest entry is okay, but someone who bonded with a middle school friend one summer while playing the original 1987 game on the Nintendo Entertainment System will have much more of his ego invested in being a fan of *Zelda*—and possibly Nintendo in general.

This is one of the reasons why nostalgia is such a powerful force in video games and in the minds of fanboys and fangirls, which should make you think of the lessons from last chapter.

ROSE-TINTED HEADS-UP DISPLAYS

The fact that we feel nostalgia for some games specifically to make us feel better and the fact that the endowment effect warps our perceptions of value suggests that our memories may not always be accurate. We may, in fact, be unconsciously biased toward remembering things that make us happy and against remembering the things that don't. This is the "rose-tinted glasses" phenomenon. Was using graph paper to make our own maps in *The Bard's Tale* really fun? Was manually entering IP addresses to connect to vanilla deathmatch games of *Quake* more of a pain than we remember? And holy cow, was *Mega Man* always this hard? It turns out that we humans have a remarkable propensity towards fooling ourselves. As I described in chapter 3 on fanboys and fangirls, we generally require less information to confirm beliefs when they are consistent with our desired state of mind, and a substantial body of research has shown that we are predisposed to remember more of the good things in life. Instead of rose-tinted glasses, gamers may view their hobby through a rose-tinted heads-up display.

Take the "fading affect bias," for example. That term describes a wrinkle in memory's landscape that makes the emotional footprints of positive memories fade more slowly than those of negative ones. Severely traumatic events aside, we're better at remembering positive memories of the everyday sort than negative ones. This and similar phenomena have been studied under many names: dissonance reduction, self-deception, ego defense, positive illusion, emotion-based coping, self-affirmation, self-serving attribution, and subjective optimization.[13] They all show that for all the platitudes about finding silver linings, what we're really good at is ignoring the clouds altogether.

And overall, that's adaptive for our species. It's kind of a psychological immune system to protect us when things turn out to be suboptimal so that we're willing to take chances and make decisions. But it also leads to nostalgic memories of how great things used to be—memories that could be disproved through the simple application of time travel, if you were so disposed. Psychologists Daniel Gilbert and Jane Ebert did a study where they had students in a photography class process and make prints of their two favorite pictures.[14] The experimenters then told the students that they had to pick one of the two prints to take home, and one to ship off across the ocean in five days along with the film negative. But some students were told that once they made their choice, it was irrevocable; others were told they'd have five days to change their minds. When, nine days later, the researchers asked both sets of students how much they liked the picture they had chosen to walk away with, the ones who were immediately locked into their choices said they liked their photos significantly more than those who were given the opportunity to change their minds. Members of the locked-in group tended to be happier with their photo and enjoyed it more. This is the psychological immune system kicking in: You can't change your choice or your past, so whether you're aware of it or not you slip on rose-tinted glasses to change your attitude and memories to match what has happened. Nostalgia could often be a by-product of the same system.

Or overly optimistic nostalgia could all be a case of bad mental aim. Some researchers claim that vividly remembered events seem so great relative to the humdrum of the present because simply remembering something feels good. In one study, researchers Jason Leboe and Tamara Ansons showed that people tend to have an "ah-ha!" moment when experiencing easy recall of information, and a quirk of the brain makes that kind of moment innately pleasurable.[15] Just think about how good it feels to have something on the tip of your tongue for a few, fumbling moments and then finally remember it. Feels good, right? What we tend to do, the researchers argued, is mistakenly attribute the pleasure not to the easy recall of the experience, but to the experience itself, which is much more salient in our minds. Some stand-out experiences obviously were pleasurable, but this kink in the human brain biases us toward erroneously remembering such events as more positive than they really were, just because they were easy to remember.

In the end, though, the rose-colored display phenomenon may be beside the point, even if it is true. This is because it's an adaptive system that leads to good mental health for most people. Usually when you're in the middle of a largely positive experience, all of the annoying little quirks and frustrating things about that experience are noticeable. But as that experience fades into memory, we forget about the minor annoyances and more vividly remember the positive stuff. This is good and fine, since nostalgia's function is to make us feel better and happier with ourselves. If willful ignorance is self-imposed bliss, it's still bliss of a sort, and that's okay.

NOSTALGIA AND GAMES: A PERFECT MATCH

Everything described so far in this chapter speaks to several reasons why the video games of today and tomorrow have the potential to elicit more nostalgia than any other medium in history—more than television, more than movies, more than music. Chief among these reasons is that video games are inherently social and are becoming more so every year. Early video games may have been experiences that we shared through gleeful shouting on the playground or chatting around the office coffee pot in much the same way experiences with movies or television shows were shared. But as we will explore in the next chapter, almost every new game that will come out this year will feature mechanics or tools that encourage players to share, compete, communicate, help, and socialize. More and more games feature leaderboards, cooperative play modes, chat, matchmaking, friends lists, competitive play modes, rankings, guilds, achievement lists, online streaming tools like Twitch.tv, level creation tools, and support for editing and sharing gameplay videos. These are all features that either create new social relationships in video games or allow us to strengthen existing relationships through easy sharing of experiences. If, as we have seen, nostalgia is most likely in the context of social relationships, today's video games are perfect for laying the foundations of tomorrow's nostalgia.

Video games are also marketed to those in the perfect demographic for nostalgia to take root. The average age of gamers is definitely rising, but according to a 2014 study by the Entertainment Software Association, about 29 percent of gamers are under 18, and another large chunk are in their early 20s.[16] And let's be honest: Nintendo has its staples of childhood, such as *Zelda*, *Mario*, and *Kirby*, but many other successful video games are targeted at people around this age. People are going to be incredibly nostalgic about *Minecraft* in a few decades. Today's young gamers are spending real amounts of time on games during the most formative years of their lives, and those are memories that they will look to in the future when they need to bridge a sense of identity between their past and present.

And that's another reason why modern games and nostalgia are a perfect match: We spend an incredible amount of time with games. Watching a movie may only take 90 minutes, and television shows may only take a dozen or so hours across the span of a season. But we sit down and spend 10, 20, or 30 hours with a typical game, and in the case of massively multiplayer games or online competitive games like *Call of Duty* or *Dota 2*, we may invest hundreds of our hours in those experiences. As of this writing, I have over 600 hours invested in the online shooter *Team Fortress 2*, and I know some people who have played *thousands* of hours. We create narratives with these games. We create histories with them. They become part of our own identity. And as we've seen, history has a huge psychological weight when we consider how much we value something.

Keep all this in mind when, not too long from now, someone tries to use your favorite game of today to sell you some product in the future. Video games will someday boost more moods and sell more arthritis cream and fiber supplements than anything else in history.

THINGS TO REMEMBER FROM THIS CHAPTER

- Nostalgia is an emotion and can be manipulated like other emotions. It's generally defined as a sentimental longing for the past, especially in reference to how things used to be better.
- Nostalgia has the benefit of helping deal with melancholy and sadness.
- Nostalgic memories almost always involve people—usually loved ones. It's a very social emotion. Feeling nostalgia put us in the mood to maintain social relationships or create new ones.
- It can also make us feel better by reminding us of who we were in our best moments from the past.
- An item's history has heaps of psychological weight. People overvalue what they own relative to people who want to buy the same thing. This is called the "endowment effect."

- The endowment effect is stronger when the history of the item is interesting or personally significant. It need not even necessarily involve us.
- Children are insanely gullible. We should take advantage of this more.
- The "rose-tinted glasses" phenomenon is real. We tend to ignore the faults in products or situations when feeling nostalgic about them and play up the good things. The "fading affect bias" is one example of this.

Part 2

Those Who Make

5

HOW DO GAMES GET US TO KEEP SCORE AND COMPETE?

"Everything is number."
　　　—Pythagoras, Greek philosopher and mathematician

Growing up, I was an arcade rat. I mean the kind of arcade where the games were coin-operated, the lights were dim, and in hindsight I suspect that the attendant was selling something besides tokens out of the back office. I practically lived at the Aladdin's Castle that was within walking distance of my home, so games like *Burger Time*, *Ms. Pac-Man*, and *Galaga* elicit their own kind of nostalgia in me. I wrote in the last chapter about how nostalgia usually centers around shared social experiences, and one thing I recall fondly is entering my initials into an arcade game's high-score list after beating my friend's score. But it was also agonizing to see my initials fall off the bottom of the list, replaced by smug strings of characters representing friends who had fired back by accruing just a few points more. Friendly rivalries led me to feed coin after coin into machines just so I could stay at the top of the list— or at least above my friends. The proof of my superior skill would be right there on the screen, at least until the arcade attendant unplugged the cabinet at the end of the night.

This scenario from my childhood is a small version of what was writ large in the 2007 independent film *King of Kong*. That movie tells the story of Steve Wiebe, an underemployed engineer making ends meet as a school teacher. Weibe gets the wild idea to beat the world record for high score on *Donkey Kong*, a Nintendo arcade game where an early iteration of Mario (then called "Jump Man") tries to rescue a Princess Peach prototype ("Pauline") while avoiding obstacles thrown by the eponymous gorilla. Wiebe's rival for the high score is Billy Mitchell, a somewhat flamboyant character who has parlayed his fame as the holder of several arcade high-score records into a career selling homemade hot sauces. After setting up an old *Donkey Kong* machine in his garage, Wiebe begins to practice obsessively in order to beat Mitchell's high score of 874,300 points. Along the way there is drama, obsession, and cries of foul play. The two players are clearly fixated on besting each other, and each does amazing things to grasp at the title of *Donkey Kong* high-score champion. The film often makes use of the VHS video footage Weibe captures to provide evidence for his scores, and one memorable scene shows his young daughter asking for help with going to the bathroom. Wiebe, who is in the middle of a promising high-score attempt, begs her to just hold it for a few minutes more. If you want to find out if Weibe prevails in his high-score chase, I recommend watching the movie. It's pretty good.

Games have evolved greatly since the coin-op days of *Donkey Kong*, but the concept of comparing our performance against others has remained, and we all have a little Steve Wiebe or Billy "The Hot Sauce King" Mitchell in us. Today, however, online leaderboards have replaced high-score tables, and we can make even more detailed comparisons via achievements, badges, or trophies. And as games have evolved to match our social nature, the prominence and frequency of such comparisons have grown. Everything we do is compared to or related to other players. Pure numbers, be they a high score from the arcade-inspired game *Geometry Wars* or a kill/death ratio from a multiplayer match of a first-person shooter like *Battlefield*, have limited meaning to us on their own. Instead, their true value comes from how they relate to the numbers other people have. And even then, not all comparisons are equal. It matters against whom you compare yourself. It's rare to gnash our teeth in frustration when we watch YouTube or Twitch.tv videos of high-level play in *Street Fighter* tournaments or insane *Spelunky* speed runs because we realize that those people are operating on another level of play. And we can pretty easily shrug off any feelings of inadequacy in a massively multiplayer game if we see that the powerful equipment someone got came from playing for a ridiculous number of hours or just getting lucky. (We may still feel jealous, but that's a topic for a later chapter.)

Why do some social comparisons drive us to try harder or invest more in a game than others? And how can we recognize when game designers have engineered their games to capitalize on these aspects of our psychology in order to keep us coming back for one more try or to get us to make in-game purchases that give us an edge against the competition? Tricks of the trade include presenting you with different comparison targets, moving the goalposts on you, and making you think you know more about the game than you do. Let's take a closer look.

WHAT FRIENDS ARE REALLY FOR

First, it's whom you're comparing yourself against that matters the most. One of the first researchers to explore this concept was legendary social psychologist Leon Festinger. He was interested in building on earlier research on group interactions, and in 1954 Festinger published an influential article called "A Theory of Social Comparison Process- es."[1] The article, which goes a long way to explaining the appeal of today's gaming leaderboards, formalized the idea that we generally de- sire accurate information about our abilities. But even when we have hard data about how well we're doing in a tennis game, a class, or our career, the information is usually of limited meaning without appropri- ate context. In such cases, Festinger argued, we invariably turn to com- paring ourselves with other people. Do I have more points than my opponent? How many people are getting an "A" in this class? Am I making as much money as Karen, who just started here six months ago? These are all important questions, because Karen seems to spend all her time playing *Clash of Clans* on her phone instead of actually work- ing. Furthermore, Festinger argued that we prefer to make those social comparisons with people who are similar to us.

Festinger's article was a good start, and later research confirmed most of his theory. The only part he was a little vague on was what exactly "similar to us" meant. Was it in terms of ability? Other charac- teristics? Demographics? Subsequent research has supported what has become known as "the related-attribution hypothesis."[2] Essentially, we prefer to compare our performance against the performance of people we know something about in terms of characteristics related to the task. For example, if I wanted to know if my kill/death ratio in *Call of Duty* is acceptable, I feel better off comparing myself against someone my age, since players in the throes of youth tend to have quicker reflexes. I also don't want to compare myself to someone playing the game on a computer with the use of a mouse and keyboard, since precision aiming with a mouse is easier than with my Xbox controller. One study, for example, showed that people tended to consider another person's hand size when guessing if they could match their performance on a test of grip strength.[3] Another found that subjects in a group of nine who completed a task sought out comparisons with people who they knew had practiced the same amount as they had.[4] This is one reason why we don't see much point in comparing our accomplishments in a game to those of people who do nothing but play it all day long. Your having awesome armor in *Diablo* or owning a massive, sprawling estate in *Farmville* is great, but I feel less inadequate if I know you played 23 hours a day for a month to get them.

The leaderboards, achievements, scores, and replays built into modern games provide a great context in which to apply social comparison theory and the way that developers can use it to keep you playing. Leaderboards that rank players according to scores represent the evolution of entering initials into high-score lists in coin-operated games, but they are of limited effectiveness unless they let you compare your scores to those of your friends instead of just to those of strangers. Pick up any game on your mobile phone, for example, and find the global rankings. Chances are you'll see a group of strangers perching at the top of the list like gods peering down at mere mortals from the absurd height of Mount Olympus. Does that motivate you to get better at the game, to keep playing, or to drop some money on an in-game purchase to improve your score? Probably not. But take a look at what smart games like *Candy Crush Saga* do: When you play a level, it shows you not the scores of haughty gods on global leaderboards, but the scores of your much more down-to-earth friends and colleagues. Hey, just 200 more points and you can beat Dave on this level. Dave is a jerk. We hate him almost as much as that slacker Karen. Does anyone actually do work in this office? The car racing series *Forza Motorsport* does something similar with its rivals system, which alerts you to the next person on your friends list whose time you're about to beat in a given race. The people on your *Candy Crush Saga* and *Forza* leaderboards are probably people you know, and, let's be honest, they're people whose lives you compare your own life to all the time. These systems also work because, in line with Festinger's social comparison theory, we tend to aspire upward and have a bias toward comparing ourselves to the person directly above us in the rankings as opposed to the person below us or even the person at the top.[5] This is why clever game developers will make use of friends lists to provide good reference points for our performance.

Another good example of a game that brings this all together is *Trials Evolution*. This side-scrolling, motorcycle-driving game is both very difficult and has a heavy emphasis on how quickly you complete each of its obstacle-laden racetracks. The left and right triggers on your controller map to the bike's throttle and brakes, but the real trick is mastering the game's simulated physics by using your left-thumb stick to control how far your little dude leans forward or back on the bike. This, along with your momentum and how much gas you give it, will determine if you crash and how quickly you zip through the track. Among the several things that the game's developer, RedLynx, really nails with *Trials Evolution* is the social competition aspect. The game is replete with leaderboards and indications of how well you're competing against others. And though there are global leaderboards available if you want to dig for them, RedLynx seems to be aware that it's more meaningful to compete against our friends and other people we know, because the default leaderboards compare us to people on our Xbox Live friends list by default. *Trials Frontier*, a mobile entry in the franchise, does the same thing with either Apple's Game Center or Android's Google Play Games app.

But you don't even have to wait until the finish line in *Trials Evolution* to compare your performance. Each time you run a track, the game shows you where your friends were on their best run by moving a little dot with their gamer tag attached along the track with you. It's amazingly effective—much more so than showing you a dot belonging to "xxXTrialzd00d42Xxx," the world record holder for that track, because he'd simply shoot off past the right edge of your screen and not offer any kind of meaningful comparison. But I personally know my sister, my co-worker, that guy I went to school with, and other people on my friends list. They provide much better reference points because I know how I compare to them in other important ways. It's invaluable to see the little dot representing their progress through a track get hung up over and over again on the same obstacle that's vexing me. Likewise, it's also useful to see when they don't get hung up, since I know that if they can get past a certain tricky part, so can I. As a result, I noticed that I was much more likely to try to shave off a few seconds and creep up a notch on the leaderboards when it was a shorter list of people important to me.

Even in the absence of specific friends to compare ourselves to, game designers could do more of this to keep us motivated—obsessed, even—with chasing high scores and rankings. They could tell you what percentile you are in among people your age, or among people who also like to play support classes, such as medic; or among people who have played more than (or less than) 50 hours of the game in the last month; or among people who prefer the sniper rifle. As we saw in chapter 3 on fanboys, it doesn't take much to make us feel like we're part of a group and to thus trigger more meaningful comparisons. Even presenting some quick biographical information ("xXSoulKillaXx" lives in your country, is age 30 to 35, and works in the hospitality industry") could make comparisons to someone more motivating than nothing at all. These demographic data are usually in the system, and simply throwing a metric like this up on a loading screen or while waiting to respawn after getting killed can motivate us to play just one more match or make one more run at a course instead of turning off the machine or going to bed.

BIG FISH, LITTLE POND

The second thing game designers often do to make you feel more pleased with yourself and your performance is to make you feel like what is often called a "big fish in a small pond." Or sometimes researchers speak about frogs and frog ponds, presumably because the metric system uses frogs. Either way, the phenomenon happens naturally when you provide a small set of familiar comparison targets from a friends list, as described above, but it can also work with strangers and abstract groupings. This has more to do more with how data are presented than whom the data describe. People who are ranked near the top of a badly performing group tend to feel better about themselves than those ranked near the bottom of a well-performing group. This is true even though your performance in the group you're at the top of is lower than anyone in the other group. Like feeling good about being the most valued player on the losing team, sometimes all it takes to make you feel like the smartest person in the room is to step into a closet full of idiots.

In fact, this "big fish, little pond effect" has been studied extensively in education, where it has been found to hold true in schools of all levels across 40 different countries.[6] Its importance is huge, because simply looking at your performance in the context of a smaller group tends to override any comparisons you may make with the world at large. Yet this quirk of psychology has its dangers, too. Many of us may be familiar with a particularly illustrative example of a big fish made small: the valedictorian of a small high school, who is literally the smartest person in her class and thus gets into a competitive university. But when she gets there, she finds that for the first time in her life she is among intellectual equals and some people who are even smarter than she is. She can't keep up with the other talented students and feels stupid as a result. She may get discouraged and drop out or change to an easier major in the face of unprecedented feelings of mediocrity. Despite the fact that she's just as smart and hard-working as she ever was, this former valedictorian was happier when that meant she was at the top of a small group instead of the middle of a large one.[7]

Ethan Zell and his colleagues Mark Alicke and Dorian Bloom at Ohio University provided additional proof of this anecdote in a study where they split groups of 10 college students into 2 teams of 5 people each.[8] The researchers then kept both teams in the same room and asked everyone to watch a series of videotaped statements. Some of the videos were of liars, they were told, and some were not. The liars and the honest speakers weren't identified, of course; it would be the subjects' job to tell them apart. Then, because psychologists are pathological liars themselves, the researchers' subjects were given bogus feedback about their performance in this task, indicating that they were ranked fifth out of the 10 people in the room. So they knew their rank, but only as it related to all 10 participants and not to their own five-person team. Students in one experimental condition, however, were given the additional information that they were the worst-performing member on their particular team of five. The researchers found that relative to the people who were just told they were "fifth out of 10" and given no feedback about their ranking in their own group, subjects had lower self-esteem when they knew they were ranked fifth in their 5-person team. This despite the fact that people in both groups were rated fifth out of 10 overall. The study showed that when people rate themselves, they think about how good they are in small groups, and they can easily be made to neglect considering how well they have done overall. The converse is also true: Even if your group is terrible, you can feel kind of good about being at the top of it. And more importantly, you can more easily be motivated to keep trying until you get to the top, even if the group sizes are arbitrary.

We can see, therefore, how games that provide comparisons to our friends naturally benefit from the big fish, little pond effect. You're ranked as the 6,458th best player out of 11,092? That's not as interesting as knowing that you're 12th out of the 45 people on your Game Center friends list, nor is it as likely to get you to keep playing the game until your rank improves. Even better would be games that let you specify levels of closeness with others to broaden your base for comparison. Tracking close personal friends or sibling rivalries separately from the people you vaguely know from a message board would really help to arouse your competitive spirit.

But smart developers take this even further by enabling you to dice up the data yourself and establish the comparison groups that are important to you. Instead of global rankings, they could show how you compare to people in your country, your town, or even your neighborhood. And mobile games could make use of GPS information to show you how you rank against the people who visited your location within the last month, so that you can get an idea of your standing among your schoolmates or co-workers. They don't even have to be friends; just giving us a smaller group to feel a part of will trigger the big fish, little pond effect and motivate us to keep playing so that we can gobble up the competition and be the biggest in our pond. Clever developers can also change the size of the pond and the fish by changing what data are presented to us. Forget always looking at total score or number of matches won. Games could make us feel special simply by pointing out accomplishments that we have in common with the cream of the crop. Getting a notification along the lines of, "You've scored 1,000 headshots— something only 10 percent of other players have done," would go a long way toward making us feel like we're part of the upper echelon.

But what happens when you get to the top of your group? Or, worse, what happens when you're in danger of sinking to the bottom? Well, then it gets a little more complicated. Let's look at the story of one singularly unimpressed athlete to see how upward and downward comparisons matter more than you may think.

LAST AND FIRST AND SECOND

McKayla Moroney is a better gymnast than you, anyone you've ever known, or anyone you could ever name without a Google search. Even then it would be debatable. At just 16 years of age, she and her teammates on the USA women's gymnastics team won gold medals in the 2012 Summer Olympics. But despite all her accomplishments, Maroney is best known to many people as that girl who was disappointed with winning second place. In the first of her final two runs in the 2012 Olympics vault competition, Moroney lined herself up and glared at the vault horse like she was going to murder its face off. She then exploded down the runway and executed an impressive maneuver that looked to me like it would involve hitting the A button, then the left trigger button, then rotating the analog stick back in a quarter circle with perfect timing. On her second run at the vault, though, it looks like she hit the B button instead, because her altitude was off and she fell on her backside with a graceless thump.

That fall and the deduction in points that came with it ruined Maroney's chance at the gold medal. She got silver. The "McKayla Moroney is not impressed" meme that swept the Internet starting in 2012 had its origin in the Olympic medals ceremony where Maroney briefly smirked as if to express her disappointment with second place. Jokers on the Internet soon started Photoshopping the image of a disappointed Maroney everywhere to illustrate how various things were as unimpressive as coming in second place in the Summer Olympics: the Eiffel Tower, the Sistine Chapel, an exquisitely tiny horse, whatever. To her credit, the normally cheerful Maroney owned the meme and even posed with President Obama as they made the famous face together.

Still, the "McKayla is not impressed" meme is emblematic of a strange thing about human psychology in the context of competition: not all rungs on a tournament ladder are equally spaced. This leads to what seems like a crazy question: Would Maroney have been happier with the bronze medal instead of the silver? Some research actually suggests she might have been, at least while she was up on the awards' stage. Cornell University's Vicki Medvec, Scott Madey, and Tom Gilovich did a study where they had trained raters watch video tapes of the 1992 Summer Olympics.[9] The raters scrutinized the facial expressions of Olympic winners, both at the conclusion of their performances and at the medals ceremony. They found that bronze medal winners looked much happier than silver winners. Because, the researchers hypothesize, the bronze medalists tended to compare themselves downward when thinking "what if . . . ," but the silver medalists made upwards comparisons. The bronze winners were thinking about how close they were to getting no medal at all, but the silver winners were thinking about how close they were to being the best of the best. If they could have had just one more chance to hit "Load Save Game" on some menu and try just one more time, they would have been much more likely to do so than a bronze winner.

Other researchers, including Stephen Garcia from the University of Michigan, have replicated this idea that the difference between first and second is bigger than anything, except maybe the distance between last place and second to last.[10] He also found that these goalposts can be moved to manipulate our interest in competition versus cooperation. Garcia and his colleagues hypothesized that people were more likely to act competitively (or at least refuse to act cooperatively) the closer they and a rival were to a meaningful standard—being ranked number two and number three out of a group, say. To test this hunch, they had subjects pretend to be company executives or poker players deciding whether they should compete or cooperate with rivals. The scenarios were structured so that cooperation with would-be opponents maximized total financial payoffs, but it would also benefit the rivals enough that subjects would be surpassed in the rankings. For example, in one study subjects were asked to role-play the part of a CEO for a company on the coveted *Fortune* 500 list. They were then told that they had a choice to enter into a joint venture with a rival company. Doing so would grow their profits by 10 percent, but it would also increase the rival company's profits by 25 percent. What's more, it would also move the rival to a higher spot on the *Fortune* 500 list than the subjects' company. Garcia found that people were often too competitive to cooperate if doing so meant sliding from first position to second—despite the fact that they ended up with less money as a result of hanging on to first place. Conversely, subjects would generally be happy to cooperate if it was only a matter of going from being 202nd to 203rd. But the researchers also found the effect present when it was a competition to stay out of last place.

Like the subjects in these studies, gamers tend to place a high value on rankings. If you're the top-ranked member of our guild in player-versus-player competition, for example, you're generally less likely to sacrifice resources or time to help out guildmates if it means being dislodged from the top spot. This has clear implications for how game makers design their systems and how we as players think about them. If competition is the tune to which developers want their players to dance, they are more likely to provide lots of information about not just rankings, but also opportunities for being at the top of different rankings. They could be first in rankings, first in wealth, first in gear, and so forth. Or, if they really want to rub it in, a game could tell you when you're about to drop to the bottom of the list. Likewise, if you find yourself in second place (or, again, second-to-last place) check your impulses to see whether it's really worth it to invest more time, money, and effort into dealing with a tiny gap that separates you from the next person up or down. Or whether the metric by which you're supposedly being judged is even important to you. You might be happier in third place after all.

And actually, any nonarbitrary goalpost will do. In golf there is the concept of par, which is the maximum number of strokes that a golfer should take to get the little ball in the little hole. Taking fewer strokes (below par) is good; taking more (above par) is bad. Researchers Devin Pope and Maurice Schweitzer examined data on 2.5 million golf putts made by professional golfers between 2004 and 2008 in order to find out if these pros were more or less careful when making a shot that would make them go over par.[11] After using statistical methods to control for all kinds of things (e.g., distance from the hole, slope, etc.), the researchers found that pro golfers indeed tried harder and were more accurate on putts that let them avoid going over par. This is irrational, because at this level of play golfers should try equally hard on every single shot of the game. Rankings in pro golf tournaments frequently change on account of a single stroke, so every shot counts. Yet the standards of "above par" and "below par" exerted an influence even among the best of the best.

Sometimes, though, segmenting ourselves and comparing ourselves to smaller groups and finding some little hill that we can stand on and call our kingdom can have drawbacks. Sometimes developers can be so intent on making us feel proud of ourselves that we can get burned, and we are amazed that we didn't know fire was even in the game.

THE DUNNING–KRUGER EFFECT

Let me describe a scenario that I think we've all been in. You pick up a competitive multiplayer game like *Hearthstone: Heroes of Warcraft*, *Starcraft II*, or the most recent *Call of Duty* game. You jam through the tutorial and the single-player campaign. Maybe you play a few skirmish matches against computer-controlled opponents—on the second-to-hardest difficulty setting, because you're totally hardcore like that. And you're better at the game than anyone on your friends list, judging by the leaderboards and because nobody will play with you anymore. You've got this game figured out, and you think you're pretty awesome. It's telling you that you're awesome!

What's the logical next step? Venture online, of course, and try your hand at ranked ladder matches, a tournament, or maybe even just some pickup games via online matchmaking. And how does that go? You get creamed. Stomped. Crushed. At the end of the match your competition has left you with a kill/death ratio in a realm of negative numbers so low that mathematicians haven't even bothered to really think about it yet because they figured nobody would ever use them. This baffles you, because by all previous accounts you're totally awesome at this game. If any of this sounds familiar, congratulations. You have encountered what psychologists call the Dunning–Kruger effect.

Named after the authors of a 1999 article by Cornell University professor of psychology David Dunning and his then graduate student Justin Kruger, the effect describes how those who aren't very good at something overestimate their skill and how those who are experts at something tend to sell themselves short.[12] This is because the more skilled you are in some complicated task, the more you understand that there are complexities and possibilities that you don't fully understand. Somewhat skilled players of a musical instrument, such as guitar, can glimpse advanced-play concepts just enough to know that they haven't mastered them. And really good guitar players understand everything the instrument is capable of better than someone who has only now figured out how to bang out the beginning of that one Green Day song. In the same way, those of us who are really bad and inexperienced at a game often lack true understanding of what's even possible. We think the limited strategies and possibilities that we know make up the whole picture, when in reality we're only seeing one corner of a huge canvas.

In their initial research, Kruger and Dunning gave students tests of logic, grammar, and humor (really; the researchers had subjects evaluate the laugh-out-loud potential of jokes from Woody Allen and Al Franken). When the researchers asked the subjects to guess at their performance on these tests, the poorest performers overestimated their achievements. For example, someone who was actually in the 12th percentile of scores (i.e., only 12% of subjects scored worse) would typically guess that they were all the way up in the 62nd percentile. That is, they thought they were better than 62 percent of people, when in reality they were much worse. Further investigation showed that the poorer performing subjects overestimated their ability simply because they weren't good enough to know how difficult the tasks were. And they didn't know it.

The deck-building game *Hearthstone: Heroes of Warcraft* provides a great illustration of the Dunning–Kruger effect. *Hearthstone* requires players to duel with (virtual) cards that have individual properties and can interact with other cards in spectacular but ultimately predictable ways. The "Timber Wolf" card, for example, doesn't require many resources to play and doesn't do much damage to your opponent. Novice players may keep it out of their deck or only play it early in the game. Expert players, however, understand the synergy that card has with other cards with the "Beast" attribute: it gives +1 to all attacks by those cards. This means that experienced players will hold the Timber Wolf card in reserve and play it at the right time for devastating effect. New players who think they're hot stuff because they flew through the tutorial or a few lower-level matches may be shocked to find out that such a strategy is even possible, much less so effective. And that's just a simple example for the sake of illustration. In addition to being able to add and subtract very quickly, the path to mastering *Hearthstone* takes players through complex subjects, such as probability, algebra, logical reasoning, and other topics that new players never even suspect.

The Dunning–Kruger effect comes up in other video games, especially competitive multiplayer ones and those that let you compare your performance against others via leaderboards. The effect is exacerbated by the fact that the single-player versions of games often allow you to be incompetent in the pursuit of fun and stroke your ego with the kind of feedback I discussed earlier in this chapter and will discuss in a later chapter on progress-related game elements. New players can soak up bullets in some shooters, such as *Gears of War*, instead of using cover effectively or choosing the right weapon for the situation. They can brute-force their way through a campaign scenario in *Starcraft II* using just cheap Marine units instead of appropriately countering the enemy's army built with advanced units. They can overwhelm low-level enemies in *World of Warcraft* instead of using teamwork and assembling a set of equipment or list of perks with the optimal resistances. In each case, these players are essentially incompetent, but the limited feedback they're getting doesn't allow them to know it. The novice bumbles along missing all that but getting the occasional lucky shot and thinks he's doing all right for himself. But the great player sees every misstep and every missed opportunity for perfect play, and beats herself up over it.

Some game developers are learning to address this paradox by forcing novice players to learn the true scope of the game. *Starcraft II*, despite the fact that I've been using it to illustrate the Dunning–Kruger effect, actually tries to address it by inviting players to complete multiplayer-oriented challenges where they learn things like unit counters, defending against rushes, and other advanced tactics. Many fighting games like the newer entries in the *Street Fighter* series also have special training modes that illustrate enigmatic concepts, such as hit boxes and frame data. This kind of tutorial helps, as do collecting and presenting community guides and videos illustrating everything a game has to offer. The Dunning–Kruger effect is difficult to avoid for new players, but those who set their minds to it can move beyond it.

So next time you find your ladder rankings aren't living up to your expectations, take a second to reflect about all the things you don't know and how your experiences so far may have been designed to make you feel more competent than you really are. Readjust your concept of how good you are relative to the field of players you're trying to break into. Then go pick up some tips from those totally awesome hardcore players who know how totally awesome they really aren't.

And while you're at it, keep in mind that smart game developers are taking advantage of several aspects of human psychology in order to get you to keep competing and keep chasing higher scores. If competition and obsession over rankings are what make games fun for you, then great! A leaderboard or high-score list can be crafted in such a way to push your buttons harder and get you to keep playing, but oftentimes differences between competitors are much less meaningful than you think.

THINGS TO REMEMBER FROM THIS CHAPTER

- In the absence of objective information, people make social comparisons to determine how well they're doing. Games facilitate this.
- Not all comparisons are equal. We prefer those who are similar to us in ways that are relevant to the task or accomplishment in question.
- The "big fish, little pond effect" (also sometimes called the "frog pond effect") describes how we feel better about our performance if it puts us near the top of a low-performing group than if the same performance puts us near the bottom of a high-performing group.
- Not all rungs on a tournament ladder are equally spaced. The difference between 1st and 2nd place is much larger, psychologically, than the difference between 101st and 102nd.
- Other relevant standards may create this effect, too, for example, par in golf.
- The Dunning–Kruger effect describes how people who are bad at something overestimate their performance, and those who are experts underestimate. Single-player campaigns and tutorials may highlight this effect by making novice players think they're better prepared for competitive play than they really are.

6

HOW DO GAMES GET US TO GRIND, COMPLETE SIDE QUESTS, AND CHASE ACHIEVEMENTS?

"A soldier will fight long and hard for a bit of colored ribbon."
—Napoleon Bonaparte

In November 2012, writer and occasional game developer Christos Reid decided to attend an event with the colorful name "Fuck This Jam." Pardon my language, but that was its name. Game jams like this one are events where game developers (mostly armature ones) come together to try to create small video games with limited time and just a few resources. It's an exercise that produces creativity out of desperation and constraint. Game jams also sometimes operate within the additional limitation of a specific theme, such as the Molyjam event where participants create something inspired by a single, sublime quote from eccentric game developer Peter Molynoux. And his quotes are indeed often weird. What kind of game would you make, for example, out of Molynoux's claims that "I have to be careful what I say, there are PR policeman in the audience with sniper rifles," or "I still have nightmares about holding German sausages over my head"? You would make a weird game, that's what kind. But in the case of the Fuck This Jam event that Reid attended, Molynoux wasn't involved. Instead, the theme was to develop a quick and dirty game based on a game mechanic that people hate, thus the first two words in the name of the event. Reid chose "grinding."

Grinding in video games refers to doing the same thing over and over again in order to slowly progress toward some goal. It's wandering through the tall grass in a *Pokémon* or *Final Fantasy* game so that you can win enough random encounters to level up your characters. It's killing the same kind of monster over and over and over again in *World of Warcraft* in the hopes that you get some rare piece of equipment to pop out of its corpse. It's driving around and around the map in *Borderlands* just so you can pop the achievement for running over 25 enemies with a vehicle. Grinding sounds like a bore—and it usually is—but gamers do it constantly.

Despite its bad rap, Reid didn't necessarily hate grinding with a white-hot burning passion. "I don't mind it," he told me. "When I do it in *World of Warcraft* (where most quests are of the 'collect ten rat tails' variety), it lets me switch off mentally and just focus on the task at hand."[1] But Reid thought the mechanic made for a good subject for the game jam, so in 15 hours over the course of two days he threw together a project he called *GRINDSTAR*. The game is simple. You play as a little knight on the left, and a monster appears on the right. Between you and the monster is a sign displaying what level you need to be in order to defeat the monster. You use your mouse to click on a conveniently labeled "GRIND" button and you level up with each click. The monster on the right patiently waits for you to finish your grind, at which point you can kill it. Congratulations, here's a little fanfare! You then move on to the next monster, which takes even more clicks to defeat than the last one. Then repeat. Forever. To try it for yourself, search for GRINDSTAR on the Internet or go to http://www.newgrounds.com/portal/view/605910.

There's no point to *GRINDSTAR* except clicking and watching numbers go up. Reid essentially made a game out of being bored and risking a repetitive strain injury. As such, it satisfied the spirit of Fuck This Jam in that it poked fun at progress-related game elements, such as progress bars, achievements, levels, and quests. It exposed to players how silly these things can be when taken to an extreme. But here's what's amazing: Despite *GRINDSTAR*'s totally transparent nature, people kept playing it. Within minutes of uploading his completed project for distribution, Reid says that one player hit level 1,000.[2] Months later, one of his friends finally hit level 10,000 by rigging the A button on his game controller to press continuously.

GRINDSTAR wasn't even the first parody of its type. Ten years earlier, *Progress Quest* aimed to lampoon then popular online games like *Everquest*. It was a text-only game where the player created a goofy character (e.g., a Half-Orc Robot Monk or a Half-Halfling Fighter/ Organist) then leaned back while the game did all the grinding for her. Satirically given the title of the world's first "zero-player role-playing game," *Progress Quest* required literally no input from the player other than to keep it running in the background. You could do this for as long as you could avoid rebooting your computer. You just occasionally checked in to see what monsters your character was killing ("a crippled ape") and what treasures it was accumulating ("some harpy mascara"). All the while, little colored bars fill up to show your meaningless progress. It was the ultimate easy grind, since it literally did the same thing over and over again and generated nonsensical, random quests like "Deliver the newspaper" or "Placate the Dervishes" that sound only slightly more absurd than the entries you can find in the quest logs of real role-playing games.

GRINDSTAR and *Progress Quest* are extreme cases rooted firmly in satire that people find funny because their absurdity speaks to truth. Gamers will frequently grind out levels, hunt for hidden collectable items, slavishly complete side quests, and keep playing long after the game stops being fun. I know I have. In early 2014, the free Apple App Store game de jour was *Make It Rain*, an app where players did little else than swipe their fingers across their iPhones to make their score go up. That's it. You just swipe for as long as you can stand it in order to see a number go up. Or, as an alternative, many mobile games like *Tiny Tower* or the *Real Racing* series will also let players spend real money to avoid grinds to reach the same ends. Why do it? To complete a quest. To gain a level. To fill a progress bar. To earn an achievement, trophy, or badge. In this chapter, I will explore some of the psychological mechanisms behind these progress-related game elements so you can better understand why they work on you. Keep reading! You're already about 16 percent done!

SCRATCHING A PSYCHOLOGICAL ITCH: AN OVERVIEW OF SELF-DETERMINATION THEORY

One of the things that I've noticed nongamers wonder about is why people play games at all. More than one newspaper reporter assigned to write about some hot new casual game like *Clash of Clans* or *Candy Crush Saga* has tracked me down for some insight. Frequently, the interviews simply start with, "So, why do people play these things, any-way?" Thankfully, many clever researchers have also thought of this question and many of them have paid special attention to things like quests, achievements, and collectables.

One of the first of these researchers was Richard Bartle, whose interest during the 1990s lay with MUDs, a genre of games that he helped create. Short for "Multi-User Dungeons," MUDs were the text-based precursors of massively multiplayer role-playing games like *Ever-quest* and *World of Warcraft*. Based on message board conversations and observations, Bartle conceived a taxonomy of MUD players defined by what motivated them to play the game.[3] Killers wanted to compete with others, Socializers played to interact with others in less violent ways, Explorers got joy from finding new areas or story material, and Achievers sought to fulfill a desire to see numbers go up. Bartle's tests of his model weren't very scientific or extensive, but the idea that players differ from each other in terms of what motivates them to keep playing was an important one that others built on.

Nick Yee, whom we will discuss much more in a later chapter on avatars, is one such person. In 2006, he surveyed 3,000 massively multi-player online game players with 40 questions based on Bartle's taxono-my. Using a statistical technique known as "factor analysis," which clumps questions together into larger concepts based on how people's answers tend to coincide, Yee found evidence for three types of gaming motivations: social, immersion, and achievement.[4] In a follow-up study a few years later, Yee also looked at the relationship between players' scores on surveys measuring these motivations and their accomplishments via *World of Warcraft*'s achievement system. [5] He found further evidence of the importance of those social, immersion, and achievement motivations based on what kinds of in-game activities *World of Warcraft* players pursued the most. Many gamers, he found, are at-tracted to achievements and quests. They play because they want to experience achievement through progress, power, accumulation, and status within a game. What's more, he could pick them out from a crowd based on their answers to some simple surveys. Other research on Yee's achievement motivator suggest that ratings of how well a game satisfies this need for achievement predict how many hours someone is likely to spend with a game. The downside, though, is that the competitive or grinding aspects of achievement may also lead them to be in a slightly worse mood.[6]

Finally, one of the most researched models of why people play video games has been proposed and tested by researchers Andrew Przybylski, Scott Rigby, and Richard Ryan. Based on a framework called "self-determination theory" (SDT), they argue people engage in voluntary behavior like play or even work to the extent that it scratches three psychological itches: the need to feel competent at what you're doing, the need to feel like you have meaningful choices when deciding how to do it, and the need to feel connected and related to others in the process. SDT calls these motivators "competence, autonomy, and relatedness."[7] Przybylski, Rigby, and Ryan claim that to the extent that these needs are met, people will play games for longer and enjoy them more in the process.[8] Satisfaction of SDT's three motivators can be achieved a number of ways, but progress-related game elements offer direct lines to each. Let's dig deeper to explore how competence, autonomy, and relatedness can each be addressed by game elements like quests, achievements, badges, and levels.

COMPETENCE: "I STABBED THAT ORC REAL GOOD"

As mentioned, competence is the need to feel that you are doing well, being effective, and developing new skills. Similar to Yee's concept of achievement motivation and Bartle's Achiever type, self-determination theory's application of competence to video games involves getting higher scores, becoming more powerful, winning, and getting feedback about how super awesome you are. Video games are stuffed with markers of competence in these areas. Completing a quest in a role-playing game gives you a sense of accomplishment, as does earning a badge for getting 100 headshots in a competitive shooter. Even filling up a progress bar and having your character level up is a signal of competence independent of whatever other perks you receive.

But some progress-related elements scratch the competence itch more satisfyingly than others. Rigby and Ryan argue that competence needs are best satisfied when goals challenge our abilities without being too easy or too daunting.[9] This agrees with research done by psychologists studying the effects of goal setting in the workplace, who have known for decades that goals are most motivating when they are specific, difficult but possible, and accompanied by feedback showing progress.[10] "Kill zombies until I tell you to stop" is not nearly as motivating as knowing you need to put down 53,594 of the walking dead for the "Zombie Genocider" achievement in *Dead Rising*. And even that goal could be made better, given how huge that number is. This is why many games break down large goals into smaller ones in order to get you started. Baking 500 pies to master your character's Cooking skill? That's a bit much. But adding additional tiers of skill and only asking me to bake 10 pies to get to the first one? Sounds good! This kind of breakdown gives the player feedback and monitoring on progress and regulation of effort toward a distant goal.[11]

The lesson of many small measures of progress over one large measure can also be applied to the user interface. Researchers have studied the effects of including a progress bar—a near ubiquitous user interface element in games—on the completion of online survey results. One study found that progress bars were very effective at getting people to complete a task if it required only a moderate amount of time and the bar filled quickly. But if a task was lengthy and the bar filled up too slowly, the presence of a progress bar actually caused more people to drop out.[12] This is why most games start you out with easy-to-achieve goals and levels, so that the first few hits of achievement come quickly. Then, when new levels or upgrades start to take a very long time, they layer in other goals that start the cycle over, like earning reputation ranks with different in-game factions or leveling up a new set of skills. In the first-person shooter *Destiny*, for example, there are multiple factions that you can earn favor with by doing quests for them, and there are multiple types of crafting materials that you can collect to upgrade each piece of equipment you own. The games most effective at getting you to keep playing are the ones that make you think you're always on the cusp of completing something, and it's difficult to just walk away and forget about it.

In fact, there's a specific name for this phenomenon: the "Zeigarnik effect." Sometime during the 1920s, Russian psychologist Bluma Zeigarnik and a group of her colleagues from the University of Berlin were having lunch at a local café. Zeigarnik then noticed something peculiar. Her waiter displayed an unusual ability to remember complex orders while they were being filled, allowing him to deliver the right combination of food to the right tables without the benefit of pen and paper. But that information vanished from memory as soon as the eats were put in place. The waiter's memory didn't seem to have much to do with sustained mental effort or chanting the undelivered orders under his breath to hold them in short-term memory. Yet when Zeigarnik went back to quiz the waiter, he said he could remember nothing of her lunch order. At the time, the orders that hadn't yet been filled just seemed to nag at his mind until they were completed. Once that was done, the orders disappeared in a puff of mental smoke.

Back in her lab, Zeigarnik and legendary psychologist Kurt Lewin pursued this idea and ran some experiments involving the completion of various tasks or puzzles. Some of the subjects performing the tasks were interrupted, and then everyone was asked to describe what tasks they had done. Like the waiter who remembered what orders still needed to go to what tables, subjects were far more likely to recall the tasks they had started but hadn't completed. This Zeigarnik effect subsequently entered the psychology lexicon to describe how we tend to find it easier to recall a task—and the details surrounding it—when we feel like we have begun to undertake it but we were unable to complete it.[13] Apparently we as humans don't like it when we begin something and don't finish it, and such circumstances create an internal tension and preoccupation with the task. Completing the task provides closure, release of the tension, and makes us happy.

Today, we see the Zeigarnik effect show up in relation to game quests, achievements, and other progression-related game elements. This is particularly true with role-playing titles where in-game journals bloom with unfinished quests, objectives, and uncharted grey areas on maps. Any *World of Warcraft* player who has collected 13 Goretusk livers as part of a quest to collect 14 can tell you how reluctant she is to leave Westfall before grinding for just one more in order to get that quest off her list. Once we begin one of these tasks, they hang around in the back of our mind and are much easier to recall than completed tasks. As such, they come to mind more easily and more quickly when we consider what to do next, especially if the game makes it easier to keep track of the accomplishment, as we discussed earlier. We also see the Zeigarnik effect happen in empire-building game series like *SimCity* or *Civilization*. Many players are familiar with the "just one more turn" effect where we can't seem to stop taking tiny, incremental steps toward completing some kind of structure, upgrade, technology, or conquest that we started 30 turns ago. University of Sheffield psychology researcher Tom Stafford notes in a 2012 article for the BBC blog *Neurohacks* that the Zeigarnik effect even explains the appeal of one of the most popular video games of all time: *Tetris*. The game incessantly drops differently shaped blocks into a field, and the player is supposed to rotate and move the blocks so that they stack up neatly. If the player creates an uninterrupted wall of blocks at the bottom of the field, he is rewarded with points and a bit of fanfare. The high points of *Tetris* games are seeing a cavity in your wall at the bottom of the screen and then having the game deal you a block that fits it perfectly so that you knock out several rows at once. *Tetris* is appealing because it presents us with rows of unfinished tasks, and then occasionally lets us finish them to erase them from both the game and our thoughts.

But what's even more insidious is when a game slips something into your quest log without your even realizing it, like some kind of reverse pickpocket. To see how this works, imagine that two people decide that their cars are filthy and each goes to the same car wash. Let's call these people Kim and Carlos. With their washes they each receive a special card that lets them earn a free car wash if they get the card stamped enough times during future visits. Kim's card says it requires 10 purchases for a free wash, but the perky girl at the counter gave her a head start with 2 free stamps. The card Carlos got doesn't have any free starter stamps, but it only requires 8 future purchases instead of 10. So both Kim and Carlos are looking at the same number of purchases to score their complimentary car cleaning: eight. Who do you think is more likely to come back enough times to fill up his or her card first? Kim or Carlos?

It turns out that it's Kim, who got saddled with a card that required 10 total stamps, but who received enough free stamps to get her 20 percent of the way toward her goal. This is thanks to a phenomenon related to the Zeigarnik effect called "the endowed-progress effect." Basically, the idea is that when you give people just a feeling of advancement toward a distant goal, they're more likely to try harder and try longer to reach that goal, even relative to people who have an equally easy goal but who got no sense of momentum off the bat. Researchers Joseph Nunes and Xavier Dreze coined the term in an article where they did the car wash experiment described above.[14] They found that 34 percent of people who got a 10-stamp card with 2 freebies ended up coming back enough to redeem the cards, compared to 19 percent of customers who started with an unstamped card requiring only 8 stamps. Nunes and Xavier also found that those endowed with the two free stamps tried to reach their goal faster by waiting less time between washes.

Why? The researchers argue that the reason for the results is that by giving out free stamps, the merchant was framing the task (i.e., buying enough car washes to get a freebie) as one that has already been undertaken. That creates tension and motivation to complete it. This has a few interesting possibilities for game design that we should keep in mind. Imagine, for example, that I'm playing through the role-playing game *Fallout: New Vegas* and I get a quest to save 10 prisoners from a nearby encampment. One way to deliver that quest to me would be to have me meet a nonplayer character and have her say, "Hey, there's 10 prisoners. Go free all 10." Off I would go, and the quest tracker would tick up "0 out of 10 prisoners rescued," and then "1 out of 10 prisoners rescued," and so on. Alternatively, if the game designer wanted to invoke the endowed-progress effect, I could first receive the quest upon opening the cell door for a pair of prisoners on the outskirts of the encampment. One of the slaves could say, "There were 12 of us that were captured! Free the others!," and my progress would start off as "2 out of 12 prisoners rescued" as the first 2 sprint off over the horizon to safety. According to everything discussed in the Nunes and Dreze study with the car washes, I'd be much more motivated to complete this quest if it were presented this way.

AUTONOMY: "I STABBED THAT ORC AND NOT THAT OTHER ONE"

What about autonomy, the second motivator in self-determination theory? That part of the theory holds that we are more satisfied with an activity when it allows us meaningful choices. Being able to choose which side quests we pursue or how to pursue them satisfies our need for autonomy. If, for example, a quest in the role-playing game *Skyrim* allows you to ally with either the rebels or the ruling class in the course of completing a chunk of the storyline, that lets us dabble in autonomy. Even something as simple as choosing an outfit for our characters in *The Sims* or the online environment of *Second Life* plays strongly into autonomy. Choices have to be real and volitional, though, and the game can't manipulate us into them. Early on in the mobile game *Kim Kardashian: Hollywood*, for example, the player is supposedly given the choice of whether or not to let the eponymous Kardashian into her store after hours. One of the dialogue options amounts to "Take a hike, we're closed," but if the player chooses this option, the Kardashian in question simply says, "Pleeeeeease?," and the player's avatar proceeds to let her in. There is no real choice. It's no more motivating than if making that choice had resulted in "Game Over."

In other games, side quests offer autonomy simply by being available but optional. Open-world games like those in the *Assassin's Creed* series are stuffed with choices about what side activities to pursue. You can take on assassination contracts, climb landmarks, hunt down treasure, collect hidden items, upgrade your gear, or any number of other things. One the most exciting experiences in my gaming history to date was stepping outside of the constrained tutorial area of Vault 101 in the role-playing game *Fallout 3*. Laid out before me was the game's post-apocalyptic but very open world. I could go anywhere I wanted and be as good or evil as I wanted. Games that give you this kind of autonomy are going to be more compelling and players will engage for longer, say Rigby and Ryan.[15] Indeed, one study by these researchers surveyed people after playing *Super Mario 64* and found that those who reported experiencing greater feelings of autonomy also said that they not only liked the game but wanted to play it more.[16]

There is another angle to autonomy, though, in that humans hate to lose options once they think they have them. This is a phenomenon that some psychologists have termed "psychological reactance."[17] Clever game designers sometimes take advantage of it. For example, the game development studio BioWare turns out complex, character-driven role-playing game franchises like *Mass Effect*, *Dragon Age*, and *Star Wars: Knights of the Old Republic*. A while back, I was playing through *Dragon Age: Origins* and found myself facing one of BioWare's signature dilemmas: With which of the nonplayer characters should I pursue a romantic interest? Should I woo the crabby but sexy Morrigan, or should I court the more pure-hearted and worldly Leliana? BioWare's inclusive attitude toward same-sex couples even would have let me pursue the roguish Zevran. But choosing one romance would require completing a set of quests that would close the door to the others. Oh, I couldn't commit! Instead I strung all three of them along as far as I could until one of them confronted me around the campfire at night and forced me to choose.

Why did I invest so much mental and emotional energy into a pointless choice between three make-believe people in a video game? Part of the reason is that humans hate to lose choices, goals, and freedoms. Or, more to the point, we hate to lose options for choice. Psychologist Jack Brehm coined the term "psychological reactance" to explain this concept.[18] A child will want the toy she showed no interest in moments earlier just because her sibling is playing with it now, but her mom and dad are also guilty of this quirk. One well-timed study showed that when Florida shoppers learned that a certain kind of laundry detergent was to be banned in their state, they rushed not only to horde the soapy goods while they could but also to start organizing caravans to import them from neighboring states.[19]

A line of research by Jiwoong Shin and Dan Ariely also provided a striking example of psychological reactance that I think directly relates to my inability to let go of romance options in *Dragon Age*.[20] Jiwoong and Ariely created a computer game where participants could choose between three doors—red, blue, or green. Players had only 100 mouse clicks to "spend" in the game by clicking to navigate between doors and then clicking in the rooms on the other side of each door. Doing so yielded a random amount of money within a certain range. The red room, for example, could pay between 3 and 9 cents for each one of the player's limited clicks, but the blue room might pay between 8 and 16 cents. Only, the players didn't know the ranges; they had to experiment to determine the optimal way to play the game and maximize their payout. But if a player ignored a certain room for 12 turns (i.e., clicks), the door to that room would shrink and eventually disappear. Gone was that option! But players could "reset" the door by exiting their current room and then clicking on the dwindling door before it disappeared completely. This act cost two clicks without generating any money, and so it was an irrational waste of clicks if used on a subpar door.

What did people tend to do? Even after discovering which room yielded the highest payout of real money, they still tended to go back and waste clicks on lower- paying doors just to keep those options open, even though they didn't intend to actually exercise them. This hurt their game performance and their earnings, but psychological reactance made them reluctant to lose those options. I think the same thing is at play when we wring our hands over closing the door to one of the quest lines relating to BioWare's trademark romances or any other mutually exclusive choices in a game, especially after the point where we have nothing to gain by drawing things out. The same could apply to choosing which warring faction to align with in *Skyrim* or whether to support Templars or Mages in *Dragon Age: Inquisition*. This kind of thing is so common in character progression and achievement as to be mundane. For example, when we accumulate enough experience points in *Dark Souls*, we can choose to spend them on upgrading weapons or increasing any number of abilities, such as dexterity or vitality. Game designers can also do the same thing by giving us irrevocable choices in narrative branches. Making choices that kill the player creates little tension, because you can usually load a saved game. But forcing a player to make a choice and pursue an objective that will result in losing one party member or closing off an entire part of the game world will cause real consternation. The research on SDT shows that players love choices in their games and will be happier when they have them, but on the flip side, players hate losing those choices. A developer with a strong vision can make this work by leveraging psychological reactance to inject gobs of hand-wringing into the experience that will be remembered for a long time.

RELATEDNESS: "THE PEASANTS WERE SUPER HAPPY WHEN I STABBED THAT ORC"

The final psychological need from SDT is relatedness. This motivator deals with the need to feel a meaningful connection with other people—usually other players, but even fictional ones like characters in a video game. We will go through much effort to feel these connections, and progress-related game elements often help us. Simply completing a quest and earning the adoration of nonplayer characters is close enough to the real thing, say Przybylski, Ryan, and Rigby.[21] Some games directly scratch the relatedness itch by having team-oriented goals and quests that require player cooperation. Any massively multiplayer game will have challenges that require groups of people to complete—sometimes dozens at a time, in the case of world events or massive dungeon raids. The whole group has the same goal—take down a raid boss in *Destiny*, for example—but each player has a very specific role to play, and each player is relying on others to do something specific. This makes you matter to other people, and it's a nice feeling when you do what's needed of you. Other games like *PlanetSide 2* feature territory control where winning a battle can mean that resources and areas are available for teammates who log in hours later. The space exploration game *Eve Online* takes relatedness to perhaps the furthest extreme, where players have to band together into corporations and other alliances to protect each other and exchange resources. I think that like many massively multiplayer online games, *Eve Online* can be more about managing social relationships and obligations than exploring space, and that makes it engrossing and satisfying to its hundreds of thousands of players.

Our collection of achievements, badges, and trophies in a game also tell other people about what games we play and how much better (or worse) we are at them. And it's not just about a longer list. It's about a more varied and interesting list that tells people that you're a varied and interesting kind of person. Your gamer score on the Xbox consoles is essentially an index of how many achievements you have earned, presented in a number that is easy to compare with other players, as are the metrics shown in iOS's Game Center app. This is one reason why I think that systems with "rarity" metrics attached to their achievements are more appealing. The digital platform Steam, for example, shows for each achievement the percentage of people on the platform who have earned it. Looking at the Steam game *Wolfenstein: The New Order* right now, I can see that I'm one of the 8.7 percent of players who managed to get the "Vaporize" achievement for maxing out the demolition skill tree. That's a lot of Nazi storm troopers blown to bits. You should be impressed.

That figure of 8.7 percent sounds pretty good to me, but some people want to stand even farther apart from the crowd. They want to chase down the ultimate achievements for the ultimate bragging rights. The notoriously punishing action-adventure game *Dark Souls 2*, for example, has one of the most difficult achievements I've seen. Players get special rewards for finishing the game without dying even once and without using any of the game's bonfires, which serve both as in-game save points and a way to quickly travel around the game world. *Dark Souls* is a game series that will kill even experienced players frequently, especially if they are not careful. Getting these special rewards requires an enormous amount of skill and knowledge about the game, but you have to get them in one run. Given how fragile your character is in *Dark Souls 2*, one tiny mistake could undo hours and hours of progress. Getting that achievement is really difficult, and even the nudges we've discussed so far seem like they would be insufficient in the face of such a challenge. And yet it's not hard to find other examples of punishingly difficult achievements that net you more controller-biting frustration than gaming pleasure. Beat this cheap boss without taking any damage. Complete the game using only the weakest weapon. But some people do it, as evidenced by YouTube videos and seeing the evidence in the achievements list of other players. Why?

An article titled "Conceptual Consumption" published in the 2009 *Annual Review of Psychology* suggests some clues.[22] The authors explore a theory which holds that people are as interested in consuming ideas, information, and concepts as they are physically consuming things—sometimes more so. People want to "possess" an experience simply because it's novel and rare, and they will sometimes forgo other more rational choices in order to do it. For some people, there's a drive to add that concept or experience to their list of "stuff I've done" just so they can have the satisfaction of a longer list. Researchers Anat Keinan and Ran Kivetz liken this to ticking items off a life's to-do list or an "experiential resume" so that they can die feeling like they've accomplished more in life.[23] These are the same kind of people, Keinan and Kivetz say, who elect to stay in hotel rooms carved out of ice instead of a Florida Marriott or to eat bacon-flavored ice cream instead of chocolate. Similarly, getting the achievement for beating *Dark Souls 2* under such absurdly difficult restrictions is a way of relating to friends and strangers that you're the kind of hardcore person who has really mastered the game. After all, that experiential resume is no good if you can't show it to anyone.

So markers of progress matter in that they can be a direct path to satisfying our basic psychological needs for competence, autonomy, and relatedness. That's why the most successful games feature role-playing game mechanics, such as leveling up weapons in first-person shooters like *Call of Duty*, quest and side missions in open-world franchises like *Assassin's Creed*, and the increasing emphasis on achievements in games like *Dead Space 3* or *Portal 2* that can be earned only through cooperative play. And within each of these uses of progress-related game elements, there are various psychological tricks to keep you running on the treadmill and to keep you wanting to finish some goal that you don't even remember starting. But progress-related elements aren't the only mechanics that can motivate people to grind. Sometimes players keep flailing wildly, even though they get no feedback, have no clear target, and have no progress bars inching their way toward completion. Players just swing in the hopes that they'll eventually hit a piñata and something cool will drop out. So let's look at the psychology of loot drops next.

THINGS TO REMEMBER FROM THIS CHAPTER

- "Self-determination theory" offers a framework for understanding why people are motivated to keep playing games. We do it to satisfy needs for "competence, autonomy, and relatedness."
- Competence relates to feeling like we're doing well and getting better.
- Autonomy is satisfied when we feel we are given meaningful decisions to make.
- Relatedness happens when we feel that we are important to others.

- The "Zeigarnik effect" and the "endowed-progress effect" describe our preoccupation with tasks that are begun but not yet finished. Think side quests here.
- "Psychological reactance" is related to how we hate to lose options once we have them. Remember how stressful it is to choose between branching storylines and romance options in some role-playing games.
- Gaming achievements/trophies and in-game possessions can be used to signal our status and accomplishments to other players. This is true even if they're outlandish and unreasonably difficult to acquire.

7

HOW DO DEVELOPERS KEEP US SO EXCITED ABOUT NEW LOOT?

"The terrible truth is that a whole lot of us begged for a Skinner Box we could crawl into, because the real world's system of rewards is so much more slow and cruel than we expected it to be."
—David Wong, novelist and Cracked.com editor[1]

"Loot" in gaming parlance is the rewards you get for defeating monsters or completing quests. It's separate from experience points or knowledge, so it includes things like treasure, gold, crafting materials, ammo, armor, or weapons. Most gamers invited to play a round of "Answer My Question or I'll Push the Button Again" would probably name the *Diablo* series as the perfect example of a loot-driven game. These action-adventure clickfests emphasize killing demons from an overhead view of gothic environments, featuring cathedrals, medieval hamlets, and hell itself. The games also emphasize improving your barbarian, demon hunter, or wizard through not only leveling up but also acquiring better equipment. Better equipment means higher numbers. Higher numbers mean being able to defeat tougher monsters to get better equipment, which means even higher numbers, and so on. Also, your character just looks cooler wearing better equipment. As in many role-playing video games, the loot drops in *Diablo* are largely random. Particularly tough enemies ("elites") and particularly resplendent treasure chests have a higher chance of dropping something good, but epic loot can come from anywhere. I once found an awesome battle-axe that served my barbarian very well for many levels, and it was hidden in an ordinary-looking barrel sitting out in an ordinary-looking hallway that I just happened to smash. Because of that find, I cracked open almost every other barrel, vase, crate, box, urn, sarcophagus, pot, rock pile, bookcase, basket, jug, casket, bone pile, hollow log, cocoon, loose stone, and chest I could find in the hope of getting something else that good.

This is what game developers often call a "core loop," or sometimes a "feedback loop." You perceive a cue that you can do a thing, you do the thing, you are rewarded for doing the thing, you do the thing again the next time you see the cue. Even after finishing the main campaign in the *Diablo* games, players will continue to replay parts of it, making runs on difficult elites and bosses in the hopes of getting them to drop better and better loot. Some players will do this for literally hundreds of hours, keeping the game and its community alive for years and providing an evergreen market for sequels, add-ons, and in-game purchases.

The 1996 debut game in the *Diablo* series was a pretty solid product and a pioneer of the loot-based game market, but 2001's *Diablo II* perfected the design. This second game in the series had the same basic design I described earlier: Move through a randomly generated environment, click on monsters to make them burst like gory piñatas, scoop up the candy/loot, and repeat. Again, some of the loot would be worthless (like equipment with no benefits to your class), and some would be of only minimal value (like a few gold pieces). But some of it would be spectacularly awesome. The game's brilliance came from how expertly it spaced out the awesome among the mediocre and worthless. Getting a weapon or piece of armor that massively improved your character happened just frequently enough to motivate players to keep playing so they could hit the next jackpot. And as we will see, the analogy to the one-armed bandits found in casinos everywhere is pretty apt.

Coupled with the rise of the World Wide Web, though, *Diablo II*'s emphasis on loot created a new problem for Blizzard. Many players wanted the awesome stuff, but they couldn't or wouldn't put in the time to get it through random drops. So some people with more money than time looked to trading with other players within multiplayer game sessions. This was often facilitated by third-party websites where one could arrange to exchange real money for virtual game items. These services ranged from just some guy on a message board to surprisingly robust and automated online stores. But they all frequently required players to find what they wanted, then release PayPal or credit card information into the wilds of the Internet. Then shoppers would have to coordinate delivery and receipt of the items, usually by meeting up with someone within the game or temporarily taking control of one of the vendor's "mule" accounts with the help of yet another player or friend. At best it was an awkward experience, and at worst it attracted scammers who would cheat or steal. Blizzard saw this, and though *Diablo*'s product managers surely felt bad for their customers when they got ripped off or had their accounts hijacked, they also probably regretted not taking in some of those profits themselves. At least a little. And so they figured they could solve both problems by offering a better product and a more trustworthy service.

This is why it was a huge deal among loot fans when Blizzard announced that 2012's long-awaited *Diablo III* would solve the problem of third-party item sales by having in-game auction houses. These virtual storefronts would let players sell their unwanted gear and safely buy exactly what they wanted from other players who created their own auctions. Need level 15 pants that are + strength and + vitality? No problem, you'll be able to choose from 35 different pairs up for sale, starting at 360 gold pieces. Pick a color. This announcement caused the community's first collective eyebrow to arch in surprise, but what made the other one join it in an expression of complete amazement was that in addition to the auction house based on the in-game currency of gold, a second auction house would be available where players could sell and buy using real-world money. As in a "give me $100 and I'll give you this stupidly awesome sword" kind of arrangement. I remember reading mixed reactions from fans and the gaming press when the auction houses were first announced, but when *Diablo III* came out they clearly worked as intended. Buying items within the game was safe and easy. Some lucky (or supremely diligent) players who managed to acquire highly desirable items even got some pocket money out of the system.

But in fixing one problem, Blizzard created an unintended consequence for what had always been the core of the *Diablo* games: the joy of the loot drop. The story of how the game developers working on *Diablo III* figured this out and how they walked away from steady revenue in order to get the game back on the right track wonderfully illustrates what it really is about the loot-drop mechanic that game developers so often use to keep us playing long after we've seen 99.9 percent of what a game has to offer. But to understand more, we first need to consider how a psychologist once taught pigeons to play ping-pong.

A PSYCHOLOGIST ONCE TAUGHT PIGEONS TO PLAY PING-PONG!

Let's play another little game called "Name any psychologist except Sigmund Freud." Some of you probably said "Sigmund Freud," in which case I urge you to review the rules of the game. Many of you, though, probably said "B. F. Skinner." He's the American psychologist made famous by his research in the field of behaviorism. Skinner is most remembered for the boxes bearing his name, which he used to train animals through a process called "operant conditioning": perform a task, get a reward, repeat. This kind of stirred things up in the psychology world at the time, since more than a few people's thinking followed the rut formed by Ivan Pavlov and his slobbering dogs. They (Pavlov's followers, not the dogs) thought that you shouldn't even try to study internal mental processes that you can't directly observe. They had concerned themselves mostly with how reflexive actions, like salivating at the smell of delicious meat powder, could be conditioned to happen in response to an unrelated stimulus, like the sound of a bell, if paired under the right conditions.

But Skinner thought that there were internal thoughts and other mental processes at work that would associate voluntary behavior with consequences. The Skinner boxes were contraptions where he could put the rewards and punishments of operant conditioning to work. Reward an animal with a treat for pressing a lever and it will press the lever more. Punish it with an electric shock and it will press it less. This is how Skinner taught those pigeons to play ping-pong: He had two of the birds face each other across an adorable little ping-pong table, then rewarded each bird with a bit of food if it managed to peck the ball past its opponent. There are videos of these avian athletes preserved on the Web if you're interested. Search for "Skinner pigeon ping-pong" on YouTube if you want to spend a few minutes giggling and clapping your hands while you watch them go at it. Training the birds to do what might have seemed like a supremely weird task took a while, since pecking ping-pong balls across tables is not something they normally do. Skinner had to use a process called "shaping" where he rewarded the birds for baby steps toward that end. Stand at the edge of the table, get a treat. Look at the ball, get a treat. Peck the ball, get a treat. Peck the ball across the line, get a treat. Keep at it and eventually you've got guys in white lab coats gathered around the table, cheering at the top of their lungs and using their grant money to bet on the 1948 Pigeon Ping-Pong World Cup. If you're curious, "Gregory Peck" eked out a victory against "Calvin Coolidge" in the last of a seven-game series. Also, I spent way too much time coming up with clever pigeon names.

At this point you can probably guess how I'm going to tie this into video games, and you may not be surprised to learn that "Skinner box" is a widely used term in the game development community. The dungeons of the *Diablo* games act as Skinner boxes. You go into them, and then you figure out what to click on to get the best rewards. It's just something you do automatically in the game when you see a chest or an elite monster. I can't even imagine having my avatar walk right past a chest in that game. It would actually stress me out a little. This is what's called a "compulsion loop": you see a trigger (the treasure chest), you perform an action (you click on it), and you get a reward (loot).

As an aside, this is also what makes people repeatedly pull out their phone to check their e-mail, Twitter, Facebook, Instagram, Pinterest, or whatever other social networking tools they're into. They hear a ding, they open the app, and they get rewarded with some new loot in the form of a message, photo, or upvote. Nir Eyal, technology consultant and author of *Hooked: How to Build Habit-Forming Products*, also notes that the most successful products add a fourth step to the compulsion loop: commitment. If a user invests time, money, personal data, or social capital in the product after getting the reward, he's more likely to start the whole loop over again the next time the trigger happens. The game developer Valve apparently understands this. The treasure chests in their free-to-play games *Team Fortress 2* and *Dota 2* require keys to open. How do you get a key? By committing real money to the game. But you can't just buy a key; you have to put a minimum of $5.00 in your "Steam Wallet" account to make the purchase. With that commitment made, you're more likely to use one of the keys (or buy one on the spot) to open the next chest you find. Games can also bank on other kinds of commitments. Facebook games that encourage players to advertise what they are playing get them to commit social capital and their online reputation. Many online games let you link to your characters' builds, loadouts, and progress, which is another form of committing social capital. Even the accumulation of loot is a kind of investment, in that if you stop playing and stop looking for the next piece to improve your loadout, you'll feel like you're throwing away your hard work.

What's really eye-opening is that you don't even have to be the one that receives the reward for operant conditioning to work. Psychologist Albert Bandura developed a model of learning called "social learning theory" and did research that shows how you can learn and become conditioned through watching what happens to others. The most famous of Bandura's experiments in this area involved kids who learned to beat the living daylights out of a doll by having them watch someone else enjoy doing so. (We'll return to Bandura and that poor doll later in the chapter on video game violence. It'll be great.) If we see others rewarded for a behavior, we internalize that lesson and it can kick off our own compulsion loop. Many games capitalize on this by broadcasting when good things happen to other players. *Diablo III*, in fact, tells players when their friends or members of their guild get a particularly good piece of loot by putting a message in the game's chat area. The name of the item is even highlighted so that you can pause what you're doing to click on it to bask in how fabulous it is. *Team Fortress 2* does something similar by telling everyone in the current match when someone is awarded a new cosmetic item or weapon.

Sorry to say, but playing loot-based games like *Diablo* means you're not that far off from a pigeon playing ping-pong. Scientists who train monkeys to press a button to get a treat using this kind of compulsion loop can get them to sit in a chair and ignore distractions, such as other monkeys or different food. They will just sit there waiting for the signal to press the button to come up on their computer screen. Remind you of anyone? Sure, one of the defining traits of humans is that our brains possess executive functions that can override this kind of conditioning if we will it, but often we decide to keep on going because we want the next reward. Compulsion loops and operant conditioning are pretty effective, which is why they're found everywhere.

But is that the end of the story? Is this the part of the loot mechanic that Blizzard broke with its auction house for *Diablo III*? Nope, because there's one other aspect of loot hunting that's more important than anything I've discussed yet: its randomness and the sense of antici-pation that comes with it.

Like slot machines payouts, loot drops in *Diablo*, *Borderlands*, *World of Warcraft*, *Destiny*, *Marvel Puzzle Quest*, *Dota 2*, and many other games are random. You may get something lame, you may get something epic, and in some games you may get nothing at all. The Japanese government went so far as to outlaw a certain kind of random-loot game mechanic called "kompu gacha," which encouraged players to spend real money in social games in order to complete sets of items through random drops.[2] The games were very profitable, but officials felt that the feedback loop was too effective—indeed, it caused some players to spend the equivalent of thousands of dollars a month—and it was too frequently used deceptively in games targeted at children. That was obviously a special case involving real money, but many game de-velopers still use random loot drops to perform a bit of psychological judo on a system in our brain that's critical for survival but that makes hunting for epic loot even more compulsive. To understand why, and to understand why *Diablo III*'s auction house was a catastrophe for the game's core mechanic, let's move over and up the evolutionary tree of life, from pigeons to monkeys. And grab a case of apple juice; the monkeys love that stuff.

UNEXPECTED DOPAMINE FREAKOUTS CAN'T PREDICT THE UNPREDICTABLE

The *Diablo* games and others like them have plenty of different kinds of loot, and much of it is predictable. Open a chest in the first-person shooter *Borderlands* and you know you're going to get some ammuni-tion, just like you'll get some gold out of every chest in *Diablo III*. Run over a medkit in an *Unreal Tournament* game and you know you're going to get health back. Those are examples of rewards given on a fixed schedule, because you get them every time you do a specific action. But the power of loot-based games relies on what's known as a "variable schedule": sometimes you open the chest or kill the monster and you get nothing, or at most nothing good. Other times, though, you get a fist full of awesome—some seemingly endless cascade of cash or some new weapon that doubles the amount of damage you can do to your enemies.

Across a variety of animals, situations, and outcomes, random rewards outperform any other kind of reward schedule in terms of getting the person (or animal) to do what you want.[3] Predictable rewards get boring. But never knowing if you're going to get something good or not? That's mesmerizing. This is because it turns out that it's not the loot itself that's so exciting to us. Of course, gamers love some equipment because it lets them do things better—having a sniper scope on your catapult is useful, so that's surely part of it. But it turns out that what really excites us is not so much the loot as it is the loot *drop*. And actually, if you want to get really specific about it, it's the *anticipation* of the loot drop.

In 1954, neuroscientists James Olds and Peter Milner were jamming electrodes into rat brains. Don't ask why; it's just a thing that neuroscientists do. One day when they inserted a wire into an area of the rat's brain called the *nucleus accumbens*, they accidentally hit on an important bit of grey matter, and the electric current in the wire caused the rodents' brain to be flooded with the neurotransmitter dopamine.[4] A collection of just 22 atoms, dopamine is a chemical that plays a huge role in regulating decision-making, particularly goal-oriented behavior and the pursuit of pleasure. When we encounter something we like— say a patch of berries or a Strong Gothic Axe of Slaughter—our brain releases dopamine. Brain cells that are sensitive to that chemical go bananas when it is present, which makes us feel good. These cells are known as dopamine receptors. Olds and Milner's rats didn't fare too well with so much dopamine, though. With their pleasure centers constantly buzzing, they ignored food, water, and even *Diablo III*. Technically they died of thirst, but in a way they were killed by ceaseless euphoria.

Now let's stick with monkeys and dopamine, but move over to Switzerland. German-born neuroscientist Wolfram Schultz was at the University of Fribourg conducting research on the relationship between the chemical dopamine and Parkinson's disease when he almost accidentally started a line of research that can be used to explain gamers' love of loot drops. Over the course of years, Schultz experimented with macaque monkeys while monitoring their dopamine receptors. Schultz and his colleagues discovered that presenting a lab monkey with a bit of fruit juice caused the creature's dopamine neurons to light up. They also discovered that when they repeatedly preceded the treat with a light or a sound, the neurons would start to fire when the monkey saw the light or heard the sound, but they would remain relatively inactive when the fruit juice showed up.[5] The cue—the light, an image on a screen, or a sound—had basically become the reward because it was so inextricably tied to the fruit juice. The system they had discovered was, at its core, about anticipation and trying to predict rewards based on what was happening in the environment.[6] You may recognize this as exactly the kind of operant conditioning via fixed reward schedules used to train the ping-pong pigeons I discussed earlier, except that now we're drilling down into the neurochemistry of it.

But things got more interesting when Schultz started to mess with the monkeys' heads. Well, he had already literally messed with their heads by inserting electrodes into them, but now he started doing things like delaying the reward after the monkey pushed the button.[7] Or diluting the fruit juice. Or withholding the reward altogether. When this happened, the monkey seemed to get upset. The predictive model in its head had failed, and this caused it some consternation. Repeated failure to deliver on the predicted treat would cause the neurons to fail to fire at all.

This makes sense from an evolutionary perspective. In his book *The Science of Happiness*,[8] Stefan Klein notes, "Whenever dopamine is released, it sets off the signal that the decision was a right one and that something good has happened." If humans can be said to have a superpower relative to other animals, it's pattern recognition. Our brains are generally sensitive to patterns and adept at making predictions based on those patterns, especially when it comes to rewards. The thing is, though, that we're most sensitive to variations between what's predicted and what actually happens. Like a *Diablo III* player finding a +5 maul to replace his +3 hammer, if a monkey in Schultz's studies was suddenly presented with something it liked a little better than the fruit juice, the dopamine receptors would flare up in ways that made previous reactions seem like dull sputters.

This is because our brains, and the brains of certain animals, such as other primates, have evolved to seek out surprising and unexpected rewards. Dopamine receptors become much more excited when something good happens if it signals a prediction error. Surprising pleasures, it turns out, are the most joyous ones of all because they highlight failures in our predictive predilections. It's like the dopamine neurons were sitting up and yelling, "Hey! There's something really good here! Let's obsess over that until I can figure out why I didn't see it coming!" And so the tiny machinery in your brain goes to work trying to make new, updated predictions. In a predictable world, that's a handy thing, because it's about figuring out how to get more good stuff by learning what leads up to it. You found delicious berries in the shade of a certain tree? Maybe they're more likely to grow there, and you'll find more of them if you always check the base of that particular kind of tree.

But we can't predict the inherently unpredictable. This is how slot machines get you, and it's how random loot drops get you. In a casino, your dopamine neurons are trying really hard to learn what precedes a jackpot in terms of what bells you hear, pictures you see, or even which cocktail waitress last walked by. I rarely gamble, but once I went on a riverboat casino just for the experience. I sat down at a video poker machine and after plunking in a few dollars, I got a lucky hand: a full house that paid out a couple hundred dollars to my small bet. Woo! At the machine next to me sat a retiree wearing a John Deere hat. He had a plastic bucket of quarters on his left and an overflowing ashtray on his right, so it seemed to me that he had been there a while. He seemed genuinely happy for my win and even offered his congratulations, but immediately after doing so he got up and started to leave. I asked him where he was going, and he said that I had used up all the luck in that row of machines; he had to move down a row if he wanted to hit his own jackpot.

This was absurd, I knew, and I'm pretty sure that he knew it at some level too. But the reward system that drives our brain is obsessed with predictions even when we're dealing with video poker machines and loot drops that other parts of our brain understand can't be predicted. The result can be what is called the "post hoc, ergo propter hoc" fallacy (Latin for "after this, therefore because of this"), which describes our bias toward assuming that two events are related just because one happens after the other. In his book *The Proteus Effect*, Nick Yee talks about this fallacy in the context of some of the amusing stories he heard while interviewing the players of massively multiplayer online role-playing games like *Everquest* and *World of Warcraft*.[9] Downed bosses or treasure chests in the games could yield magnificent loot, but it was random, and the very best prizes were exceedingly rare. They dropped in as few as 1 or 2 percent of cases. And yet people had a hard time believing that these drops were completely random. The prediction systems in players' brains led them to believe in all kinds of superstitions about what had caused the good loot drops to happen, or made them more likely to happen. Players reported thinking that they could make these valued items more likely to appear if they faced a certain cardinal direction, wore certain lucky charms, or had a certain character enter the dungeon first. This happens in the *Diablo* games, prompting one exasperated community manager on the official forums to tell fans, "Streaks of bad luck are going to happen, and we all go through them. The danger lies in the spread of misinformation, which in turn can inspire players to alter their in-game habits in ways that actually have no influence over what items they find."

My favorite example of such misinformation and altered habits from Yee's book involves a bug in *Dungeons & Dragons Online* that allowed players to use the "Diplomacy" skill on treasure chests. Normally this would be disallowed since negotiating with, flattering, and sweetening up an inanimate object like a treasure chest makes no sense. But a bug in the game allowed players to do it anyway. Using the skill had no effect on anything, but the post hoc, ergo propter hoc fallacy led players to become convinced that using the skill in this way would increase the odds of their getting more treasure. Our minds will seize on anything to avoid feeling like it can't predict when good things—and good loot—are going to happen. And yet it gets excited every time a prediction goes wrong.

WHAT THE *DIABLO III* AUCTION HOUSES FAILED TO PREDICT

So let's return to the auction house in *Diablo III* and see why Blizzard actually had a problem on its hands even after it created a safe, reliable way to buy and sell equipment. The game's predecessor, *Diablo II*, was really good at keeping players around and hunting for loot because of the compulsion loops and dopamine freakouts discussed above. Everything was built around that loop of finding a treasure chest or elite enemy that you knew could drop something good, then clicking on it, repeatedly, to see what popped out. This process played off our brain's reward system, which has evolved to pay special attention to beneficial but unexpected rewards. The loot rewards were engineered to be just frequent enough to prevent our brains from calming the heck down and moving on to another game.

But *Diablo III*'s auction houses unraveled that loot loop, because making a run to the auction house was a far more efficient way to get really good equipment. Once players flooded the economy with tons of items, the laws of economics took hold and prices plummeted. For a trivial amount of gold, you could hit the auction house, completely swap out every piece of equipment you had on you for something better, and venture back out in just a few minutes. This meant that equipment drops lost much of their meaning, as did the sight of treasure chests and elite monsters that players had been conditioned to associate with them. Loot was just money in a slightly less convenient form, destined to be sold to an in-game merchant or, at best, in the auction house. For sure, particularly rare loot for those with characters at the highest level was still valuable and sought after. But those drops were exceedingly rare and not experienced by the majority of players. Even worse, much of the loot wouldn't even be usable because the character was the wrong class or not at a high enough level. It's always annoying to find a rare upgrade for a class you don't even play. Getting loot in *Diablo III* of almost any kind didn't confer any immediate benefit, and the process of listing and selling even a valuable piece of loot on the auction house was too far removed from the visual and gameplay cues that signaled it to be very motivating. This new system turned an epic quest for fabulous treasures into a quick jaunt to the department store, and you'd just repeat the trip whenever the game started to get difficult or you thought you passed some minimum level requirement for the next tier of gear. As a result, people were playing the auction house instead of the game to get better gear. It wasn't nearly as much fun.

But you have to hand it to the developers at Blizzard because they didn't bury their heads in the sand. In fact, they were willing to disregard all the work they had sunk into building the auction houses and fix things. And remember that Blizzard took a cut of every sale in the real-money version of the auction house. That means that even if the system was bad for the game, they were making money off it. In September 2013, John Hight (production developer at Blizzard) and Josh Mosqueira (*Diablo III*'s lead game developer) appeared in a YouTube video to discuss a pair of sweeping changes meant to bring *Diablo III* back to its core.[10] "When we originally set up the auction house," said Hight, "it was supposed to be a safe and convenient way for you to trade items. And in that respect it was very successful, but it became a double-edged sword." Mosqueira jumped in to note that *Diablo*'s core premise should be simple but compelling: Kill monsters to get cool loot. "The auction houses," he concluded, "just made that experience way too convenient and really short-circuited our core reward loop."

This announcement went along with another important change that had been previously announced and was code-named "Loot 2.0." The idea was that the game would drop less loot in the form of items, but it would be smarter about what it dropped. It would be much more unusual, for example, to get a shiny new piece of equipment that was unusable because it was for the wrong class, was restricted to characters at a higher level, or had a useless attribute like +233 Intelligence on a Barbarian's battle-axe. Because even though highly intelligent barbarians are great at dinner parties, big vocabularies aren't much good for hacking up the hordes of hell. The result of Loot 2.0 and the razing of the auction houses was that instead of a steady stream of junk, loot drops meant something again. They were rewards that players were much more likely to need and want since one-stop shopping at the auction house was a thing of the past. You have to admire Blizzard for doing this, both because it displayed a solid understanding of the psychology behind why loot works and because the real-money auction house had been earning them revenue. On top of that, gutting the auction house necessitated other substantial adjustment to the game's economy that required a lot of time and effort. But in the end, I suppose they just decided that a better game—not to mention a more addictive one—was the right call. Chalk this one up to using psychology for good.

THINGS TO REMEMBER FROM THIS CHAPTER

- Well-established theories about the timing of rewards do a pretty good job of explaining why gamers love loot drops.

- The random nature of loot drops is essential. It works because the prediction systems in our brains want us to pay special attention to failed predictions.
- The "post hoc, ergo propter hoc" fallacy describes how we tend to think that two things are related just because we see one happening after the other. This can lead to some amusing superstitions and rituals.
- Seriously, one time these psychologists taught pigeons to play ping-pong. They got paid for this.
- The *Diablo III* auction houses hurt the game's core loot loop because they downplayed the importance of randomness.

Part 3

Those Who Sell

8

HOW DO GAMES MAKE US FEEL IMMERSED IN IMAGINARY WORLDS?

"Your mind makes it real."

—Morpheus

Anyone else out there remember the 1982 movie *Tron*? It flopped at the box office, but it's beloved by nerds because of one very powerful idea: proto-gamer Kevin Flynn (played by Jeff Bridges) gets zapped into a world where the video games he had programmed are very much real and all around him. He's literally in the game. At the time the movie was released, video games were just crude collections of beeps, boops, and pixels that were supposed to be dragons but looked more like ducks. Any delusions of being pulled into their imaginary worlds required the suspension of so much disbelief as to risk internal injury. Yet here was Kevin Flynn leaving the real world behind so he could battle in digital arenas, zip around on light cycles, and sling a glowing Frisbee at a compound-interest program that just wanted to work at a savings-and-loan company. It was amazing, and the 10-year-old me wanted nothing more than to experience that kind of immersion within a game world. Fortunately, the much older me almost can thanks to how far technology and game design have come. (If you're too young to remember seeing *Tron* as a kid, refer to Neo and *The Matrix*. Close enough.)

"Immersion" is a common part of marketing material for new video games, and gamers love to talk about how titles such as *Skyrim* or

Grand Theft Auto make them feel like they're really present in a world where they can do all kinds of stupid (but awesome) stuff. Developers of these games often design with immersion in mind, crafting dynamic settings full of objects that you can interact with for no other reason than it makes the game world feel more real and authentic. Why spend 200 hours coding a system that lets players roll a hundred cheese wheels down a mountain and then suplex a mime into a hot dog cart? BECAUSE REALISM.

Yet immersion in the context of entertainment media isn't a new idea. Psychologists were studying it for decades before video games became popular. It's just that instead of video games they were studying how media consumers are pulled into the imaginary worlds created by books, radio, television, and movies. Also, these researchers didn't call it "immersion." They still don't. They call it "spatial presence" or sometimes just "presence," for short. The truth is that there are more types of presence than there are Pokémon. A survey of the literature turns up "social presence," "telepresence," and "self-presence," just to name a few, but the one that's closest to what most people describe as being immersed in a video game world is called "spatial presence." (I'll use that term and the shorter "presence" interchangeably in this chapter.) Spatial presence is the psychological state brought on when you forget that the world you're experiencing is created by technology. You forget about the controller, the edges of the screen, the neighbor's dog, and the other person in the room yelling, "Hey! Are you even listening to me?" I should also point out that researchers typically think of immersion as something different from presence. They usually describe immersion as paying close attention to a game or being surrounded by it, but when you experience presence it feels like you're actually in the game world, like Kevin Flynn and the world of *Tron*.

Many of us are familiar with this feeling of presence from firsthand experience, but it's been examined scientifically. Experiencing spatial presence has been empirically linked, for example, to how much people enjoy the media in question. People experiencing spatial presence also generally feel that their interactions with the game were easier, more intuitive, and user-friendly.[1] One 2013 study published in the journal *Cyberpsychology, Behavior, and Social Networking*, for example, looked at how much spatial presence people experienced while playing the role-playing game *The Elder Scrolls: Oblivion*.[2] It found that enjoyment of the game and spatial presence were strongly correlated across many game sessions. Another study examined the interaction between and among presence, skill, and psychological flow—that feeling that you're "in the zone."[3] The study found that the more presence players felt while playing the racing game *Need for Speed*, the more likely they were to experience psychological flow when their skill was matched to the challenge of the game. Yet another study has shown that people playing the platforming game *Super Mario 64* were more likely to experience spatial presence when they felt skilled at the game.[4] And, as we'll soon see, spatial presence is strongly related to our ability to understand, envision, and navigate the complex virtual environments that are part of many modern games.

So though many of us have a pretty good idea of what spatial presence is and how it affects our experience with a game based on our own experiences, the larger question of how it happens remains. What characteristics of video games are likely to elicit spatial presence? Some designers and researchers, such as Mike Abrash, who has pioneered the technology development at Valve Software and Oculus VR, argue that presence is attainable only through the use of sophisticated virtual reality (VR) technology. It happens when head-mounted virtual reality systems like the Oculus Rift fill your field of view, react to your head movements, and surround you with sound. "Presence is an incredibly powerful sensation," Abrash told the audience of game developers during a presentation on virtual reality at the 2014 Steam Dev Days conference.[5] "And it's unique to virtual reality. There's no way to create it in any other medium." Oculus VR spent millions of dollars developing its Oculus Rift virtual reality headset to do these kinds of things, and the results are impressive. Donning the Oculus Rift headset and standing on the edge of a virtual precipice will likely trigger very real feelings of peril, according to Jeremy Bailenson, who runs a virtual reality lab at Stanford University.[6] One of his favorite demonstrations for members of the press visiting his labs is to have them put on a sophisticated virtual reality headset so that they feel like they're standing in a simple, blank room. With a few taps on a keyboard, Bailenson then drops the virtual floor out from underneath the visitors in a cascade of tiles and watches their reaction. He has quickly learned to be ready to catch visitors whose legs buckle in a reflexive response to the sensation. This is the kind of spatial presence that virtual reality hardware can bring.

On the other hand, many other game designers and researchers argue that such bleeding-edge technology isn't necessary to create presence. Players, they say, can be transported to a game world through crafty design and game content that pique the player's interest without the use of anything as sophisticated as virtual reality headsets. As we will see later in this chapter, the reasons why even small, independent games can create presence have little to do with the cutting-edge technology or virtual reality.

So which camp is right? Is technology or game design more important for getting players to forget about the real world and journey to fictional realms? Psychologists have studied this question, and their research on presence is illuminating. But before we dive into the technology versus design question, it's worth taking a moment to better understand the concept of presence and what happens in the heads of players experiencing it.

"WHOA. HOW DID I GET HERE?": A MODEL OF SPATIAL PRESENCE

In 2007, a group of European researchers led by Matthias Hofer, Werner Wirth (both from the University of Zurich, in Switzerland), and Tilo Hartman (from the Hanover University of Music and Drama, in Germany) aimed to test the process by which spatial presence happens.[7] Donning pith helmets (let's assume), the researchers hunted down university students in the wilds of Portugal and Switzerland. Once captured and sedated (again, let's assume), the research subjects were put in front of a computer running a program with the slightly sinister name of the "House of Learning." Within the program's virtual environment was a 2-story manor with 10 rooms full of displays about the life of Wolfgang Amadeus Mozart. The hapless subjects explored the house and its displays about the famous classical composer for 10 minutes before being tagged, given a questionnaire, and released back into the wild. Each room in the House of Learning contained an average of zero cyberdemons, so even though it wasn't exactly a video game, it suited the researchers' purpose: to test their model of how spatial presence in a virtual reality environment is achieved.

This was just one study in a research program that several members of the team had been working on for years. It suggests that presence is achieved after two broad steps. First, players (or media users of any kind) form a mental representation or map of the virtual space or world being presented to them. Second, players begin to favor the game world as their primary point of reference for where they are—or as the researchers put it, "their primary ego reference frame."

Let's break those two steps down. The process starts with players forming a mental model of the game's make-believe space by looking at various cues (images, movement, sounds, and so forth) and then forming assumptions about the world that they may bring to the table. Then, once that mental image of the game world is created, the player must decide, either consciously or unconsciously, whether she feels like she's in that imagined world or in the real one. Of course, it's worth noting that this isn't necessarily a conscious decision with the prefrontal cortex's stamp of approval on it. It can be a subconscious, on the sly, slipped into sideways, and entered and exited constantly.

But this process obviously doesn't happen with every video game, and it doesn't happen for every gamer every time. Research on presence, including the study described above, confirms that there are a few basic tricks that technology and game content can facilitate to create a baseline of spatial presence. Let's start with the technology side of the equation.

VIRTUAL REALITY GETS LUCKEY: THE IMPORTANCE OF TECHNOLOGY

Palmer Luckey's story sounds quite like that of a typical geek wunderkind. Smart and curious, he was interested in electronics from an early age, especially as it related to video games. Luckey was a hardcore gamer who was always looking for—and sometimes creating—technology to improve his gaming experiences. He explored many different technologies, but by age 18 he was obsessively tinkering in his parents' Long Beach, California, garage to create something in his new, favorite gadget category: virtual reality headsets. Luckey had amassed a collection of such head-mounted displays (HMDs) but wasn't satisfied with any of them. But according to an interview he gave to *Wired* magazine in 2014, Luckey desired more spatial presence out of the devices and wanted to smooth out major roadblocks to that sensation, such as screen flickering, nauseating delays between head movements and head tracking, image blurring, and general image quality.[8] So Luckey kept tinkering until one day he announced to a virtual reality enthusiast message board that he had completed a HMD prototype that improved on all these areas.

Lucky for Luckey (I've waited so long to make that pun), his post caught the attention of id Software's John Carmack. If you were trying to identify the one person most responsible for pushing gaming hardware forward in the mid-1990s and early 2000s, you could build a very strong case for Carmack. id Software, which Carmack had co-founded and where he led technology developments, had popularized the first-person perspective in video games with *Wolfenstein 3D* and *Doom*. Later Carmack and his colleagues at id would push advances in 3D graphics cards, 3D acceleration, computer networking, and other areas of gaming with the *Quake* series. Carmack was used to being on the cutting edge, and though he suspected that virtual reality could be the next big thing, it needed people like Palmer Luckey to solve certain fundamental problems with the technology. He wrote to Luckey asking if he could have one of the HMD prototypes. The star-struck Luckey, who had grown up a fan of Carmack's and of id's games, eagerly agreed.

The same Wired.com article[9] describes how Carmack made improvements to the prototype and started cranking out code to run on it, including a version of the game *Doom 3*. More importantly, he started showing off the unit to people in the technology and video games business. Things progressed quickly, and in short order Luckey scrambled to create a company (which he called Oculus VR) and to start a crowdfunding project on Kickstarter.com to raise enough money to get things going for real. The Kickstarter fundraising drive was obscenely successful. It generated just under $2.5 million for the young Luckey and his new business partners, the ranks of which eventually included Carmack himself. The company continued to make improvements to its HMD and to gain fame in the gaming community. Facebook founder Mark Zuckerberg was so amazed by the Oculus Rift's ability to create spatial presence that he had Facebook buy the Oculus VR company for an incredible two billion-with-a-*B* dollars in 2014.[10]

As I write this, the Oculus Rift has not yet been released as a commercial product. Sony and other companies are getting into the HMD product category, so it remains to be seen who—if anyone—will be successful in that space. But the ultimate success or failure of any HMD is irrelevant to our discussion of spatial presence. Regardless of its performance in the marketplace, the Oculus Rift and other devices like it illustrate many of the ways technology can create presence, regardless of platform. Let's take a closer look at why.

Per Wirth's two-step model described above, a game will create spatial presence to the extent that it either makes it easier to form a rich mental model of a virtual world or makes it easier to lose track of the technology between us and that world so that we can adopt it as our primary reference point for where we are. A rich mental image of a game space depends primarily on the vividness of the sensory information coming out of the medium. In video games, this depends on the quality of the graphics, sound, and even haptic feedback such as you get from rumble controllers.

Some of the earliest research on spatial presence looked at simple factors, such as the size and resolution of the screen used.[11] Adopters of technology like 3D televisions and the Nintendo 3DS handheld platform would be smugly pleased to know that adding that third dimension to an image generally facilitates presence, specifically because it makes the medium that much more vivid. And virtual reality head-mounted displays like the Oculus Rift that completely wrap the user's field of view in 3D graphics will do even more to create vivid sensory information. In the case of the Oculus Rift, the technology mediating the experience will literally disappear when it is moved outside of even your peripheral vision. Oculus Rift developer Mike Abrash said in his 2014 Steam DevDays presentation that presence is much easier to experience when the display is high-resolution (e.g., 1080p is better than 720p) and offers as wide an angle view as possible.[12]

Other researchers have spoken of the importance of how a piece of media engages our senses when creating a rich mental model.[13] Seeing an ogre lumbering toward you in a game is good. Also hearing its thunderous footsteps is better. But feeling your controller rumble with each stride in addition to all that is the best. Virtual reality headsets not only hit you with immersive visuals and directional sound, but they also track your head and body movements to adjust the display according to your orientation in the real world. Some developers are even experimenting with an outward-facing camera that could see what your hands are doing and copy that feedback into the game world. But this kind of convergence of sensory information is possible with other technology. The company NaturalPoint makes a system called "TrackIR" where a screen-mounted tracker uses input from reflectors that you clip to a hat or headset. This tracks players' head movements and changes the on-screen view accordingly. Or take the Playstation 4 game *Infamous: Second Son*, which uses a clever trick with the speaker and gyroscope in the game controller to funnel several sensory channels into one experience. At one point in the game, your character uses a can of spray paint to tag a brick wall. To begin the process, the player must change his grip on the controller to mimic holding a can of spray paint, then shake it like he were priming it for use. The speaker embedded in the game controller makes clacking sounds like a ball bearing inside a spray can, and the tag pattern emerges on the screen as the player waves the controller around. The sensory experiences from visuals, motion, and sound all work together.

Paul Skalski from Cleveland State University explored this role of game controllers in presence and argued that controllers are more "natural" to the extent that they closely match the actions that you perform in the game and allow you to focus on the game instead of the technology in your hand.[14] Swinging a Nintendo Wii controller like a tennis racket in a game of *Wii Sports*, for example, is a very natural control scheme, as is using a driving wheel in a car racing game. Using the W, S, A, and D keys on a keyboard to control movement in a first-person shooter, however, is not nearly as natural, especially for those not used to it. Skalski and his colleagues suspected that more-natural controllers were more likely to foster spatial presence, so they put it to the test. In one study, they had volunteers play *Tiger Woods PGA Tour 07* with either a Wii controller, which required players to control their golfers by swinging the controller like a real golf club, or a gamepad, which required them to use buttons and thumb pads. Similarly, another follow-up study described in the same article had subjects play the racing game *Need for Speed Underground 2* with a keyboard, a gamepad, a joystick, or a steering wheel. In both studies, Skalski and his pals found that players not only enjoyed the games more when playing with a more-natural controller (e.g., the Wii controller or the steering wheel), but also they reported greater feelings of spatial presence. Why? Skalski argued that using more-natural controllers made it easier for players to retrieve mental models of how the real world worked, since they were familiar with the devices (a golf club or a car) that those controllers represented. Using button-based controllers or keyboards requires us to do a little mental work to imagine the golf swing or the steering correction. And the less work our minds have to do in constructing the mental model, the better. But creating a rich mental model and becoming immersed in it isn't about the hardware. The way it shows us the content is key, too.

Controllers and sensory channels aside, if we are to form a detailed picture of a physical space from what we see on a computer screen or even a 3D display, we need a little help. The medium has to contribute to this little mental dance by providing what cognitive psychologists call spatial cues. Early games like *Wizardry: Proving Grounds of the Mad Overlord* and *Wolfenstein 3D* used simple cues, such as converging lines, that created an illusion of depth. You knew you were looking down a hallway in these games because the lines seemed to converge on a vanishing point in the distance. Since then, game developers have started using additional tricks, such as dynamic lighting, depth-of-field manipulations, and parallax scrolling, where elements in the background scroll slower than the foreground. And, of course, environments where you can move in all three dimensions provide better visual cues for world-building than do environments like 2D side scrollers. Most of us have seen optical illusions on 2D media like paper or computer screens that trick our brain into perceiving that one line is longer than another, even though it's not, and the illusion is caused by converging lines or the old cinematography trick of forced perspective.[15] Or the way our eyes and brains use contrast to perceive color can make a bright white square appear to turn grey when the color of the space around it changes. Technology that is effective in creating spatial presence does so because it hijacks our perceptual systems in similar ways. It engages with our brain from the bottom up at a very low level—as low as reality itself does. All these perceptual cues and brain hacks work together to draw a clear picture of how the game world is shaped, and the richer and more immersive that mental model is, the more likely people are to forget about the real world and use the virtual one as their primary reference point for where they are.

But are cutting-edge technology and virtual reality the only path to presence? Have you never felt transported into a game based on simpler technology? Or have you ever felt pulled into the world created by a good book or movie, for that matter? I know I have, and to understand how, let's set aside head-mounted virtual reality displays, billion-dollar buyouts, and perceptual illusions. Instead, let's visit two ordinary houses in the Pacific Northwest of the United States—one of them real and the other one virtual. Oh, and we'll need to make a quick stop at the ruins of a sunken, underwater paradise while we're at it.

GONE TO RAPTURE, *GONE HOME*: THE IMPORTANCE OF GAME DESIGN AND CONTENT

Steve Gaynor began his journey into the big leagues of game development years before Palmer Luckey started tinkering with virtual reality headsets. Gaynor started down his career path in 2005, working in various quality assurance departments where he tested code and looked for bugs in games still under development. Not fulfilled by poking around in the virtual worlds created by others, Gaynor spent his free time playing with development tools to create amateur levels in the first-person shooter game *F.E.A.R.* That experience helped Gaynor pull himself up out of quality assurance and into a job designing real levels for the *F.E.A.R.* franchise at Houston-based TimeGate Studios. Instead of documenting geometry errors and crash bugs, Gaynor was designing his own little slices of a game world. After that, opportunities took him back to the San Francisco Bay area to do more work as a level designer at 2K Marin, which had recently been tasked with creating the sequel to the immensely popular *Bioshock* game.

I feel any discussion of presence in video games would be incomplete without diving into *Bioshock*, since it exemplifies the concept so well. *Bioshock* takes place in the ruined, undersea city of Rapture. It's a setting that seems like something a college sophomore clutching a copy of Ayn Rand's *Atlas Shrugged* with one too many beers in him might come up with. But as weird as that sounds, the concept works, and many gamers—including me—consider their first steps off the bathysphere and into Rapture to be one of the most gobsmacking moments in gaming history. The *Bioshock* game was so intricately detailed and

Indian Prairie Public Library

Checked Out Items 9/26/2016 16:02
XXXXXXXXXX8144

Item Title	Due Date
31946005937930	10/17/2016

Getting gamers : the psychology of video games and their impact on the people who play them

Amount Outstanding: $0.40

catalog.ippl.info

artfully made that their environments didn't feel like levels or maps the way most other first-person shooters had up until then. Rapture felt like a coherent world that you could explore and experience.

Appropriately enough, 2K Marin's sequel to *Bioshock* was named *Bioshock 2*. Gaynor was assigned to help design the very first area that players visit after starting the game: the dilapidated ruins of Rapture's Adonis Luxury Resort. This is an area that's like a checklist for the *Bioshock* design ethos of immersion and environmental storytelling. The dilapidated hotel feels like something that was once beautiful but that had been wrecked through neglect and unchecked ambition. Pink coral and fronds cover much of the walkways, and the local lunatics had defaced those walls not already dripping with seawater. Many of the intricate details serve no other purpose than to make the hallways feel like a part of a bigger society. Advertisements, furniture, even bathrooms all told a story about the fall of Rapture. Like the first *Bioshock* game, it was far more detailed and more realistic than most gamers were used to at the time.

Gaynor got a chance to continue that emphasis on detailed world-building and player engagement in his first job as a lead designer on *Minerva's Den*, the downloadable expansion for *Bioshock 2*, then as a lead level designer in the early days of the game's spiritual successor, *Bioshock Infinite*. But despite working on one of the industry's most beloved franchises, Gaynor announced in December 2010 that he and two former co-workers, Johnnemann Nordhagen and Karla Zimonja, were breaking away to form an independent game development company called the Fullbright Company. The trio secured a small house in Portland, Oregon, that they would not only work out of but also live in. And to make things even cozier, Gaynor's wife also lived there. The Fullbright Company's first project, later revealed as *Gone Home*, would apply lessons learned from *Bioshock*. Like the house the company operated out of in Portland, its setting was about as far from a fantastical underwater city as you could get.

Instead of giving you a fully populated city or a sprawling, sunken ruin to explore, *Gone Home* plops you into the role of a young woman returning from a long trip to find that her family's new but otherwise unremarkable house is empty. There's just a cryptic note from the protagonist's younger sister that kicks off your investigation into what the hell happened. It's an incredibly detailed world, and the gameplay consists entirely of exploring the house from a first-person perspective, picking up and inspecting objects to glean the information you need to complete the game's story. Despite how different it is from big-budget, open-world games or the virtual reality glitz of the Oculus Rift, *Gone Home* is the most immersive game I've ever played. It's a textbook case of how research on the psychology of spatial presence can be harnessed and put to work creating game environments that make you lose track of the technology between you and them, to the point where you really feel like you're there.

What psychology? I'm glad you asked! Yes, you did. I heard you. So let's get back to our friends Matthias Hofer, Werner Wirth, and Tilo Hartman, who formulated that two-step process of spatial presence described earlier. The vivid, deep, and convincing presentation of a game world created by technology is important, but the researchers also identified additional aspects of a medium that are important for drawing us in. And it just so happens that *Gone Home* provides textbook examples of how they work.

It's critical to spatial presence that the world created by the game behaves consistently and in line with what we expect. All of a game's impressive visuals can be undermined, for example, if it makes inconsistent use of them or if things within the game don't behave as we expect them to. Research on spatial presence in media shows that incongruous elements undermine the development of that mental model of the game world.[16] This means you don't want to see anything that reminds you that "oh, yeah, this is a video game." *Gone Home*, for example, has a sparse user interface that doesn't put floating numbers up on the screen, or even a compass to show you what direction you're facing. Games like *Skyrim* and those in the *Far Cry* series have similarly limited user interfaces so that there's very little to trigger thoughts that this is an artificial environment. Intrusive heads-up displays, damage numbers appearing over enemies' heads, achievement notifications, messages notifications, load screens, and tutorial messages frequently undermine immersion. This is also why in-game advertising is so distracting: Seeing 25 instances of the new Adam Sandler movie while trying to infiltrate a terrorist training camp kind of pulls you out of it. Though I should note that in instances where advertising is not incongruous with the game world, it could actually help to have real ads. Playing a NASCAAR game, for example, wouldn't feel right without seeing logos smeared all over everything, and the outfield walls in a baseball game look more realistic when covered in ads for real sports drinks.

Yet everything in *Gone Home* looks like it belongs in the kind of house you're exploring. One of the game's hooks is that it happens within a small area, but that environment is extremely detailed. You can pick up and inspect almost everything—highlighters, magazines, ticket stubs, knickknacks, reminders that your parents still have sex, whatever. What's more, you can rotate the item and inspect it up close. The game artists even carefully replicated different people's handwriting where appropriate. And this isn't a world of identical objects that are copied and pasted into the world just to fill it up. Most of *Gone Home*'s in-game flotsam is unique.

It's also worth noting that the game world has to persist if presence is to be maintained. It can't up and go away, which is exactly what happens every time you hit a "Loading" screen, an "Insert Disk 2" prompt, or a "Disconnected from server" warning. It seems like a small thing, but spatial presence is much more likely when games either avoid pausing to load new areas or find clever ways of disguising it when it does have to happen. The science fiction game *Mass Effect*'s interminable elevator rides were the butt of jokes among fans, but they did mask the loading of new game areas and often gave players the chance to overhear realistic (and often amusing) small talk between Commander Shepard and crew members as they passed the time. Other games like *The Last of Us* flow smoothly from area to area, only showing us a loading screen when we start the game up. The budget and labor limitations under which *Gone Home* was made resulted in an entire game world that could be experienced without interruption.

Finally, interactivity is vital to creating spatial presence in video games. The more things you can interact with in a predictable way, the easier it is to create that mental model. Perhaps more importantly, the easier it is for your mind to fall into the habit of assuming that the game world is your primary point of reference for your location—the very definition of spatial presence. I'm a little embarrassed to admit it, but back in 1996, I was amazed to find out that you could flush the men's room toilets in *Duke Nukem 3D*. ASTOUNDING! Some years later while playing the action-adventure game *Shenmu* on the Segal Dream-cast, I was delighted to find out that I could put my character's personal quest for revenge on indefinite hold while I forced him to play with a kitten in a cardboard box. The webcomic Penny Arcade immortalized this moment in a strip where the hero proclaimed, "I am Ryo Hazuki. I will avenge my father's death . . . Right after I play with this kitten! And drink this soda! And play with these toys!" Thankfully, the kinds of interactivity we get out games have come a long way since then and tend to matter much more. In *Gone Home*, for example, you can pick up, rotate, inspect, and place almost any object in the game. Notes are even presented as hand-written on lined notebook paper with little doodles in the margins. Steve Gaynor says that he and his team chose 1995 as the setting for their game because it represented the latest time period they could think of where such items wouldn't have been replaced by e-mails and text messages. [17]

Interacting with the game as you expect to is one thing, but Matthias Hoffer, who was the primary author on the "House of Mozart" study described above, wrote at length about a critical concept he and his colleagues call "involvement." [18] More than simple attention or even interaction, involvement is an intense and prolonged focus on and mental processing of the game world. It's finding a way to scale a mountain, exploring the shattered remains of a downtown shopping district, or figuring out the safest way to ransack a nobleman's mansion. It's the end result of seeing what a game has to offer, thinking about it, and putting it to use over the course of a play session.

Involvement also includes deliberate exploration of a game's mechanics, which is why game designs with heavy focus on systems often make us feel really present in their game worlds. "Systems" in game design parlance refers to a set of rules for how the game behaves and what you can do in it. For example, foraging for materials and items to increase your crafting skills in role-playing games like *Skyrim* or *Far Cry 4* is a major part of why those games are so absorbing. It's not just what you see or how you see it or even that you're interacting with it. It's that the game systems and gameplay are taking up your mental resources and thoughts over a prolonged period of time.

This is a two-way street, though. One of the important things to understand about involvement and its relationship to spatial presence is that it hinges on a player's motivation to get involved. This is where something that Hofer and his colleagues call "domain-specific interests" comes into play. This concept relates to how much you're into the subject matter, setting, themes, or other aspects of the game. Do you live in Southern California? If so, *Grand Theft Auto V* will be more immersive for you because of all the familiar landmarks, cultural references, and in-jokes specific to that region. Do you think cyberpunk is like the dumbest thing ever? Well, the *Deus Ex* games may have a hard time pulling you into that kind of world. The same could be said for subject matter (World War II and *Sniper Elite*), settings (zombie apocalypses and *DayZ*), or even thematic elements (*Bioshock*'s take on Ayn Rand's philosophy of objectivism). If something about the game piques a specific interest of the player, Hofer's research shows that it will lead to increased involvement, which leads to losing yourself in that game world.

It's also worth circling back around to the development of our mental representation of a world and noting that domain-specific interest can make that process easier. Being really into Clint Eastwood's run of spaghetti Western films or modern military hardware will make it much easier to fill in the blanks and make assumptions about the worlds you encounter in *Red Dead Redemption* or *Call of Duty: Advanced Warfare*. Even if the game doesn't present players with every little detail of the world, they will draw from their own stores of knowledge to increase the vividness of the mental model.

Similarly, *Gone Home* is very easy to become involved with. The game is set in the mid-1990s, a time that many in its target audience remember quite well and to which they will bring their own wealth of memory. And as we saw in chapter 4 on nostalgia in games, this emotion is likely to get people to pay attention, feel good, and want to be involved in a piece of media. In fact, the game demands involvement, because very little is spelled out for the player, who has to piece together scraps of the game's narrative through information gleaned from all those intricately modeled objects, notes, and other clues. You have to search for sources of information, figure out from whose perspective that information originated, how it fits in chronologically, how reliable it is, and many other factors. The clues are often vague, so much of the game's enjoyment comes from letting them tumble around in your mind and constructing a narrative that makes sense. And because there are no zombies or Nazis or Nazi zombies, there are no shooting sequences or traversal puzzles to interrupt this involvement. It's all the game has, and its design doesn't try to distract you from it.

So, in the end, is the technology or the game design more important to eliciting presence in video games? Based on what I've learned while researching this chapter, I won't equivocate: I think that technology probably carries the most weight. Simply putting on a head-mounted display and experiencing a well-crafted virtual environment can trick your brain into reacting as if you were really in that space. It doesn't even have to be anything more detailed than an empty room. But just picking one aspect of games—either technology or design—to rely on for presence would be short-sighted. Both are important, and game developers use both to make games that pull you in to their world. The coupling of technology such as virtual reality, high-resolution screens, natural controllers, motion tracking, and surround sound with the right game design is a very effective foundation for spatial presence. The game worlds that we will fall into the most easily and never want to leave will be the ones that are built with all the tools and materials game designers have available.

THINGS TO REMEMBER FROM THIS CHAPTER

- What most gamers call "immersion" psychologists call "spatial presence," because they like being difficult about these kinds of things.
- Spatial presence happens when we stop paying attention to the technology between us and the virtual world of the game.
- It is facilitated by creating a rich and complete mental representation of the game world for us and then by us adopting that as our primary point of reference for where we "are."
- The more vivid, detailed, and familiar the mental model of the world is, the greater the potential for spatial presence. Both technology and game design choices can help this.
- Technology can do it by tricking your brain on the same level as reality with visual and auditory cues about the environment.
- It can also help by providing controls that feel natural and require inputs that are expected for the activity you're supposedly doing.
- Game design helps create a rich mental model by using game worlds that our imagination and familiarity with the setting can help fill in.

- A consistent, unbroken, and interactive presentation of the game world also helps, as does the lack of unrealistic intrusions that break the illusion.
- Games that encourage involvement help, too. In this context, involvement means intense and prolonged focus on and mental processing of the game world.

WHY DO WE GO CRAZY FOR DIGITAL GAME SALES?

"We are all gamers here, and we started thinking, what is the best way to make promos more entertaining and make them more similar to the games? . . . We basically created a game out of buying games."
—Oleg Klapovsky, GOG.com's vice president of marketing[1]

In 2011, the department store chain JCPenney announced that they had hired Ron Johnson to become its new chief executive. Johnson was coming off a streak of retail makeover successes with Target and Apple, so the venerable but struggling JCPenney was looking to him for a similar feat with its department stores. Right away Johnson announced that much like he had done with Apple's retail operations, he wanted to make JCPenney a fun place to visit and poke around until you decided to buy something.[2] So new policies were introduced, stores were redesigned, and a small army of clerks was mobilized on store floors to make the changes.

Sounds like a good idea, but Johnson also made plans to change something subtle yet fundamental about the typical JCPenney's shopping experience. Shortly after arriving, he noticed that three-quarters of everything the company sold had been discounted by at least 50 percent. Shirts, belts, shoes, small appliances, bedding—whatever it was, the company's standard operating procedure was to slash prices during sales events or offer deep discounts to shoppers who came prepared with the right coupons. Maybe both. Many items were somehow perpetually marked down throughout the year, which stretched the defini-

tion of "sales event" into unlikely shapes.[3] Johnson thought such decep-
tive pricing practices were incompatible with the company's new image,
and he felt that they undermined an honest relationship with customers. So on February 1, 2012, Johnson initiated a "Fair and Square Every
Day" pricing practice across every one of the company's hundreds of
locations.

Fair and square pricing meant several things that JCPenney customers weren't used to. One of them had to do with the end of "charm
prices" that ended in ".99." So a shirt that cost $11.99 changed to
$12.00. But the big change was that Johnson largely did away with sales,
coupons, and bargain hunting. Everything in the store would be marked
with what the company thought was a full but fair price. You wouldn't
need a coupon to get discounts, and you could walk into a store today
without fear of having missed a sale that happened yesterday. To kick
off the change, the company ran ads where JCPenney customers did
their   best   Darth   Vader   impersonations   by   screaming
"NOOOOOOOOoooooo!" at overlapping markdown stickers and rivers
of coupons pouring out of their mailbox. The tagline for the ad was
"Enough is enough."

But that turned out to be wrong. Enough is not enough. For JCPenney customers, too much is enough, but only after you've reduced the
price just enough. Otherwise, enough is just too much. The point being
that lifelong JCPenney customers had not only come to expect sales,
coupons, and bargain hunts, they had also come to enjoy them. It didn't
matter that $35 was the fair price for a pair of jeans. People wanted
jeans that were marked $50 plus the satisfaction of getting them while
they were $15 off for a limited time. They wanted to feel like they had
more control over how much they paid because they waited for a sale
and stacked a pair of 10-percent- off coupons. They wanted the thrill of
getting something while the getting was good, even if it was a hassle.
Johnson had, in short, neglected the psychology of bargain hunting.
Sales at JCPenney stores tanked as a result. To be fair, analysts with the
benefit of hindsight point to additional reasons why the fair and square
pricing initiative failed: ham-handed implementation, a failure to pilot-
test in a small number of stores, and failure to listen to feedback from
employees. But the psychology of bargains was a big part. Sales went
down 32 percent—THIRTY-TWO PERCENT—in the fourth quarter

of 2012 alone, and as a result Johnson was kicked out and the new management brought back sales and coupons.[4]

People shopping for video games often act in just the same way as JCPenney customers who are shopping for back-to-school clothes and blenders. Many of us love sales, and the video game industry has come up with some pretty ingenious and effective ways to present them to us. The consumer psychology literature is stuffed with studies about pricing and sales for every kind of product, but the video game market is special in how purchases are increasingly digital. You can buy or even rent games through the magic of the Internet, which lets you download or stream them straight to your console or computer. And for mobile games on phones and tablets, digital is the only way to buy.

This kind of digital-only sales is largely new territory, and though some of the ways you're used to thinking about sales may be relevant, some don't apply as directly or cover all the ways that you can be marketed to in this new world. Digital sales have created some new opportunities for publishers and retailers to use psychology to get you to buy their stuff. According to a report by the Entertainment Software Association, 52 percent of game sales in 2014 were in digital format.[5] Steam, the leading digital distribution platform on the personal computer, has twice-a-year sales events that many gamers simultaneously anticipate because of great bargains and dread because they buy more games than they will ever play. But Steam is far from alone. The Humble Bundle company offers weekly combinations of games where customers pay only what they want (as low as a penny), but they get to support charities in doing so and get additional games thrown in if they beat the current average price. GOG (formerly "Good Old Games" for its emphasis on the kinds of titles I discussed in chapter 4 on nostalgia) runs "Insomnia Sales" where it slashes prices on one game at a time and refuses to move on to the next until a certain number are sold. But neither does it wait around for you if you don't jump on a deal while the jumping is good. And, of course, although mobile games frequently use free-to-play models and in-game purchases that I will discuss in a later chapter, virtual storefronts for Apple and Android mobile platforms also have sales events and think carefully about how they present their products.

So let's take a look at some of the most common psychological sales tricks that you may find yourself up against the next time you scroll and click in search of a new game to buy. To start, let's look at how even the savviest gamer is much like a shopper jogging into one of the big JCPenney sales events of yesteryear.

ARTIFICIAL SCARCITY AND PSYCHOLOGICAL REACTANCE

Sales aren't usually perpetual. That's pretty much right there in the definition of "sale," if you look it up. Bargains are often only "while supplies last," and the research is pretty clear that "available for a limited time" is a super-effective sales pitch because we value things more that are rare or otherwise have limited availability. For example, Bandai's 1987 game *Stadium Events* is one of the most sought-after games for collectors of the Nintendo Entertainment System. In 2010, a woman sold a copy of the game on eBay for $13,105, essentially by accident. She had included it with a box of Nintendo games that she had found in her garage and had no idea why the bidding had gone so high when she checked on her new listing the next morning. Why was *Stadium Events* so valuable? Right around the time of its release, Nintendo pulled all copies of the game and destroyed them so that they could promote a different track-and-field game instead. But a few copies of *Stadium Events* managed to escape into the wild, making it one of the rarest game cartridges in existence. For that reason alone it is worth so much to collectors. It's certainly not because it's a great game.

This mentality isn't limited to obsessive collectors, though. Valuing something because it's rare is just one of those decision-making shortcuts that sticks with us because it offers such a good tradeoff between accuracy and mental effort over a lifetime. Psychologist Stephen Worchel and his colleagues illustrated this with a study involving cookies, but not those that websites deal in.[6] The researchers told subjects that they were participating in an experiment measuring people's preferences for various consumer items. At a certain point in the spiel, the experimenter jabbed at a secret button under the desk. Psychologists love secret buttons, but instead of opening a trap door underneath the subject as usual, this one summoned a second experimenter bearing a jar of cookies. Depending on the experimental condition to which the subject had been assigned, this second experimenter delivered either a jar full of 10 cookies or an almost empty jar with just 2 cookies. Subjects were then asked to retrieve a cookie from the jar, take a bite, and then share their thoughts on taste, attractiveness, and what the cookies should be priced at. Relative to those who picked a treat from the mostly full jar, people drawing from a jar with only two cookies found them more delicious, more desirable, and worthy of a higher price. This happened despite the fact that the contents of both jars were exactly the same and came from a larger stash of just one brand of supermarket cookies. The perceived rarity of the cookies was influencing not only their perceived value but also their taste and appeal.

GOG.com uses this scarcity phenomenon to good effect during their semiregular Insomnia Sales. During these events, the digital storefront displays one game at a time with deep discounts. You might be able to get 80 percent off the classic game *System Shock 2*, for example. The catch is that there's something like a health bar for the promotion that ticks down a little whenever someone takes advantage of it. When the bar empties, it's time for the next sale item. For popular titles with steep discounts, the bar plummets to zero in a matter of minutes or even seconds, so shoppers are motivated to never take their tired eyes off the website lest they miss something. Thus the "insomnia" hook to the sale. It's not difficult to imagine that someone will frantically click "Buy Now" to snag a title for which they would normally be skeptical or lukewarm when they see supply leaking away. They don't want to miss out on what looks like a good game for cheap.

This overvaluation of rare things also happens in other kinds of digital game sales. Despite delivering games that are no more than streams of infinitely available 1s and 0s, digital retailers capitalize on the scarcity effect because the bias applies to opportunities just as it does to physical goods. This artificial scarcity is the reason why "for a limited time!" offers are as effective as "while supplies last!" deals. The Humble Bundle website, for example, runs weekly specials where it packages up several games for an extremely low price—as low as you want to pay, in fact. Along with every deal is a timer that counts down the hours that the opportunity will be available, along with a "time is running out!" warning. Steam uses a similar timer for its daily deals, and the bargains in its biannual sales events turn over on regular 24-hour or 8-hour schedules.

The threat of losing an opportunity to do something also triggers another psychological effect that I discussed in the chapter on quests and goals: psychological reactance. In short, we tend to value scarce things more highly, and the idea of losing them often makes us see them as better than more readily available alternatives. In one study of the effect, a group of psychologists studied Florida housewives' reactions to the banning of laundry detergents containing environmentally unfriendly phosphates.[7] Not only did those facing such loss of choice buy more of the product (both more than they did before learning about the upcoming ban and relative to a control group), but they also rated the phosphate-laden soaps as much more effective than the government-mandated alternative. This is a by-product of how the human mind has evolved to be more averse to losing something than gaining something of equal value, since we feel ownership of an opportunity even if we haven't taken it yet. Many of us behave like those Florida housewives when we stare at a Steam Daily Deal or an Xbox Marketplace sale that's about to slip away. Simply knowing that we are going to lose the opportunity to buy something makes us averse to missing it. What if it never goes on sale again? In reality, games almost always do go on sale again, but that doesn't help in the heat of the moment when you're staring down the possibility of missing out. You could spend the same money you're spending on digital sales in any number of ways. You could buy other games, even if they are fewer in number. You could buy something else. But artificial scarcity and psychological reactance may be making you think that you'll get more total enjoyment out of the ones that will soon be unavailable.

There's an additional psychological trick that complements scarcity, and it's much easier to pull off in a digital environment than in a physical one. It has to do with the fact that you don't always know what the next game to go on sale will be. And you don't know if it will be good. You just know it's going to be something.

RANDOM REWARD SCHEDULES: WHAT'S ON SALE NOW? WHAT ABOUT . . . NOW?

One of the first topics covered in a Psychology 101 class is likely to be reward and punishment schedules. If your goal is to get people to adopt and then repeat behaviors, giving them rewards is key, but the scheduling of those rewards is also critical. If you give someone a food pellet every tenth time they press a lever, that's essentially a "fixed-interval schedule." But if you randomly give or withhold a pellet after each lever press, that's called a "random or variable-reward schedule." Random schedules are generally the most effective way to get people to keep slapping that lever. You may remember all this from the chapter on loot drops, and that's no accident. Sales are real-life loot to gamers.

Seeing a game you've wanted to buy show up in the Daily Deals on Steam or as a special on EA's Origin service of the same type is like getting a food pellet. It's a reward you get for checking the storefront. In fact, during biannual Steam sales, checking the store at noon every day to see the new batch of deals is my favorite thing about the event—second only to checking back every eight hours or so for the handful of flash deals. I'm sure the owners of the storefronts have the slate of deals worked out ahead of time, but the selection of games seems random to me. And the store managers usually space things out masterfully, making sure that I come back to the site throughout the day to see if I'm going to get a reward in the form of a great deal. That's what makes the sales so compelling, and digital sales can rely on random rewards more easily than brick-and-mortar establishments because they can rotate entire inventories in and out instantly without redlining prices, changing displays, and slapping on new stickers. As a side note, the online retailer Woot.com has made a business out of random reward schedules and the scarcity effect. The site offers limited-time discounts on seemingly random things across various categories. Amazon.com (which owns Woot) does the same thing with its daily "Gold Box deals" on random assortments of video games and other retail oddities.

Sometimes, though, a big slab of sales has limited appeal, and it can even backfire on the retailers a little. What do you do when you excitedly check a digital storefront for a batch of sales and find out that you either don't want some of them or you already own some of them?

FEWER HUMBLE BUNDLES ARE MORE

I've mentioned the Humble Bundle sales a few times already. Its offerings are much more diverse now, but the program started off a few years ago as a collection—a bundle, if you will—of games by independent developers that you could buy as a package at whatever price you wanted. One bundle in 2012, for example, included *Amnesia*, *Limbo*, *Psychonauts*, *Superbrothers: Sword & Sworcery EP*, and *Bastion*. Shoppers could pay $1 for that bundle or $100, but either way some proceeds went to charity.

The Humble Bundle has become a big success because of the appealing mixture of philanthropy and gimme, gimme, gimme. But though the pay-what-you-want and bundling concepts are great together, a simple psychological phenomenon often kept people in the early days from spending as much as they might have and thus giving as much money to charity. To see how, let's talk about dinnerware. Yaaaay! Dinnerware!

Christopher Hsee from the University of Chicago conducted an experiment where he asked a bunch of research subjects to imagine they were visiting a discount store to buy a dinnerware set.[8] Think dining plates, bowls, cups, saucers, and that kind of thing. Hsee told the subjects that there were only two sets left on the clearance table: Set A and Set B. The contents of each are described below:

Dinnerware Set A:

- 8 dinner plates
- 8 bowls
- 8 dessert plates
- 8 cups, but 2 of them broken
- 8 saucers, but 7 of them broken

Dinnerware Set B:

- 8 dinner plates
- 8 bowls
- 8 dessert plates
- 0 cups
- 0 saucers

Your above-average powers of observation have no doubt revealed to you that Set A has everything Set B has, plus more. Sure, some of the items in that "more" are broken, but some are whole. Hsee asked each would-be shopper to take a look at the table with the two sets and say how much they would pay for Set A and how much for Set B. The averages were about $32 for Set A and $30 for Set B. As you would expect, shoppers were willing to pay a little more for the additional, unbroken cups and saucers in Set A.

Unsurprising, I know. But here's the thing: Hsee had two additional experimental groups of shoppers in what he called "separate evaluation conditions." One group considered just Set A without ever seeing Set B, and the other did the same for Set B without ever laying eyes on Set A. When the experimenter asked these people how much they'd pay for the one dinnerware set they were shown, the pricing pattern flipped: people averaged a value of about $23 for Set A but $30 for Set B. That's weird, right? People seeing Set B were willing to pay more than those seeing Set A. This was despite the fact that Set A had additional, unbroken pieces.

Hsee explains this "less is more" phenomenon by saying that during separate evaluation mode, we estimate the value of options—clothes, video games bundles, dinnerware sets, whatever—by comparing them to a reference point for that category. In the example above, the reference point is "a complete, 40-piece dinnerware set," but only for Set A. Those looking only at Set B have a different reference point: a 24-piece set. We then tend to devalue options that compare unfavorably to that reference point. Set A compared unfavorably to the reference point of a 40-piece set because it had only 31 unbroken pieces. Set B's comparison against its own reference point was neutral because it had 24 of the 24 pieces.

Hsee's influential article[9] included another example that can make this idea clearer: A 10-ounce cup only partially filled with 8 ounces of ice cream was valued less than a 5-ounce cup overflowing with 7 ounces of ice cream. This despite the fact that the larger cup had 1 ounce more ice cream in it than the smaller cup. Why? Because 8 ounces in a 10-ounce cup feels like someone is skimping. Lame. But 7 ounces in a 5-ounce cup? OH, MY GAWD, that dude just piled it on. I love this place! Ice cream party!

Once again, how a choice is framed matters enough to overrule purely logical thinking, at least much the time. Human brains don't like to think about value or prices in isolation. They seek out reference points—40-piece dinnerware sets or 10-ounce cups—and think about how close the deal comes to that reference point. So let's go back to the

Humble Bundle and say I was looking at the contents of the bundle I mentioned earlier: *Amnesia: Dark Descent*, *Limbo*, *Psychonauts*, *Superbrothers*: *Sword & Sworcery EP*, and *Bastion*. Those are all good games, but I already own *Psychonauts* and *Amnesia*, so they don't have any value to me. They're like broken teacups. This "three out of five" comparison will drive down my valuation of the bundle. And because I set my own price, I may have even been willing to pay as much or more for just a three-game bundle featuring just the titles I wanted. The same thing could happen with the Steam bundles I discussed earlier, or with bundles on any digital download service.

One possible solution to this would be to let Humble Bundle shoppers build their own bundles, humbly. A "get any five games from this list for whatever you want to pay" offer might generate higher prices. Or maybe it could be as simple as letting users uncheck a box next to the name of individual games they already own or don't want, so that those titles disappear from the screen, leaving only a set of desired games from which shoppers will form new reference points. Either of those would be ideal, but the Humble Bundle folks also came up with the idea of allowing you to give away gift copies of bundled games if you don't want them. It's almost as good, since it does give the unwanted games some value.

I know it's hard to believe that we're that easily manipulated in such a counterintuitive manner, but sometimes it's nice to realize that marketers are using psychology to our advantage and to their own. Of course, you can be sure that they will not always wield their knowledge of psychology for good. Sometimes they play games with their games that are specifically designed to draw you in a little before pulling you in all the way.

COMMITMENT AND CONSISTENCY: "I'D BUY IT, I CAN BUY IT, I'M BUYING IT"

As a rule, people like to appear consistent. Once someone makes a commitment or states a preference, some amount of mental inertia sets in and they feel pressure to keep their behaviors in line with their thoughts. In his excellent book *Influence: Science and Practice*, Robert Cialdini describes a trip to an introductory class on "transcendental meditation" that he and a friend attended on a lark.[10] When the instructor offered to teach an advanced course on how to perform such wonders as floating and walking through walls, Cialdini's friend tore into him and exposed his claims as impossible flimflam. Amazingly, many people in the audience who listened to Cialdini's friend still proceeded to plunk down $75 for the advanced course, despite evidence that it was all a sham. They had taken the time to attend, after all, and thus they had signaled a belief in what was being sold no matter the evidence. It was easier to believe in what they had done than to change the past. If this makes you think of the part of chapter 3 on fanboys where I discussed our desire to avoid cognitive dissonance, you paid pretty good attention. It's a very similar thing happening here.

So, with that in mind, ever notice how Steam will e-mail you when something from your wish list goes on sale, including during the big sales events? I throw stuff on there all the time to keep track of what I want to buy during sales, and when I get a notification I feel like a commitment is being called in. Steam even has a "Friend Activity" page where you can see what other people have added to their wish list, so you know that others might be watching when you add something to yours. Steam also banks on your commitment when you vote on Community Choice polls during its sales, assuming you don't already own the game you vote for. These are little contests where you get to vote on which game you think should go on sale next. Actively involving yourself, hoping for a certain outcome, and forming an intention means that you're more likely to buy the game if it wins in the poll. And having your choice actually win feels like a reward—like you won a little contest—so you're more likely to associate good feelings with that game.

Our bias toward consistency also comes into play with another topic I introduced in the chapter on progress-related game mechanics: the endowed-progress effect. To recap, once we begin progress toward a goal, we tend to want to complete it because it creates a mental tension. Information about such goals and related tasks are easier to remember and come to mind more readily. In 2013, Valve introduced a new element to its Summer Steam sale that uses this quirk of human nature: trading cards. The event was called the "Steam Summer Getaway Sale" and shoppers received a random trading card for every $10 they spent. It bears mentioning that these were not physical cards. They were just virtual cards viewable within the Steam software. The 10 imaginary cards could be combined to create an imaginary set, which you could combine to get other benefits. Just know that shoppers were tasked with completing a set of 10 cards through buying stuff.

Most people got at least a couple of cards in the course of buying games, and thus without really meaning to they had begun progress toward the goal of completing a set of trading cards. In line with the research I discussed on the endowed-progress effect,[11] some people felt sufficiently motivated to buy more games in order to complete their set, or at least try to trade cards with other shoppers. Adding a game to their shopping cart during the Summer Getaway Sale displayed a progress bar showing how much more they needed to spend to get their next card. Just showing someone that they've begun progress toward that goal is enough to create some mental tension over not having yet reached it. It was also clever of Steam to show the progress before checkout so that shoppers had one more reason to complete the transaction. Of course, once they got the card, the effect happened again because they've now started checking off what they had collected from the 10-card set needed to craft the Summer Getaway Badge. So double whammy. That's out of a three-whammy set. Get just one more whammy to complete the set.

So these are all subtle tricks about commitment, artificial scarcity, and surprise deals that you may now recognize when you see them in your next game. They're the kinds of experiences that Ron Johnson underestimated when he dumped them from JCPenney's pricing handbook. But there's one other psychological trick that's more straightforward and deals directly with what's literally at the bottom line: price.

GETTING DRAGGED DOWN BY PRICE-ANCHORING

Pricing is one of the most basic tools in the salesperson's kit, and it's often of prime consideration for people with a potentially expensive hobby like gaming. When you look at a page for a sales event or the inventory of an online store, you can be sure that a lot of work went into the placement of price information, the size of fonts, and the emphasis of certain details. One of the simplest yet most effective tricks is to get you to notice a number other than the price of the item before giving you information about the actual cost of a game or the size of a discount during a sale. In price negotiation, the "lowball" offer is the classic example of this same concept: Open with a really low offer and you'll set the stage so that what you're actually willing to pay looks higher in comparison. The simple presence of particularly high or low number can subconsciously affect your evaluation of the sale price. In psychological parlance, this is called "anchoring."

As a simple but elegant example, consider an experiment done by psychological wizards (seriously, I think they were actual wizards) Amos Tversky and Daniel Kahneman.[12] The researchers asked one group of subjects to estimate the product of these numbers:

8 x 7 x 6 x 5 x 4 x 3 x 2 x 1

And then they asked another group to estimate this product:

1 x 2 x 3 x 4 x 5 x 6 x 7 x 8

Those of you with a grade school education and the benefit of seeing both lines at the same time know that because of how multiplication works those products are equal. Yet the average estimate for the group that was only given the problem starting with "8" was 2,250, and those who saw a "1" at the beginning of the problem had an average estimate of just 512. Why? Because one group anchored on the higher number that they saw first while reading left to right, and the other anchored on a lower number. (Both sides were far off from the correct answer of 40,320, in case you were wondering.) Kahneman and Tversky were also able to activate anchoring by framing a question in terms of a large or small number, even if they were ridiculous. For example, they asked one group of people these questions: "Was Gandhi more or less than 144 years old when he died? How old was Gandhi when he died?" When a second group was asked only, "How old was Gandhi when he died?," and didn't hear the 144 number, they guessed Gandhi was much younger at the time of his demise because they didn't anchor.[13]

Anchoring is an incredibly robust phenomenon, to the point where the source of the numbers in question can be absurd. Kahneman and Tversky were also able to prime people with large or small numbers by spinning a wheel of fortune that was rigged to stop on either 10 or 65.[14] Similarly, behavioral economist Dan Ariely and his colleagues conducted a study where they used anchoring in an auction simply by having bidders write down the last two digits of their Social Security number.[15] Those whose numbers ended in the 80s and above actually were willing to pay up to 346 percent more for things like wine and chocolates than those whose Social Security numbers ended in the 20s or below.

We see the anchoring effect being put to use all the time during sales. During their biannual Steam Sales, Valve offers bundles of games that you can get for a deep discount. For just $69.99 you can get every game id Software made, or every game from Rockstar, or every game featuring squirrels. Look closely at one of those promotions, and you'll see that the marketing gurus for Steam readily list the retail value of the bundle if you paid full price for all games individually. It might look something like this:

Individual Price: $194.79
Package Price: $69.99

The top number showing what the games would cost if bought individually is your anchor. Seeing that number will cause many people to set their perceptions of the bundle's value much higher than if they had seen the sale price first, or a breakdown of individual prices.

As an aside from anchoring, this bundling strategy also works because it obscures the true value of the games in the package. William Poundstone, author of *Priceless: The Myth of Fair Value (and How to Take Advantage of It)*, calls this the "value meal" strategy when describing the psychology of restaurant menu design.[16] How much cheaper is it to get the bundle than just the individual items? What about if I supersize it? With curly fries? Oh, forget it. Give me the No. 3 Value Meal with a Coke. Likewise, I might look at a massive bundle of digitally distributed games and think about how much I could get those older games for elsewhere. Could I find them for sale used, and for how much? Could I rent or borrow any of them? Is the discount big enough to make up for buying extra copies of games I already own? And how much is it worth to me to have those games available through Steam so that I don't have to dig out my old boxes and CD keys? It's a psychological truism that we have limited cognitive processing power at any one time, and when our brains are tied up considering these questions, we've got fewer cycles to devote to thinking how much we want to actually play some of the games in the bundle. We'd rather just latch on to a signal of value rather than doing the mental legwork. In most of life's little situations, these shortcuts work well enough. It's just that situations can be engineered to take advantage of them.

Indeed, any time you see an "original price" next to a sale price, the retailers are banking on your substituting an anchor for this kind of value estimation. Amazon.com does it with game sales by showing the original price first, but with a line through it. You also see it in sales pitches that advertise "starting at . . ." prices. Sony's PlayStation Now service, for example, lets users rent access to games through the magic of streaming them through the Internet. They offer several increasingly expensive options depending on how long you want to rent the game. Spending $4.99 to rent the game for just four hours might be the cheapest option, even though most people will want the game for longer than that and will need to pay more to do that. But when they browse the PlayStation store, they will see a big button saying, "Rent from $4.99." Since it's so much larger and brighter than the rest of the image, most people will notice the $4.99 figure first, which anchors their perception of the cost of the service and makes them more likely to click through to get the details than if they had seen "Up to $29.99."

Let's look at one more example of how anchoring worms its way into all kinds of unexpected places, but one that seems obvious once you understand the concept. The phenomenon also affects our perceptions of discounts depending on whether they are presented as percentages (e.g., "25% off") or specific amounts off (e.g., "$5 off"). For example, which of the following sounds better to you?

Buy *The Sims* for 80% off: $6.99
or . . .
Buy *The Sims* for $28 off: $6.99

Same price, but thanks to anchoring the 80-percent-off figure seems like a larger discount than $28 off simply because the number is bigger. This is why you see sales on Steam, Origin, and other digital distribution platforms emphasize discounts as percentages instead of absolute dollars. They may also show the dollar discount or make it easy to calculate, but the percentage off is almost always highlighted by specific design choices of font, color, background, or placement. Notice, though, that this effect can flip for high-priced items like computers. Taking 25 percent off a $2,000 iMac is not quite as appealing as a $500 discount, for example. But since we're talking about relatively cheap items like games, percentages get used to the best effect.

As I said earlier, there are all kinds of additional nuances to pricing that have been studied by marketing professionals and consumer psychologists. The ones I have discussed above are just some of them that you are most likely to encounter when buying games during big digital distribution sale events. In psychology, forewarned doesn't necessarily mean forearmed in terms of being totally immune to these effects, but maybe you'll be able to mitigate them somewhat the next time you set out to bulk up your gaming backlog at a big sale. Then again, don't worry about it too much. Like the shoppers turning a trip to JCPenney into a game, half the fun might be screaming "SAAAALE!" and flinging credit cards at your screen. Whatever makes you happy.

THINGS TO REMEMBER FROM THIS CHAPTER

- Consumers have irrational attitudes toward sales. Many find value in bargain hunting beyond simply what they're saving.
- Artificial scarcity is often used to make people want something simply because the "rare means valuable" shortcut we often use for decision-making. For digital goods, this is employed by making the opportunity to buy limited.
- "Psychological reactance" makes us overvalue something when we think we're about to lose the opportunity to buy it.
- Surprise sales events and digging for bargains is a real-life loot drop. All the same lessons about randomness of rewards apply.
- The "less-is-more bias" describes how we may adopt reference points for the value of something and then have that reference point bias our valuation. Favoring 6 ounces of frozen yogurt overflowing in a 4-ounce cup versus 8 ounces at the bottom of a 10-ounce cup is an example.
- People don't like inconsistencies between their stated intentions and actions. Wish lists and preorders use precommitment to buy in order to get more sales.
- "Anchoring" is a robust psychological phenomenon that makes you biased toward the first or most salient number that you see in a sales

pitch. This is often used to raise your estimate of how much something is worth or how big a discount is.

HOW DO GAMES AND APPS GET YOU WITH IN-GAME PURCHASES?

"It's the oldest marketing gimmick in the book. When you hear 'free' you reach for your wallet."

—Chris Anderson, writer and entrepreneur[1]

Academic and game designer Ian Bogost once annihilated tens of thousands of cows just to make a point about Facebook games. In early 2010, Bogost, a professor at the Georgia Institute of Technology who explores video games and culture, was thinking about how to prepare for a debate at New York University where he would be cast in the role of "guy who hates casual social games." Bogost would be up against other game designers and academics who argued that these kinds of games, which were particularly popular on Facebook, were the future of the industry and that those making them were to be lauded for their contributions. You know the kind of game that I'm talking about here: things like *Farmville* and *Cityville*, which are free to install and play, but which also erect barriers to gameplay that players are encouraged to circumvent by either paying real money or capturing and using the attention of their friends as another kind of currency.

In a 2010 Game Developer's Conference presentation in San Francisco, Bogost described how he didn't like this kind of game.[2] Like many others, he had been unhappy about the fact that Zynga's *Farmville* had been given an award for "best new social/online game" at a recent Game Developer's Conference. These weren't games, many people like Bogost thought. They were simple Skinner boxes that enticed players to download them for free, and then exploited those same players with cheap psychology in order to squeeze out a trickle of money. Many people obviously loved these games, but their critics said that they represented a dangerous and ultimately unfulfilling direction for the gaming industry to take whether or not their players realized it. It was the beginning of the schism between "premium" games—those that charged players a fee up front and delivered a complete game with no strings attached—and "free-to- play" games that offered downloads for free (or in some cases for very cheap) but were designed to incentivize players into micropayments and other in-game purchases. Incidentally, I think the terms "micropayment" or "microtransaction" are no longer accurate. There is nothing "micro" about many of the transactions that free-to-play games offer. Players are frequently pitched offers with $20 price tags, and some games even sell items that cost $100 or more.

Let me briefly discuss an example you may have heard about. In early 2014, EA released the poster child for this kind of product in the form of *Dungeon Keeper Mobile*. A recasting of the classic 1997 *Dungeon Keeper* strategy game in a free-to-play mold, *Dungeon Keeper Mobile* demanded in-game purchases from players in order to complete even fundamental gameplay. Want your imp to clear out a 1 x 1 block of dirt so that you can build a new structure? That's going to take 24 hours unless you pay money to speed it up. The player's guide during the opening tutorial is literally the devil, who seems to understand the controversy associated with this kind of mechanic. At one point he dryly notes, "Occasionally, tasks may test your patience, but who says money can't buy time? I have quite the polarizing solution to make that timer disappear." No kidding. The devil then teaches the player how to spend money to make the game playable. To be fair, most free-to-play games don't go this far, but *Dungeon Keeper Mobile* was reviled by critics as the worst that the business model had to offer, so much so that publisher Electronic Arts recanted and updated the game to make it less demanding of players' wallets and purses. Criticisms and perceptions of predatory play continued throughout the mobile game scene, however. In January 2014, Apple struck a deal with the Federal Trade Commission to refund $32 million to customers of its App Store whose children had unwittingly (or, let's be honest, sometimes wittingly but uncaringly) racked up in-game purchases without their parents' permission.[3]

But let's return to 2010 and Ian Bogost's preparations for his debate at New York University. Thinking that satire would make his points better than anything else, Bogost spent four days prior to the event creating a game he called *Cow Clicker*. It was a complete game that tightly embraced the entire design ethos that Bogost was critical of. *Cow Clicker* was built around in-game purchases, social networking, pointless grinding, timers, virtual currencies, and showing off vanity items. As such, the game was meant to lampoon the popular Facebook games of the day, and Bogost spent most of his time at the debate simply walking the audience through it. This seemed to make his point quite well. Wanting to spread the message wider, Bogost launched the game for real on Facebook soon after the debate as a combination of social commentary and academic experiment.

The final version of *Cow Clicker* presented players with a pasture, sitting in the middle of which was a cute, big-headed, and somewhat dead-eyed cow. Here is the gameplay of *Cow Clicker* in its entirety:

Step 1: You click on the cow.
Step 2: Listen to your cow moo and observe the helpful "You clicked your cow" message.
Step 3: Wait six hours.
Step 4: Return to Step 1.

That's it. There was almost nothing else to do within the game. I say "almost" because in order to skewer the design of social games, Bogost included ways for you to purchase and spend in-game currency. Now go ahead and guess what the virtual, in-game money for *Cow Clicker* was called. Seriously, guess. I'm not writing any more until you guess. That's right: it was called "mooney." It turns out that puns were also a big part of the *Cow Clicker* design ethos. Players could spend 15 mooney to reduce the time they had to wait before clicking their cow again, which many players did. One could also spend mooney on a huge stable (no pun intended) of cosmetic replacements for the default bovine. There were pink cows, plaid cows, emo cows, zombie cows, communist cows, ninja cows, and more. You could buy any of them, and your friends could admire your excellent taste and purchasing power. And friends were important for other reasons. They could be invited to join your

Cow Clicker pasture so that you could see each other's cows, and also the more cows in a pasture, the more mooney everyone would earn each time they were clicked. Bogost had created an absurd and pointless game, but crucial to his aim of exposing what he saw as the dangers of social games, he had also created a real, legitimate product that players could pay for and spend money on. If he was going to poke Zynga in the eye, he was set on using a real stick.

But then something weird happened: People started to really like the game. As player counts rose into the thousands and then tens of thousands, Bogost realized that he had something of a Frankenstein's monster on his hands. What's worse, it was starting to lumber along and shake down villagers for cash. For sure, many players were engaging with the game ironically, sharing the status of their cow clicking to their Facebook timelines as an in-joke about the banality of social games and writing five-star reviews of *Cow Clicker* extolling its virtues as satire. One person even wrote a strategy guide that was as tongue-in-cheek as it was short. But there were also many people who played in their virtual cow pasture without being in on the joke. They earnestly clicked cows, sent out requests, and bought cosmetic items. They sent its creator feedback and feature requests. Bogost even started getting e-mails from companies offering to help him monetize *Cow Clicker* better by inserting ads or promotional offers.

For a while, Bogost kept the experiment going by adding new content, achievements, and features. But over time those who had installed and played the game as part of the in-joke trailed off, and what was mostly left was a group of people who were really enjoying the game. Not only that, they were spending significant amounts of money on it. In one attempt at using extreme absurdity to poke at *Cow Clicker* players, Bogost put the "Stargrazer" up for sale. This cosmetic cow cost the equivalent of $25, but it was simply the default cow switched to face the other direction. People bought it.

Eventually, though, it became just too much, and Bogost realized that his life was being consumed by the parody he had created. Players weren't getting the message, or if they did they didn't care. So Bogost decided to destroy his creation. In July 2011, he announced that a timer for the impending "Cowpocalypse" had begun counting down. Perversely, every time a player clicked on his or her cow, the timer accelerated, but players could reset it by spending more mooney. Several last-minute rallies bought *Cow Clicker* some extra time, but eventually the Cowpocalypse came. In a final joke, Bogost didn't destroy the cows or shut down the game, but rather had all the cows raptured to cow heaven, leaving behind just the shadow marking where they had once stood in players' pastures. Technically *Cow Clicker* is still running. I just clicked my cow. But there is no satisfying moo and no cute little cow to view—just void and empty space.

It sometimes amazes me that people will spend so much in these little games that they download for free and use to fill in the corners of their lives at bus stops and waiting rooms. Every month, more than 9,000 new apps are added to the Apple App store, many of them free-to-play games.[4] *Candy Crush Saga* made more money in the first quarter of 2014 by selling in-game items like lollypop hammers and extra lives than Nintendo made from selling all of its physical game disks combined during the same time period.[5] For sure, most people don't ever buy anything for free-to-play games. It's tough to get an exact number, but one estimate presented at the 2014 Mobile Gaming Conference is that about 98.5 percent of players never spend anything on their free games.[6] The remaining 1.5 percent of players pay something, with an even smaller fraction of those acting as what many game developers call "whales," a term borrowed from the gambling industry.

Whales are the big spenders who drop huge amounts of money into a game. A 2013 *New York Times* article profiled Jorge Yao, who for an impressive six months held the title of the world's best *Clash of Clans* player.[7] This is a free-to-play game that lets players build encampments and go out on raids against other players for prizes and points. It's consistently in the list of top earners in the Apple App Store and the Google Play store, thanks to the fact that players can use real money to purchase virtual currency in the form of gems. Yao, who was feeling a certain amount of ennui after moving to Philadelphia to start an unfulfilling job, turned to *Clash of Clans* for entertainment. He took it much further than most players, though, scheduling the game into his daily routine to maximize his rankings. At one point, he told the *New York Times* reporter, he was wrapping multiple iPads in Zip-Lock baggies so that he could juggle accounts and play the game in the shower. That's dedication, but it took more than just dedication to stay on top. At one point Yao was spending $250 a week on gems, the game's virtual currency.

Big spenders like Yao and his counterparts in other games exist, but the real question I want to address in this chapter has less to do with the outliers on that distribution. It's more about when the rest of us are likely to spend money in a free-to-play game supported by in-game purchases or microtransactions, because, whales aside, many of us are tempted to plop down the occasional bit of real money for in-game advantages or virtual belongings. Are there things about the way that these games are typically designed or the sales tactics that they use that rely on basic human psychology to make a sale? Are there things that go beyond the typical sales tricks and techniques that I've discussed so far for other business models? Yes, there are. But before I get into them, it's worth considering the basic question of why free-to-play games are so popular in the first place and why they account for the vast majority of downloads relative to premium or paid games.

FREE IS THE MAGIC IRRATIONAL NUMBER

When you decide you want a new game to play on your mobile device, you have many choices. The Apple App Store and the Google Play store constantly introduce new products, and even the simplest views can show you dozens at a time. Most of them don't cost anything, and that trend is accelerating. A 2014 study by Gartner predicted that 95 percent of apps in these stores will be free by 2017.[8] Games on the PC have a similar embarrassment of free riches. Steam and Origin both have thriving free-to-play sections. Consoles are also starting to give stuff away, often otherwise full-priced games to entice players to sign up for subscription services, such as Xbox Live and PlayStation Plus.

If you're as big a fan of dumb questions as I am, you may wonder, "Why do people like free stuff so much?" But the better question is why so many people will choose free games when for just a bit more money—often as little as a dollar or two—they could often get a game with deeper gameplay, better design, better production values, and no demands to pay their way around arbitrary obstacles a few minutes in. Or, in the case of free-to-play games that do have exceptional production values, you may wonder why their developers decided to include in-game purchases instead of just charging $4.99 or $9.99 for the game without them? Whether it's poor quality or aggravating monetization tricks, free-to-play games are going to have a severe downside in the eyes of many. For sure, there are free-to-play games out there that are both high-quality and treat their players well. *Hearthstone: Heroes of Warcraft* is an example, as are some PC games, like *League of Legends* or *Dota 2*. In this section I'm talking about the not-so-good kind, which is more common. Why do customers download free games in situations when they should know that they would get more enjoyment in total out of a premium game, even after taking the price into account?

To answer that question, let's talk about chocolate. Chocolate!

In 2007, Kristina Shampanier, Nina Mazar, and Dan Ariely published a study in *Marketing Science* that examined the weird and ultimately irrational way that people think about zero as a price.[9] They performed several studies to look at the issue from different angles, but the general experimental design was that they set up a makeshift shop on the campus of MIT where they offered to sell students one of two chocolates. Visitors to their booth could buy either a mundane Hershey's Kiss or a decadent Lindt truffle. For those not familiar with Lindt confections, the point is that it's a high-quality chocolate. The little bite-size truffles that these researchers used cost about 30 cents each when bought in bulk. Hershey's Kisses are about the same size and are okay as far as chocolate goes, but most people wouldn't use words like "luxury" or "premium" to describe them. Right now I could go on Amazon.com and buy them for about 4 cents each in bulk.

The setup for one of the experiments included in this study was that the researchers put up a sign that said, "One chocolate per customer," and started out by offering to sell either a Lindt truffle for 15 cents or a Hershey's Kiss for 1 cent. A good deal either way, but given the quality of the truffle, the majority (69%) of people who bought something bought the higher-quality product. The researchers explained this unsurprising result from an economist's perspective, citing a predictable relationship between how much pleasure people would get from eating a chocolate minus how much displeasure they'd experience from spending money. The Lindt would result in, say, 30 pleasure points but would cost 15 cents. The Hershey's Kiss would only give 5 pleasure points, but cost just 1 cent. Rational people should subtract the expected pain points (from spending money) from the expected pleasure points (from eating the chocolate) and choose whichever option left them with more pleasure. Thus, the Lindt was the better choice because it netted 15 pleasure points (30 minus 15), but the Hershey's Kiss netted the subject only 4 pleasure points (5 minus 1). Rationality and chocolate wedded together in delicious, thoughtful bliss.

But after a while the researchers did something tricky. They lowered the price of each chocolate by 1 cent. So the Lindt truffle was now 14 cents, the Hershey's Kiss was free. One was free-to-play (well, free-to-eat), the other premium. But they were still the same chocolates and both had their price changed by the same amount, so the ratios of pleasure to costs were the same. Any totally rational person would continue to prefer the Lindt because it should still net more pleasure. But that's not what happened. When the Hershey's Kiss was free, people's preferences completely flipped: 69 percent of those who took something chose the low-quality but free Hershey's Kiss.

And lest you think that this particular brand of irrationality is limited to products made of corn syrup and cocoa powder, Shampanier and her colleagues also did an experiment involving Amazon.com gift cards.[10] Consider this question: Would you rather buy a $10 gift card for $1 or a $20 gift card for $8? Most people (64%) in the study opted for the $20 card, correctly noting that it would lead to a net gain of $12 but the other would net them only $9. But then the researchers lowered the price of each gift card by $1 so that the choice was between a free $10 card and buying a $20 card for $7. Given these choices, every single one of their subjects chose the free $10 card, even though the $20 card for $7 would have given them $3 more in credit.

We actually see this kind of response to free offers everywhere. When Ben & Jerry's stores celebrate Free Ice Cream Day by giving out free cones, people will wait in line for 45 minutes just to get something that would cost only a few dollars any other day or at any other ice cream store. Each year on Free Comic Book Day, many comic book stores pull in crowds of shoppers that will rush tables in order to get comics that normally only cost a few dollars. When free entry to the national museums in the United Kingdom was introduced in 2001, attendance doubled.[11] And, of course, the online marketplaces for downloadable games are loaded with games that are free to download and try, even if they eventually try to make money off you in other ways. And if that marketplace activity is any indication, more people seem to prefer free-to-play games than premium games that come with up-front costs. Why the abnormally large reaction to an offer of something for free?

One possible reason has to do with what is known as "prospect theory." Pioneered by Daniel Kahneman and Amos Tversky, one of the main tenets of the theory is that people dislike losses more than they like gains of proportional value. This loss aversion makes us sensitive to any losses in a given transaction, even very small ones, like 1 cent. Habit and mental shortcuts are at work here, not necessarily rational evaluation. Kahneman and Tversky also did research to show that because of loss aversion people react very differently to bets on a sure thing, such as a guaranteed win or a guaranteed loss. Those absolutes are given disproportionate weight in our decision-making. So when we see a potential transaction with no cost, we overvalue it because there is literally no chance of a bad decision. Maybe another decision would be better, but maybe not. But there's no way that the Hershey's Kiss or the free-to-play downloadable game isn't worth zero to try out. Free is overvalued because it avoids any chance of loss, which we hate more than we love the possibility of getting a similar gain.

Shampanier and her colleagues argue that this "no downsides" feature of the free option creates what psychologists call "positive affect," which is just a fancy way of saying that "it makes us happy." People have a positive emotional reaction to an option that is free of risk and cost, then they use the fact that it makes them happy as a decision-making shortcut when deciding what chocolate to choose or what kind of game to download. When Shampanier measured general feelings of happiness among subjects choosing between the chocolate options, she found a big spike in those considering the free option. Then, to test whether or not people went on to use that positive affect to make a decision, the researchers did another experiment where they forced subjects to think explicitly in terms of how much pleasure they would get from eating the fancy Lindt chocolate and how much happier they might be if they got the Hershey's chocolate for free. The idea was that by bringing this logical approach to the fore of their attention, subjects would be less swayed by the irrational delight of a zero price tag. And that's exactly what happened: Those who had to think carefully about their reasons still preferred the free chocolate, but the effect was weaker.

Our irrational treatment of zero as a price can be used for good, too. Many cities around the world have outright banned plastic shopping bags because of their environmental costs and their contribution to litter problems relative to reusable bags. Other cities have employed a softer touch by mandating a tiny charge for each plastic bag a shopper carries out of the store. In either case, the idea is to encourage shoppers to bring and reuse their own bags. Researchers in Argentina took advantage of a rare opportunity for a naturally occurring experiment when the local equivalent of 2.5-cent plastic-bag fees were rolled out in late 2012.[12] The fees were levied in some supermarkets in Buenos Aires, but not others. Thus the researchers were able to examine how many people brought their own, reusable shopping bags depending on whether they could have their groceries bagged for free or for a small fee. The results were stark: Between 10 percent and 20 percent brought their own bags when plastic bags were free, but as many as 60 percent brought them when they had to pay just a few cents for the plastic alternative.

This effect has also shown up in one interesting little experiment of a video game. In October 2014, Lucas Redwood, developer of mobile games like *You Must Build a Boat* and the unfortunately named *10000000*, released a game called *Smarter Than You*. It's essentially an online rock/paper/scissors game where you and your opponent make a choice and have the option of trying to bluff each other. At the end of each match, the game gives players the option to "tip" each other by making an in-app purchase. At the tap of a button, you can give your opponent $.99, $1.99, or $2.99 in real money. This is done for no other reason than being nice.

In an interview with Pocket Gamer, Redwood admitted to skepticism about whether the tipping component would catch on when he released the game.[13] And indeed it didn't. In that same interview Redwood noted that fewer than two thousand players tipped at all, and almost all of them only gave $.99. So he tried something new: He made tipping free. Well, practically free. He added a monetization option where people could tip their opponents by watching a 15-second video advertisement. Watching ads in exchange for rewards is a common feature in free-to-play games, but the twist here was that you suffered through the ad and your opponent got the benefit. The results were amazing. "When given the opportunity, 85 percent of people will choose to watch the ad, solely to benefit their opponent," Redwood told Pocket Gamer.[14] The tipping behavior that cost no money was more popular than the nominal $.99 option—far more so than you might expect based on a linear relationship between dollar cost and benefit.

So whatever the reasons may be, zero is a magical number as far as price is concerned. This, of course, helps explain why there are so many free-to-play games out there and why developers keep making them. Low-risk and free-risk makes us happy, which is used as a mental short-cut to otherwise difficult decision-making about what game to try out. So let us now skip ahead to the point where the other shoe drops and our "free" game starts to try to get money out of us. Under what conditions are we more likely to make an impulsive, in-app purchase?

IMPULSE PURCHASES AND EGO DEPLETION

Back in the dark ages of the 1990s and early 2000s you would have to actually get in some kind of vehicle and drive to a store to buy games and expansion packs on disks. Before you could play them you'd have to go back home, unwrap the packaging, and run "setup.exe" or put the disk into your PlayStation. Things are different now, of course. Not only can you download all that stuff online, but games also give out new content in dribs and drabs, offering new levels, new cosmetic items, and in-game power-ups to help you get past a particularly difficult or boring part of the game. If you've got a credit card, you can make the needed microtransactions in literally seconds without even having to set the game aside.

But with that convenience comes the potential for impulse purchases. Most of us have made impulsive purchases of some kind outside of games, usually from a sales rack meant to grab our attention as we're waiting in line or on the basis of Amazon's observation that "other customers who bought Monty Python and the Holy Grail also bought barbeque sauce!" The widespread use of credit cards beginning in the 1970s made these kinds of unplanned purchases easy, and, as we will see, using a credit card makes impulse purchases more likely thanks to certain mental quirks. What's more, the way in-game purchases are handled and the way sales pitches are designed in modern video games—especially casual games played on mobile devices and Face-book—encourage us to buy stuff when we might not have planned to.

For sure, the vast majority of people who download any free-to-play game don't ever make any purchase. As noted earlier, only about 1.5 percent of players buy anything. But that number includes children who don't have access to credit cards, which I doubt describes most of you reading this book. Again, it's hard to get completely accurate numbers, but cut out the kids and the percentage of people making purchases should creep up. And when you're talking about millions of players, even a small percentage is a substantial number in absolute terms. So we're left with some important questions: Can titles that encourage in-game purchases target people who are susceptible to impulse purchases? Do they?

The answer to both questions is yes. To see why, let's start with a brief overview of research on the psychology of impulse purchases. It will involve configuring a new computer and spying on people while they do their laundry.

When consumer psychologists first started studying impulsive buying decisions back in the 1950s, they had a seemingly strange way of doing it. Mostly they looked at different categories of products and tried to decide if it was an impulse item or not. A bottle of Pepsi Cola? That's an impulse purchase, because you don't really need it. A gallon of communist repellant? Well, during the 1950s that was pretty much a staple like sugar and flour, so not an impulse purchase. From there researchers started to look at environmental factors, such as product location within the store, packaging characteristics, and a product's texture or scent. Eventually, though, the researchers wised up to the fact that any product could be purchased impulsively no matter which grocery store aisle it was in and that the really interesting stuff was going on inside shoppers' heads. Impulse purchases were then characterized as a sudden urge to buy something immediately, without thought given to either the consequences or cost of the action. And so began the examination of the processes going on within the minds of impulse shoppers. Note, though, that impulse shopping is distinct from compulsive shopping or compulsive buying, which are terms the literature generally reserves for an actual psychological disorder. Compulsive shopping is generally considered to keep company with other obsessive/compulsive behaviors that I'm not addressing here.

One thread of impulse shopping research that I think is most relevant to games deals with the fact that resisting impulse purchases takes willpower. A number of studies have looked at the relationship between personality and this kind of behavior. Most of them suggest a negative relationship between conscientiousness and impulse purchases.[15] In personality psychology, conscientiousness is just what it sounds like: a personality trait that describes how much people concern themselves with details, how thorough they are in their work, and how much they tend to make premeditated actions. People high in conscientiousness, it turns out, tend not to make as many impulse purchases as those who are low on the trait. They plan out their shopping, make budgets, and stick to them. Another personality trait found to be tied to impulse purchases is how people tend to either flip out or remain calm in the face of stress. This trait was called "neuroticism" by early researchers, but over time they have gravitated toward the somewhat less judgmental term "emotional stability." People high in emotional stability also tend not to make impulse purchases, but those who are low may find themselves more susceptible to impulsive reactions based on emotion.[16] There has also been some research to support the idea that emotions can have an effect on our shopping, and that some people may use impulse purchases as a kind of boost to their mood.[17]

But no matter who you are and no matter how a deck of personality traits is stacked in your favor, resisting that bag of candy in the checkout line or that experience point booster in a mobile game's virtual storefront takes willpower. Some of the most interesting research on impulse purchases is taking place in the context of willpower and how our behaviors before and during a shopping experience can affect how much willpower we have to resist impulses. We all have this ability to substitute a desired behavior (walking or clicking away from the potential purchase) for an undesirable one (giving in and buying it when we know we shouldn't). Sometimes it's hard and sometimes it's not.

The reason has to do with the fact that willpower is a finite resource that can be depleted by a variety of mental activities, according to Roy Baumeister and John Tierny, authors of *Willpower: Rediscovering the Greatest Human Strength*.[18] The energy that we use for self-regulation is like a pool of blue mana in a video game: You only have so much, it drains when you use it, but it will refill over time. Baumeister is also partial to the "it's like a muscle that gets tired and needs to rest" metaphor in his book and other writings. This works just as well, but we are talking about video games here, so let's go with the mana metaphor.

When your willpower/mana is depleted, you become far more likely to fail at self-regulation, and you either make indulgent choices or just roll with the status quo by making no choice at all. You're also more likely to give up on tasks that require sustained effort or attention. Beaumeister and his colleagues call this state "ego depletion" in a slight nod to that old rascal Sigmund Freud, who was one of the first psychologists to talk about self-regulation of short-sighted impulses by what he called the "ego."

Ego depletion can be created by almost any kind of mental activity that requires control of thought or emotion. One of the simplest ways of poking holes in the lining of a person's willpower pool is simply to tell her not to think about white bears. Go on. Try it. Don't think about a white bear. You just thought of a white bear, didn't you? Well, stop. If done for long enough, this kind of effortful focusing of thoughts will drain your ability to self-regulate behavior. In one of the earliest studies on the topic, subjects who tried not to think of white bears for just six minutes were asked to solve a set of anagrams—letters that could be unscrambled to form a word.[19] Relative to a control group who was free to think of white bears or anything else they liked, those who were ego-depleted gave up on the task more quickly. If you're skeptical of the white bear task, I'll tell you that similar effects have been found by having subjects repress facial expressions while watching sad or funny videos,[20] memorizing numbers,[21] doing complicated math problems,[22] faking enthusiasm for boring speeches,[23] making complicated decisions about how to spend money,[24] and more.

Other research has found that ego depletion has huge effects on what choices we make after engaging in mentally draining tasks, especially if there is an emotional component to the choice. In one study, subjects devoted a substantial amount of their mental resources to memorizing a seven-digit number.[25] This task takes significant effort and attention, as you probably know if you've ever tried to memorize a phone number without writing it down. After doing this, subjects were invited to consider two options for a snack: either a slice of decadent chocolate cake or a sensible fruit cup. Those who had their self-regulation resources drained by remembering a long string of numbers were more likely to give in to temptation and choose the cake.

Another study had subjects perform a task that many gamers might be familiar with: using a website to custom-build a computer.[26] Subjects used Dell.com to make a series of choices about how to configure a computer in terms of its processor, memory, monitor, mouse, keyboard, hard drive, and video card. To make sure they were taking it seriously, the researchers required subjects to deliberate and be able to articulate explanations for their choices. If you've ever used a website like this to configure a complicated purchase and compare all possible options, you know how mentally draining it can be. After they completed their long series of choices, subjects were asked to complete another task that would require concentration and effortful thought: solving more of those anagram word puzzles. (Psychologists love asking people to solve anagrams for some reason. It's eiwdr.) Relative to those in control groups, the subjects who had gone through the demanding process of configuring Dell computers gave up on completing the anagrams sooner. Three other experiments reported in that same article showed that simply considering options and making choices among consumer goods and college courses made people give up sooner on difficult math problems, procrastinate more, and generally allow decisions to be made for them. This was all because they had already used up too much of their mental energy and willpower.

It's not hard to imagine how this concept of ego depletion and self-regulation could apply to impulse shopping. Kathleen Vohs from the University of Minnesota has done several studies on ego depletion and impulse purchases, all of which have implications for how we are likely to react to the kinds of sales pitches we see in mobile games. In one study,[27] they used the "don't think of white bears" trick to deplete self-regulation resources. Researchers then gave subjects $10 and invited them to look through some items that the local university bookstore was considering adding to their stock. Subjects could keep all $10 or they could buy any of the 22 different products, such as candy, gum, playing cards, and coffee mugs. Relative to those who didn't have their self-regulation impulses drained, these subjects made more impulse purchases of items they hadn't planned on buying when they started the experiment. The effect was even stronger among those with personality traits related to impulse purchases.

The implications that this research on ego depletion has for microtransactions in video games is that the timing of the sales pitch can have a big impact on whether or not you fall for it. "Playing a video game is likely to use up a lot of these resources," said Ron Faber, when I contacted him via e-mail about the subject. He co-authored the study about impulse purchases that I described above, and he goes on to say, "If playing a game requires concentration, you are using up attentional and cognitive resources. If it is exciting or scary, you may be using up emotional resources. In each case, this will make subsequent self-control more difficult."

Indeed, even the simplest games require attention, focus, and cognitive effort, which leaves you with fewer resources for regulating impulsive purchases or other decisions you may not have planned on when you started playing. Clever game designers will capitalize on this. Presenting an option to buy damage boosters and offering a rematch after losing a long match in *Marvel Puzzle Quest*, for example, should be more effective than before the match, simply because the mental resources used to play the game are the same mental resources needed to resist making that purchase. Not only that, negative mood after a loss might make buying the booster even more appealing, since retrying that match and trouncing our opponent should alleviate our mood. This trick should even work for spamming friends for requests for help and to play a casual game cooperatively. Many casual games offer rewards for sending invites out to friends and contacts, regardless of whether they find such spam annoying. A mentally depleted player should be more likely to just tap through default options to get their rewards without thinking about it.

Similar to the subjects assembling a Dell computer in the experiment described above, players who have just finished a lengthy character-creation process in a role-playing game or a tutorial in any kind of game might be more susceptible to buying downloadable content or paying to unlock additional character customizations than if they saw those offers before character creation. Timing matters to the extent that a game can hit you when your resources have been spent. This is even true in retail games of the nonretail variety. When I bought *Destiny* at a big-box store, the clerk tried to sell me on prepurchasing a code for a season pass that would get me downloadable content as it was released in the upcoming months. That's not an effective time to hit me with the sales pitch. A much better time would be in-game, right after I had completed a mentally demanding raid or multiplayer match. If you want to curb impulsive spending, pay attention to the timing of every sales prompt you're responding to. Step away, take a rest to let your self-regulation resources regenerate, and think again if you want to spend any money.

And you know what? Maybe you still do, and that's obviously fine. Not all purchases are impulsive or the cause of later regret. The theory of ego depletion and self-regulation that I've discussed above is set within the wider context of goal-oriented behavior and motivation. It assumes that people have a desired behavior and they need to use willpower to make sure that behavior happens instead of something they don't want, like spending money they don't have to speed up the construction of a unit in *Clash of Clans*. But if you're intending to spend money on those microtransactions in order to support the developer or enjoy the game more, we can't fairly call it an impulse purchase. Some research on *Ghost Recon Online* players presented by Nick Yee and Nicholas Ducheneaut at the 2014 Game Developer's Conference actually suggests that the biggest spenders in a game are sometimes the most rational and least impulsive.[28]

But even in the cases where you decide to buy something without being impulsive, you may still spend more than you intend to. The virtual currencies that games frequently use create additional cases cases of psychological trickery.

FUNNY MONEY

If you've ever tried to make an in-game purchase, you know that you can't just pull out your credit card and charge 99 cents to it. In fact, the game probably took pains during the tutorial to teach you how to use a virtual currency, such as gems, coins, Smurfberries, donuts, crystals, shards, bux, or whatever other name won out in a focus group during game development. Okay, fine, so you have to convert real money into fake currency before you can spend it. Here's where you run into the second problem: rushing the build orders on that new barracks will cost you 50 diamonds (or whatever), but you can't just buy 50 diamonds. At a minimum they're sold in packs of 600 for $5—or at maximum, 20,000 for $100, which is helpfully labeled "Best value." So you're in for five bucks because you need that barracks built right now. So you charge $5 on your credit card, and a few seconds later you have a fully functional barracks and 550 leftover diamonds.

This is all a recipe for overspending in the very near future. You're now much more likely to put in another $5 down the line.

One of the most practical pieces of advice I've heard for dealing with debt is to freeze your credit cards in a cup of ice. That way you can get at them if you have an emergency, such as an unexpected car repair, but the hassle involved with thawing them may keep you from trivial purchases that you don't truly need to make. The advice is well placed because a long history of research starting back in the 1970s shows that people tend to spend more with credit cards than they do with cash or even checks. In 1977, Elizabeth Hirschman, a professor of marketing at New York University, had her research assistants ambush more than 4,000 shoppers coming out of a department store.[29] The researchers asked if they could inspect the shoppers' sales receipts, and sure enough they found that those people who used credit cards tended to both buy more items and spend more money relative to shoppers using cash.

You may be thinking that people who made larger purchases just didn't have that much cash on hand and resorted to credit cards. That's a good thought, but subsequent research has found that it's not necessarily the case. For example, one study designed a silent auction where subjects bid on tickets to a basketball game played by the Boston Celtics or a baseball game played by the Boston Red Sox.[30] It was the kind of auction where subjects wrote down how much they'd be willing to pay, and then if they won they were called to come in to cough up the money and pick up the tickets. Before bidding, some subjects were told that they would ultimately have to pay in cash, but others were told they would have to use a credit card. Those expecting to pay with credit card submitted auction bids that were, on average, twice as large as those who expected to hand over cash money.

Why does this happen? It has to do with how much less painful it is to use a credit card relative to paying cash. In their watershed article "The Red and the Black: Mental Accounting of Savings and Debt," researchers Drazen Prelec (an experimental psychologist) and George Lowenstein (an economist) came up with a theory about how people experience the pain of purchases.[31] Prelec and Lowenstein argued that any purchase decision is based on whether the expected pleasure would outweigh the expected pain. The discomfort—Prelec and Lowenstein go so far as to call it "pain"—of parting with money can diminish the pleasure of the purchase, possibly enough for us to regret or even avoid the purchase in the first place. But one thing that can reduce the discomfort of payment is to disconnect the purchase from thoughts about the payment. Using credit cards creates this kind of disconnect in at least two ways.

First, credit cards disconnect payment from pain by putting time between the two. When you swipe a credit card (or bump your smartphone against an Apple Pay or Google Wallet device) you don't become any less wealthy. No money is taken from your possession until you pay the bill. Sure, eventually you get slapped in the face with the credit card debt, but the time between the purchase and the payment means it factors in much less when you're making your decision. Other forms of payment, like drafting against bank accounts or electing to have someone to send a bill later, have the same effect.

Perhaps counterintuitively, prepayment or purchasing store credit (e.g., with a refillable gift card) can have the same effect because the pain of paying has already taken place when you loaded up the gift card with $20. The payment happens before the purchase instead of after in this case, but the two are still separated by time. Spending that $20 worth of credit later is usually considered a separate transaction—one involving much less discomfort than paying cash. In one clever experiment on this concept, Dilip Soman from the University of Toronto sent research assistants into a laundromat to spy on people to see if they tried to save money by combining white clothes and colored clothes in the same load. [32] This was right before the laundromat chain moved from coin-operated machines to ones that required customers to first fill up a reusable card with prepaid credit. Once the laundromat made the switch to the card-operated machines, Soman sent his researchers back in to see if the prepayment method made them more or less frugal. He found that the switch to prepaid cards meant that about 20 percent more people separated their whites and colors, meaning that they did more loads and spent more money. Another study found that people who were given a $50 gift card were more likely to spend more on items from a catalog than were those given a $50 bill. [33]

The second way that credit cards reduce the pain of consumption is that they don't explicitly make you think about how much you're paying. Most of us just sign the receipt and go on our way. In fact, many places don't even give you a paper receipt for small purchases anymore. Researchers call this quality "transparency." Cash is the most transparent, and thus the most painful to spend because the amount we spend is more easily seen and remembered. Hirschman's surveys of department store shoppers back in 1977, for example, found that those using credit cards were more likely to misremember how much they spent.[34] In a different study from the laundromat one described above, Soman found that having subjects in a mock shopping exercise use checks and cash made them much more likely to remember how much their purchases would cost, as opposed to those who pretended to use credit cards.[35]

In-game currencies are to credit cards what credit cards are to cash. That is, they are even less transparent and more temporally separated from the pain of payment. When you spend 10 gold coins on a cosmetic item in *Jetpack Joyride* or 10 moonies on a pirate cow in *Cow Clicker*, the fact that the game forces you to prepurchase the coins or moonies in bulk guarantees that the pain of making that purchase is separated in time from the joy of using them to get what you want from the game. In fact, it's doubly removed since you used a credit card to buy the virtual money in the first place! What's more, the act of spending those coins, diamonds, or spacebux is far more transparent than spending cash to buy a coffee or candy bar at a convenience store. How much did those five diamonds cost? Who knows. You'll never find a game that offers a simple conversion rate of "1 gold coin = 1 cent." This is because the game developers know better than to make the math that easy and thus make the expenses that transparent. Instead, figuring out how many dollars' worth of Smurfberries you're spending is going to take a calculator and a minute or two of thought to figure out, and most of us aren't going to do that. Thus, once we possess the virtual currency, the painful part is over. Spending it is frictionless, mostly painless, and completely divorced from any feeling of spending real money.

What's more, you usually have some virtual currency left over. The bundles and costs of items are generally structured so that you can never spend every last scrap of your virtual currency. So when you run low on gems and want something that costs five more than you have, you have to buy more. But once again you have to buy 50 at a time and suddenly you have 45 gems just sitting around feeling like they're free and already paid for. Because they are.

But though discrete, in-game purchases are currently the most popular business model for free-to-play games, it's not the only one. What about recurring subscriptions that let you access premium content and features? Or, for that matter, what about subscriptions for non–free-to-play games like *World of Warcraft* or gaming services like Xbox Live? Are there psychological tricks that game developers use to get us to subscribe and stay subscribed? You bet there are. Let's take a look at those in the next chapter.

THINGS TO REMEMBER FROM THIS CHAPTER

- *Cow Clicker* had a lot of stupid puns. Most of them were pretty funny.
- People treat a price of zero (that is, free) in a special, particularly irrational way. This may be because it appears to represent no risk or chance of loss in a transaction. We are biased to favor sure things.
- Some theories hold that self-control is a pool of mental energy from which we have to draw to make decisions, perform cognitively demanding tasks, and control our behavior. If it's depleted, we become susceptible to accepting the status quo or making hedonistic choices.
- Thus the timing of sales pitches matters. You're more likely to make impulse purchases when your reservoir of self-control is low. This can happen after a series of choices or cognitively demanding tasks.
- Decoupling loss of real money from purchases makes separating us from our money less painful. This happens with credit cards, store credit, and virtual currencies like those found in games.
- Transparency refers to how little the method of payment masks how much you're spending. Cash is high-transparency; in-game currencies are low-transparency. The latter leads to more spending.

11

HOW DO GAMES KEEP PLAYERS PAYING?

"At this point, I'm essentially trying to talk myself out of dropping $300 on an MMO. But the notion of paying once for a game that normally has a monthly fee associated with it is incredibly appealing."
— Jeff Gerstmann of GiantBomb.com, regarding his decision to buy a lifetime subscription to *Star Trek Online*[1]

If you've ever paid a monthly fee for an online game, you have a couple of computer nerds named Kelton Finn and John Taylor to thank for it. Back in 1980—which was almost the 1970s, according to my math—Finn and Taylor were students at the University of Virginia. They were fans of the tabletop role-playing game *Dungeons & Dragons* and wanted to see if they could bring some of what was fun about that experience to the burgeoning technology of computers. There had been simple text adventures for computers, but Finn and Taylor wanted to emulate the experience of crawling through a dungeon and exploring dangerous territory with other human players. So over their summer vacation they created *Dungeons of Kesmai*, which let up to six players on a network explore dungeons drawn with simple ASCII computer characters. Not quite "massively" multiplayer, but it was a start.[2]

Dungeons of Kesmai was quite popular on campus, but Finn and Taylor soon developed higher ambitions. They formed a company and started work on a sequel, which they called *Island of Kesmai*. It turns out, you see, that the dungeon was on an island. This stuff practically writes itself. The new game was a much improved version of the first, allowing more players to connect and play in a bigger world. A deal was made with Compuserve, the leading provider of Internet service of the day, and in 1985 *Islands of Kesmai* became the first commercial online game. Technically it didn't cost anything to play, but anyone who wanted to join in had to pay up to $12 per hour just to access the Compuserve service. That's far more expensive than the $12 to $15 per month most of us are used to.

Islands of Kesmai was succeeded by other titles from other developers with which you may be more familiar—*Neverwinter Nights* (1991, up to $8 per hour using the Internet service provider America Online), *Ultima Online* (1997, $10 per month), *Everquest* (1999, $9.89 per month), and *World of Warcraft* (2004, $14.99 per month).[3] Despite the recent success of free-to-play games that rely on in-game purchases, it's a big marketplace and some subscription-based games still exist and thrive. Many free-to-play games also offer a hybrid approach. *Dungeons & Dragons Online*, which would have blown Finn's and Taylor's minds if you showed it to them in 1980, is free-to-play and supported by in-game microtransactions. But players can also pay monthly fees to become a premium member and earn additional in-game rewards, boosts, and discounts.

In previous chapters, I discussed some of the psychology that drives our purchase of games that have a one-time cost, and I covered games that rely on in-game or in-app purchases. So now let's turn our attention to a third business model: subscription-based games and the occasional game that charges by the minute or by the hour. There are also game-related services like Xbox Live and Playstation Plus that require subscriptions, so I will include them. It should not surprise you much at this point to hear that those marketing, promoting, and selling these subscriptions employ a few basic psychological tricks to increase their numbers.

THE STATUS QUO EFFECT: PAYING WITHOUT PLAYING

Marketers and publishers know that once they have you as a paying customer, the hardest part of that relationship is over and you're more likely to stick around than not. Many of us have been surprised when one day we looked up and realized that we've been paying for a subscription-based online game like *World of Warcraft* when we haven't logged on for months. Or maybe we're reading our e-mail and we get a cheerful note from Microsoft saying that our Xbox Live Gold account has automatically renewed and the charge applied to our credit card. We think, "I should really cancel that," but we don't actually get around to it. A month or a year later, we get the notice again and think the same thing again. Why is that?

Before I explain, let's talk about 401(k) savings plans. Because, you know, kids today love talking about 401(k) savings plans. For those who don't know, these savings plans are common in the United States and they let employees automatically sock away part of each paycheck for retirement. Besides simply setting money aside for one's golden years, these plans offer other benefits, such as paying lower taxes on that money and sometimes even receiving matching contributions from employers. In the long run, it's like free money, so participating in these savings plans is generally a smart thing to do if you don't want to die of old age on the job. But they're voluntary, so younger workers lacking a long-term perspective don't always sign up for them and would rather waste that money on video games, fancy coffee drinks, or *Minecraft* T-shirts.

Consider these two groups of employees and the percentage of each group that signed up to participate in a 401(k) savings plan:

Group A: 49% participated in a savings plan
Group B: 86% participated in a savings plan

That's a big difference, right? Can you guess why only 49 percent of people in Group A decided to save for retirement but a comparatively larger 86 percent of Group B members decided to save? Maybe Group B is full of MBAs, economists, or self-aware computers who are more rational than the drunken chimps in Group A? Nope. Maybe Group A is full of young whippersnappers unconcerned with retirement and Group B is a pile of old geezers? A better guess, but still incorrect. The explanation comes down to paperwork.

These groups were actual subjects in a 2001 study by Brigitte Madrian and Dennis Shea, two economists interested in what happened when a tiny but important change was made to the paperwork related to the 401(k) plan.[4] The only difference between the groups was that the forms for Group A required new hires to actively sign up for the savings plan, but the forms for Group B automatically enrolled new hires into the savings plan unless they overrode that decision. In other words, people tended to go with the default choice: "Don't Participate" for Group A and "Participate" for Group B. The suckers in Group A saved less because they couldn't be bothered to check one box on one form.

Default choices can also save lives in the case of the box that people check (or don't check) on organ donation forms. In Austria, the organ donation rate in the case of accidental death is 99.9 percent, but in neighboring Germany it's only 12 percent. The reason, according to one study,[5] is that in countries like Austria, Belgium, and France the default selection on the organ donation form is "Yes," meaning that citizens have to opt out of the commitment. In Germany, Denmark, and the United Kingdom citizens have to explicitly opt in to being an organ donor. There may also be some cultural issues at play, but a simple change to the paperwork means that thousands and thousands of un-used eyeballs, hearts, and livers are being donated to medicine and to people who need them.

Psychologists have a term for this reluctance to change from our previous or default decisions: "the status quo bias."[6] It is in no way limited to the world of financial planning. Indeed, it shows up every-where. Those in charge of television programming use the status quo bias to glide viewers from one show to the next, using an established hit with a strong viewership to build an audience for whatever comes after it. Networks frequently take it to the point where viewers move seam-lessly from the end of one show to a quick intro to the next without even pausing for a commercial break. Because once they start, many people will continue to watch the same channel even though switching to something else is trivially easy.

This is, of course, the same reason why gaming companies prefer that you sign up for an automatically renewing service instead of using prepaid subscription or point cards. You could, for example, pay for your Xbox Live Gold or PlayStation Plus subscription with a prepaid gift card. But once the subscription period lapses, it takes too much effort and action for you to go out and buy another card and enter the code, at least compared to just sitting back and letting the subscription renew and charge your credit card, which is the status quo bias in action. This is also reason that rental services like Netflix or GameFly offer "free trials" that will roll into paid subscriptions if you don't actively cancel. They even spin it as a benefit: "If you are enjoying Netflix, do nothing and your membership will automatically continue." Thanks for looking out for me, Netflix!

But it's also important to be aware that the default choices you're presented with when signing up for a new service can also be programmed to take advantage of the status quo bias. The next time you sign up for something that has multiple tiers of subscription options, pause to take a close look. Often, the most expensive or second most expensive will be the option checked by default. That's not an accident and it's not arbitrary. Technology is sufficiently advanced so that the website could easily have had no plan chosen by default and could instead require you to make your choice in order to proceed. Instead, they're taking advantage of the "status quo effect" and probably getting more people for the $12.95 plan instead of the $7.95 one.

Similarly, "opt out" options are popular among marketers because many people don't bother with the almost effortless task of unchecking some boxes so that they don't receive e-mail spam or avoid installing some obnoxious toolbar in their Web browser. The updater for my computer's Java software, for example, asks if I want to install the Ask.com Web browser toolbar whenever I update Java. Of course, the "Install the Ask Toolbar and make Ask my default search provider" option is checked by default, and if the updater pops up while my daughter is using the computer, I'm sure to have to shake my tiny fist at the computer and undo some changes.

The status quo effect gets even more potent when the task you're faced with is more cognitively demanding. Subjects in one study[7] were asked to make difficult calls about whether a tennis ball was in or out of bounds, but for each trial one of the two possible calls was randomly made the de facto default choice. You can probably head me off at the pass and figure out that people tended to stick with the randomly assigned default choice, even more so when the call was difficult. Even considering going against a default choice seemed to increase the activity in the prefrontal cortex (an area associated with decision-making) and increased exchanges between that area and the subthalamic nucleus, a chunk of grey matter associated with motivated behavior. In other words, evaluating something besides a default option literally requires more mental energy.

But the status quo effect can work to our benefit, as we saw in the 401(k) savings example above. Many games feature built-in tutorials, tooltips, or other pointers for novice players. Often these assists can be turned off, but they are almost always on by default because even if a game makes players aware of them, most would probably not bother turning them on if they were off by default. Frustration would ensue. For example, the *Guitar Hero* and *Rock Band* games don't present tutorials to new players by default. This always seemed weird to me, and I swear I made it through most of the first *Guitar Hero* without ever knowing about advanced moves, such as hammer-ons and pull-offs, because I had skipped the tutorial.

So beneficial situations aside, how do you guard against the status quo effect when you don't want it unduly influencing your behavior? For starters you can use prepaid subscription cards instead of automatically renewing subscriptions. I renew my Xbox Live Gold membership each year by using such a card, which has the added benefit of letting me buy the cards when they're on sale and hold on to them until needed. Plus I don't have to change my credit card every time one of these services is hacked.

Beyond prepaid cards and canceling free trials before they morph into a paid subscription, just make sure you take the time to look carefully at default options the next time you're filling something out or agreeing to a terms of service. Especially when it's a cognitively demanding or confusing task, because that's when you're most likely to succumb to the status quo effect. Consider: Are those default choices what's best for you? Maybe not.

THE FLAT-RATE BIAS

Back in April 2010, Scottish game developer Realtime Worlds announced the pricing model for its upcoming online game, *All Points Bulletin* (or *APB* for short). Many people were looking forward to the futuristic cops versus robbers game, but the announcement about the pricing contained a surprise. *APB* would cost $50 to buy off the shelf, which would also get you 50 hours of playtime. After that first 50 hours, you'd have to buy additional time at the rate of $6.99 for 20 hours or $9.99 for unlimited hours over the next month.

Upon hearing this, the rage was palpable on some forums. For sure, this was partially over the fact that *APB* was to have any monthly fee at all, despite that being par for the massively multiplayer online (MMO) course (free-to-play MMOs were just starting to work their way into Western markets at the time). But there seemed to be two other targets of the virtual hand-wringing. First, the playtime included with the retail product was doled out in hours rather than the traditional 30 days of unlimited play. Second, the $6.99 for 20 hours of game time seemed a bitter pill to swallow, apparently because people didn't want to pay by the hour. The game's traditional (and by "traditional" I mean games like *World of Warcraft*) monthly subscription option seemed to be overlooked by those complaining about the pay-by-the-hour pricing. To them, it seemed like a rip-off waiting to happen, even though for many casual players the hourly rate would save them money.

Why is that? Why are we averse to metered, pay-as-you-go pricing when all-you-can-eat options are available? As it sometimes turns out, psychology holds the answer. But let's get there by way of a discussion about cell phones.

A few years ago I needed a new cell phone, but my wife forced me to admit that I didn't really need anything fancy. So I went shopping and, being a completely rational decision maker and a bit of a cheapskate, I selected one of those pay-as-you-go phones where you buy prepaid minutes. The phone cost $35 to buy off the shelf, and I would be charged 10 cents per minute for calls and 20 cents per text message. The phone came with $35 worth of credit, and after that I would have to pay per use. Sound familiar? It's not too far off from *APB*'s initial pricing plans.

I could have easily gone for a $60-a-month plan that let me spend unlimited hours on the phone, only taking breaks to send unlimited text messages. Or I could have sought out a plan that gave me hundreds of minutes per month, which equates to practically unlimited minutes for my purposes. And I would have had plenty of company, since most of us overpay for cell phone use. A 2009 article in the *Los Angeles Times*[8] reported on a study showing that the average user was paying more than $3.00 a minute when accounting for how much per month they paid and how many of their plan's minutes they left unused at the end of a billing period. Another study published in the journal *Information Economics and Policy* found that about 65 percent of telecommunications customers would save more money with a pay-per-use rate than the flat rate they had chosen.[9] But not me. Hooray my superior rationality! Bravo!

Only my decision never felt right, and using the phone stressed me out a little. Not a lot, but enough to affect how I felt about it. Because I knew that every time I flipped that thing open to make a call I would have to pay 10 cents a minute. Long chats with my sister in another state were unthinkable. I kept calls as short as possible. I groaned when people asked me to text them, and when traveling I'd actually stalk my wife on Facebook until she comes online so I can ask her to call me on her phone.

The reason for my discomfort is something called "the flat-rate bias." Generally, people from Western cultures like flat rates and don't like being on a meter (Eastern cultures show much lower preferences for flat rates). Research on the topic started in the telecommunications industry during in the early 1990s, and in 2006 researchers Anja Lambrecht and Bernd Skiera expanded the topic into the digital age.[10] In the process, they peeled back some of the specific reasons why the flat-rate bias exists by surveying and examining payment information for more than 10,000 European customers of an Internet access provider. Three reasons for the flat-rate bias were identified.

The first two reasons for the flat-rate bias combine to make a potent predisposition. First, people overestimate how much they think they will use a service, such as Internet service, cellular phone service, or an online multiplayer game. When Lambrecht and Skiera asked customers to estimate how much data they thought they would use (e.g., "700 MB to 800 MB") and then later compared those estimates to actual usage, they found that customers consistently overestimated how much time and data they would spend using the Internet. This wasn't particularly surprising, since other research has found that consumers consistently overestimate how much they will use a product or service, especially for things we value, such as going to the gym or getting better at a game. But the second reason for the flat-rate bias discovered by Lambrecht and Skiera was that people used the pricing structure as insurance against unexpected spikes in usage. Subjects choosing flat rates were more likely to agree with statements like "For the security of knowing that my Internet access costs will never go above the amount agreed upon, I'm willing to pay a little more than average." So we expect to use more than we do and think that we need insurance against possible overuse.

Lambrecht and Skiera also found evidence for what they called the "taxi meter effect." The concept should be familiar to anyone who has sat in the back of a taxi watching with increasing displeasure as the meter ticked up with each passing second. Many of us prefer to rent cars or pay a flat rate for taxi trips instead of enduring the ticking meter. The taxi meter effect is a specific manifestation of a larger concept that researchers Drazen Prelec and George Lowenstein describe as a mental accounting strategy.[11] I talked a bit about this in the chapter on microtransactions. The idea is that since a flat-fee payment is made all at once, the pain or displeasure of making that withdrawal from our mental account is also borne all at once. But once made, we tend to ignore it while enjoying our purchase. It becomes decoupled, as Prelec and Lowenstein say, much in the same way that credit cards decouple the pain of paying from the joy of getting something new. Metered payments, on the other hand, reduce our enjoyment of a taxi ride or an MMO, because we frequently experience the displeasure of payment at the time of the event—or at least as often as we look at our watch or the ticking taxi meter.

In fact, all those little withdrawals may feel like they add up to more than the total amount for the flat rate. It's like if 5 + 5 came to 12. As part of their groundbreaking research that eventually resulted in a Nobel Prize, psychologists Daniel Kahneman and Amos Tversky found what they called a "law of diminishing sensitivity."[12] Basically, this describes how the amount we wince relative to the amount of something that is lost eventually flattens out. If you graphed it for a random person with "Pain" on the y-axis and "Magnitude of Cost" on the x-axis, the slope would be steep at first but then quickly level out as costs increase. So, for example, we experience a bigger jump in displeasure between a loss of $5 and a loss of $10 than we experience between losses of $1,005 and $1,010. It's why we'll feel great about saving 30 cents on a tube of toothpaste, but probably won't bother to drive across the street in order to save $3—10 times as much—on a flat-screen TV.

Diminishing sensitivity has implications for the taxi meter effect and our preference for flat-rate game subscriptions over pay-as-you-go models. Specifically, we experience greater subjective pain from multiple losses than we do to one big loss of equal value because evaluation of the losses is constantly being reset. Each additional tick of the meter is likely to be seen as a separate cost, which adds up to more pain than a one-time cost. Similarly, each hour we spend in a game with an hourly rate is experienced individually. Under those circumstances, it can be agonizing to wait for a guildmate to shuffle items around in their inventory, much less step away from the keyboard to grab a bite to eat. We'd rather have one big cut that seems less painful overall than endure a thousand cuts as the minutes fall away one by one. This is what led video game personality Jeff Gerstmann to spend $300 on a lifetime subscription to *Star Trek Online*, as related in quote at the top of this chapter.[13] It looks ridiculous at first glance, but if he assumed he would play the game a lot, it makes much more sense.

As a side note, diminishing sensitivity to losses is also the reason that rent-by-mail services like GameFly are so appealing relative to renting games one at a time. It's preferable to sweep all our costs into one big, monthly pile and feel like we have "unlimited" rentals for that price than it would be to rent one game at a time by the day or even by the week. The same is true for Netflix and DVDs. Yet how many of us have let games or DVDs sit around for days or weeks before getting to them?

So, armed now with this information about the flat-rate bias and diminishing sensitivity, let's circle back to one of the *APB* pricings described in that April 2010 press release, particularly that "$6.99 for 20 hours" option. Realtime Worlds never released any sales data, but my guess is that most people didn't go that route because of the flat-rate bias. It'll just be too painful to feel every individual hour pass away and think that it's another prepaid hour gone forever. In contrast, people who paid just a little more can feel comparatively less pain because they experience just one loss instead of a parade of many smaller losses that feel like they add up to more. As an aside, it's worth noting that *APB* wasn't able to succeed under any paid subscription plan. In late 2010, the game shut down and launched again the next year as *APB: Reloaded*, a free-to-play game supported by in-game purchases. See previous chapter, I guess.

I also think this flat-rate bias partially explains the aversions people feel to free-to-play games that hit them up for microtransactions too frequently. If I need to buy a booster card or a power-up in order to beat every level, those individual, small expenses start to feel like ticks of a taxi meter. I may, as a result, start looking for games that allow me to just pay one flat rate and get the whole game. Games are much more effective when they straddle a middle ground by letting you get by in most levels, but then put up gates or difficult encounters to get you to reset your mental budgets between expenses.

Finally, one of the reasons we may find it hard to walk away from a subscription-based game that we've spent months or even years with is that if we stop, it feels like all that work and time will be abandoned. You got all that great gear, all those levels, all those fancy skills. You're just going to walk away from it? Back in 2010, the Norwegian company Funcom, the publisher of the MMO game *The Age of Conan*, sent out a note to all customers saying, "As part of our maintenance your account is now flagged to have your characters below level 20 deleted as part of maintenance." The e-mail went on to advise customers to "reactivate your account now to ensure that your characters progress and names stay intact." This is a rather more in-your-face version of the kind of loss aversion that threatens us when we consider walking away from an online game with a persistent world, or even the massive plot we've built up in free-to-play games, such as *Farmville* or *Clash of Clans*. Leaving things alone may mean that all that work you put in goes to waste. Weighing those sunk costs of time and money from the past in your decision to renew your subscription today is irrational. Those costs are gone and can never be recovered. But humans have evolved to obsess over the downside of every decision and be averse to losses, so your troll shaman in *World of Warcraft* or your acres of strawberries in *Farmville* will usually live to see another billing cycle.

But then again, maybe what's really important to determining if I'm going to keep playing a game is what my friends are doing. In many ways, we don't even need the help of marketing professionals. We'll do their job for them if given half a chance. Let's explore how we market to ourselves in the next chapter.

THINGS TO REMEMBER FROM THIS CHAPTER

- We are biased in favor of accepting default options when given a set of choices. This is known as the "status quo effect." This is used to get you to renew subscriptions without thinking about it.

- Seriously, have you considered contributing to a 401(k) retirement plan or something similar? You really should. It makes the status quo effect work in your favor.
- People prefer flat rates and all-you-can-eat pricing options because the sum of each individual payment hurts more than one big payment of equal value. This is sometimes called the "taxi meter effect."
- This is related to the law of diminishing sensitivity. The relationship between pain and cost flattens out as costs increase. For example, the difference between $1 and $2 is more painful than the difference between $1,000 and $1,001.
- The fact that we hate to lose things more than we like gaining things of equivalent value is also often used to keep us paying subscriptions (cf., loss aversion, psychological reactance, the endowment effect).

12

HOW DO GAMES GET PLAYERS TO MARKET TO EACH OTHER?

"Tell me who your friends are, and I'll tell you who you are."
—Proverb, author unknown

Facebook experiments on you. You know that, right? In the summer of 2014 the social networking giant came under heavy criticism for a study it published based on one of these experiments because of the way it manipulated users' emotions.[1] Conducted by a scientist in the employ of Facebook and two other academics, the study tweaked the news feeds of 689,003 users to show posts from friends that had either more positive or more negative emotional content. This was accomplished by having a computer analyze certain words and phrases within the posts and categorize them as either "happy" or "sad." Ah, there's nothing better at recognizing humanity's joy and sorrow than the cold, mechanical circuitry of a computer. I like to think that they used an actual robot that sat in a cubicle rapidly scanning pictures of babies, political screeds, and poorly composed selfies. Upon finishing the data analysis, it slumped its metal shoulders and said, "I CAN CATEGORIZE, BUT I CAN NOT . . . FEEL." Science is awesome.

Anyway, the point of the Facebook experiment was to extend research from the well-established phenomenon of emotional contagion to the realm of social networking sites. Psychologists have known from decades of lab research that if you put people together in a room, their emotional states can transfer from one person to another. Being around happy or depressed people can make you happy or depressed.[2] One study, for example, showed that college freshmen who were unlucky enough to get paired with a mildly depressed roommate were more likely to become glum themselves.[3] The Facebook researchers wanted to see if the same thing could happen in online spaces through social networking tools. So for one week in January 2012 they deliberately hid either positive- or negative-sounding posts made by users' friends, thereby making their news feeds either more cheerful or more mopey. The researchers then gathered more than 3 million total posts that participants themselves made and used that same poor robot to code the emotional tone of those posts. The robot indeed found that emotional contagion happens on Facebook, as evidenced by the fact that people who saw more negative posts made slightly more negative posts themselves, and vice versa for those who saw more positive posts. Your emotional state, they concluded, can be affected by what you see your friends do and say on Facebook.[4] And Facebook can control the throttle on those emotion-inducing posts.

Well, sort of. It's worth noting the small magnitude of the emotional contagion effects found in this study. Most people need not worry about being thrown into mania or depression simply because someone they went to high school with complained about the weather or posted a picture of a particularly fantastic desert. If it wasn't for the massive number of data points in this study, the differences between the groups might not have been detectable at all. But that's not really the point of this story, and it's not what earned Facebook so much criticism and scrutiny. The issue was that the Facebook users in this study didn't even know they were participating. Facebook has some vague hand-waving language in their end-user license agreement about the fact that all users agree to participate in this kind of thing as one of many tradeoffs for using the service, but the facts are that nobody reads those agreements and nobody was told that Facebook was trying to manipulate their thoughts and emotions. Nor were they debriefed afterward, as is standard ethical practice among psychological researchers almost everywhere. This alarmed some people, who took to their blogs and editorial columns to decry the sneaky, conniving, puppet masters who had thrown away the trust users had placed in Facebook. "The study has troubling implications for Facebook's ability to manipulate the user experience for a variety of ends," wrote one commenter on Forbes.com.[5]

And though these critics may have some valid complaints (I personally think they do), the larger picture is that Facebook isn't unique. We are constantly affected by things we see our friends do online. Our opinions, judgments, and perceptions about video games, for example, are nudged by everything we see in our friends' activity feeds on Steam, their scores on Apple's Game Center leaderboards, and even the number of stars given out by strangers in the reviews posted on Amazon.com or the App store. What's more, many companies manipulate what we see in order to shape our opinions and get us to do the work of marketing their games among ourselves. To understand how, let's jaunt back to the 1950s and observe how one social psychologist was easily able to make a room full of people tell him that up was down and short was long.

SOCIAL PROOF: "*DUKE NUKEM* LONGER THAN LINE A," SAYS YOUTUBE STREAMER

Imagine that it's 1951 and you're a student at Swarthmore College in Pennsylvania. Also imagine that you're a white male between the ages of 17 and 25. Sorry if that's weird for you, but like I said: private, elite college in the early 1950s. Your parents are well educated, strong-minded, and expect you to follow in their footsteps. So far so good, because your academic standing is well above average and you even did a semester abroad in Europe. Very impressive, very worldly. You've agreed to participate in a study about visual perception, and upon arriving at the classroom where the study is to take place you see a group of seven other fellow Swarthmore students already seated in two neat rows of chairs.

You take an empty chair in the back row and the experimenter gets started. PowerPoint not having been invented yet, he directs everyone's attention to a set of large paper cards resting against a stand at the front of the classroom. The experimenter explains that on the left is a card with a vertical line on it. You can see that this is true. On the right is another card with three lines that are similar, but two of them are of different lengths than the one on the left and the third is the same length. The lines are labeled 1, 2, and 3. Your task, the experimenter says, is to identify which of the three lines on the right is the same length as the line on the left. This strikes you as a pretty stupid task since the answer is obvious, but whatever. The sooner you finish up here the sooner you can get back to whatever young men in the 1950s enjoyed doing. Probably snapping your suspenders and saying, "Gee willikers, daddy-o!" or something. I don't know. The records are unclear.

Indeed, the task proves to be as simple as you thought. The experimenter presents the first sets of lines and your classmates take turns announcing that line 2 is indeed the one that's the same length as the one on the left. When it comes your turn to announce your answer, you agree that yes, it's obviously line 2. On the next set everybody correctly notes that it's line 1. Now it's line 2 again. Now line 3.

Wait, what? Line 3? Why is everyone saying that line 3 is the one that's the same as the one on the left in this new set? You lean forward and squint. Line 3 is clearly not the correct answer. It seems to your eyes to be shorter, not the same length. But six fellow classmates in a row have said something different than what your eyes are telling you, and now it's your turn to give an answer. "Uh," you begin, looking at the line illustrations at the front of the class. "Line . . . 3?" The experimenter writes something on his clipboard but then just goes on to reveal the next set of lines. Again, the people around you begin to unanimously give answers that appear to be wrong despite the evidence of your eyes. And again, you agree with them when the time comes. Who are you to argue, anyway?

Social psychologist Soloman Asch and his research assistant Pikachu ran exactly this kind of experiment at Swarthmore College.[6] He ran many versions of it, in fact, but the setup was generally as described above, except that the seven other people in the classroom weren't really other research subjects. Unbeknownst to the one real subject in each trial, the other students were actors cooperating with the experimenter. Their job was to give obviously wrong answers to see what each of the 122 real subjects would do. The majority of them—up to 75 percent in some versions of the experiment—conformed to the opinions of the crowd and gave obviously incorrect answers at least once. What's more, in postexperiment debriefing interviews, subjects often rationalized their choices by saying that their initial observations must have been wrong if everyone else was saying the opposite. They weren't just pretending to see things differently. They really did.

These studies tie in with many other things we know about human nature when it comes to conformity, submission to authority, and peer pressure. We're often willing to look to our peers or even complete strangers to define reality for us. Why do you think TV shows like the *Big Bang Theory* have a laugh track? Why do you think Starbucks baristas seed their tip jars with a few dollars and loose change before the coffee shop even opens? Why do you think video game publishers and their public relations companies obsess over initial review scores and even occasionally try to suppress negative reviews out of the gate?

The latter actually happened after the release of *Duke Nukem Forever* in 2011. The game was infamous in gaming circles for repeated delays that resulted in a 15-year development cycle and some big talk that turned out to be hollow. Given this and lackluster impressions reported by those who had played it prerelease, *Duke Nukem Forever* seemed like a punching bag waiting to be socked upon release. And indeed, when the game came out, most critics trashed it in their reviews. Metacritic, a review aggregation site, soon figured that it had an average review score of 54 percent, which is where it still stands as of this writing.[7] Relative to other games, that's bad. Really bad. These negative, early reviews displeased James Redner of the Redner Group, which was acting as the PR company for *Duke Nukem Forever* and which had been tasked with the job of hyping it up. In a fit of annoyance and bad judgment, James Redner took to the company's official Twitter account and responded, "too many went too far with their reviews . . . we [are] reviewing who gets games next time and who doesn't based on today's venom."[8] Disregard for grammar and punctuation aside, the implication was clear: Those who gave the game negative reviews could be locked out of future access to games and information, but those who gave positive reviews could get more access. To his credit, Redner soon realized his mistake and posted a public apology to Twitter, saying he spoke out of emotion and should have contacted the authors of nasty reviews privately. And to the credit of *Duke Nukem Forever*'s publisher, Redner Group was dropped as its PR company, and the publisher also disavowed itself of any responsibility for the tweet.[9]

But was it understandable for Redner to freak out over early reviews of the game? Could all those early reviewers be like the actors in Soloman Asch's experiments in that they were influencing the opinions of everyone who subsequently considered buying the game? Even if *Duke Nukem Forever* is a bad example, given a history that primed many people to dislike it, could the pebbles from early reviews cause similar avalanches of poor opinion for other games?

We don't have to guess at an answer to this question. Matthew Salganik, Peter Dodds, and Duncan Watts published a study in a 2006 issue of *Science* where they demonstrated how to manipulate a market for music downloads simply by controlling the flow of information about what other customers were doing.[10] The researchers recruited more than 14,000 subjects online and gave them a list of unfamiliar songs and bands. While listening to the songs, subjects rated them on a scale much like the 1 to 5 star-rating scales used by places like Amazon, iTunes, or Google Play. Subjects were also given a chance to download any songs they liked. And that about covers it for subjects in the control condition. They were given no additional information about how popular any given song was. But those in the experimental conditions were. Their lists of songs had information—accurate information—about how often the other songs had been downloaded and what their 1 to 5 ratings were. The experimenters even set up eight different experimental "worlds" where download counts and ratings were allowed to evolve independently. Think of them as alternate universes where "I've Got the Fink" by Fred Finkledinger may become popular in one universe but flopped in another. Also note how bad I am at making up fake names for songs and artists.

The experimenters found what they expected: Having social information about a song's rating and how many times it had been downloaded affected how much more popular or unpopular it became. There also tended to be much greater polarization in song popularity relative to the control group full of subjects who had no access to social information. Popular songs in the experimental groups tended to be extremely popular, and unpopular songs were likewise extremely unpopular. In a follow-up study, the experimenters discovered they could exacerbate these effects by rank-ordering the songs by current download count, just like you would see in many "Top 50 Downloaded" or "What's Hot" list of games, books, movies, or other media. In that case, a given song would become even more popular or unpopular. This is presumably because people would mostly confine their sampling to the top lists, which would ensure that those songs in the list remained there. Interestingly, the eight different alternate universes that the experimenters set up organically evolved their own unique lists of hits and bombs. A certain song might rise to the top in one group of subjects but languish in another just because a group of early listeners who either liked it or disliked it influenced subsequent listeners with their early rating and downloading.

But in this study Salganik and his colleagues let the markets for their songs grow naturally and without interference. Could someone influence the fate of a particular piece of media by presenting fake social information and artificially inflating or deflating its popularity? You bet they could. To demonstrate this, another study used ratings and social information in a context many video game fans should be familiar with: a website comment section. You probably use or at least have encountered a message board with an upvote/downvote system that lets users rate each other's comments. If your post contains a thoughtful argument, a witty jab, or a picture of a cat eating a slice of watermelon, then you could get points from other readers in the form of upvotes. If you say something dumb, use crass language, or repost that picture of the cat eating watermelon after someone else had already posted it just yesterday, then you could get hit with downvotes. A post's score is simply the number of upvotes minus the number of downvotes.

Lev Munchik, Sinan Aral, and Sean Taylor wondered what impact early upvotes or downvotes would have on the long-term scores of posts in such environments. Could early upvotes or downvotes cause what they called "social herding" of subsequent readers such that a given post was forever blessed or doomed? To find out, they partnered with a large news aggregation website (they didn't specify which one) and subtly manipulated 101,281 individual user comments over the course of five months. Each post was either left alone (the all-important control group), seeded with a single upvote the instant it was created, or similarly saddled with a downvote. Then they sat back and watched what the site's users did.

In five months, readers made 308,515 upvotes or downvotes. The seeding of posts with upvotes worked as expected: Upon seeing the initial upvote, subsequent users were more likely to bestow the post with another upvote. Again, like the music download study, this trickle turned into a steady stream more often than not. Posts seeded with an upvote had, on average, a 25 percent increase in their total score (calculated by subtracting the number of downvotes from the number of upvotes) and were 30 percent more likely to get more than 10 points, which the researchers characterized as extremely high scores for that particular website. Get upvotes early on and your comment was headed for the hall of fame, it seems.

This is why James Redner was so upset about early review scores for *Duke Nukem Forever*, and why every PR company, video game publisher, developer, and even some fans get emotional when their game does either very well or very poorly out of the gate. Early evaluations matter quite a bit when they are captured, quantified, and made available to others. What other people are doing and saying can actually affect your perception of what something looks like or how good you think it is. To combat this (or take advantage of it, depending on the circumstances) game publishers and PR companies sometimes pay to send high-profile game reviewers to lavish launch parties. It's also why publishers have started working with makers of popular "let's play" YouTube videos and Twitch streamers who can start providing social information even faster than reviewers working with written words or edited videos.

In the case of the 2014 action-adventure game *Middle Earth: Shadow of Mordor*, the PR company in charge of that game's promotion leading up to launch went so far as to offer certain reviewers and YouTube personalities early access to the game, but only if they agreed to contracts that sound like they were written by a time-traveling Soloman Asch. Amenable YouTube reviewers got access to the game a week early, but they reportedly had to abide by restrictive terms in the contract that would help ensure that only positive reviews were presented.[11] "Videos will promote positive sentiment about the game," said the contract, according to The Escapist's Jim Sterling after he acquired a copy.[12] The contract supposedly went on to tell reviewers that they were not to show any "bugs or glitches" and that they should focus on the story and the game's unique characteristics. Essentially they instructed streamers and reviewers on how to write a positive review, and, according to Sterling, the PR company was unlikely to send out any copies of the game to anyone who didn't sign the contract.

Other times, though, publishers and developers try to deal with the effects of early social information on firmer ethical ground. They may request the delay of reviews so that reviewers get experiences with a game that are more typical of what regular players will get when the game is out for everyone. This is happening more and more with games requiring release-day updates, but also with games that rely on masses of players coming online together after release day. The game developer Bungie, for example, urged reviewers to wait until the 2014 online game *Destiny* was out before giving their impressions. The company also urged customers to treat any early reviews as preliminary since those reviewers couldn't play the inherently multiplayer game as it was intended when there were only a few people worldwide who had prerelease access. "For us, this is a first—a new experience," wrote a company spokesperson on the official Bungie.net message boards. "It's a bit of a risk, too. We fully anticipate seeing day-one reviews from folks who decide to kick the tires, but don't have the time or patience to take our ride for a nice, long road trip." The last thing they wanted was for potential customers to be scared away by negative (and ultimately unfair) first impressions.

This kind of social information can also be hijacked and used against game companies, though. When Electronic Arts released the strategy game *Spore* in 2008, it included SecuROM, a digital rights management system that many felt was too restrictive and anticonsumer. You could, in essence, only install the game on three computers, and you had to let it authenticate with SecuROM servers via the Internet every few days. In response, a loose campaign formed just days after the game's release, and thousands of people flooded Amazon.com's *Spore* page with one-star reviews. Even as I write this years later, 2,598 of the game's 3,335 Amazon reviews are only one-star. Cliff Harris, who used to work at the company that developed *Spore*, went on record in one interview as saying, "From a PR point of view, this is a disaster."[13] The bombardment of early one-star reviews hurt the game's overall reception.

So we often look to other people for information about what to think, and even if we don't, they can still influence us. But it turns out that we're not only affected by people when they do or say something. Sometimes we can be driven to pick up a game or even spend money on it just by looking at someone. And some people are more influential in this regard than others, especially in social games, such as those often played on mobile platforms.

SOCIAL WHALE ENGAGEMENT: NOW LEGAL IN 50 STATES

In October 2014, I was invited to give a talk at the Mobile Games Forum in Seattle, Washington. Always up for a trip to Seattle, I agreed to give a lecture that took largely the form of an earlier chapter in this book about how social comparisons and information framing in leaderboards and high scores can motivate players to compete with each other. One thing was clear, though: I was a bit of an outlier as far as the conference program went. As the name suggests, the Mobile Games Forum focuses on mobile and social games. A handful of the other presenters talked about game design, but there seemed to be many people in business casual attire and smart haircuts going on about topics like monetization, reach, player acquisition, marketing, brand development, pipeline management, analytics, market relevance, tracking, customer loyalty, funnel analysis, products as services, and penetrating Asian markets. People working in mobile games, in other words, seemed awfully interested in how players engage with each other and how they can be co-opted to market games to each other. It was fascinating.

Dmitri Williams, CEO of the consulting company Ninja Metrics, thinks this concept of player engagement with other players is pretty important. Williams, who holds a Ph.D. in communications, has authored dozens of academic articles about the psychology of video games and how players communicate and disseminate information to each other. Along with another academic, Jaideep Srivastava, Williams founded Ninja Metrics to help game developers and publishers compete in the mobile gaming market. One of the concepts that they emphasize is "social value." Game publishers and marketers have traditionally focused on how much money a gamer generates by making purchases for herself. That's important, but Williams and his colleagues note that customers can also be valuable because they get other players to spend money. On the Ninja Metrics website they call this "social value," and people who get many others to spend money are called "social whales."[14] If someone only spends $5 on a mobile game but gets three of his otherwise frugal friends to spend $10 each, then he is worth more than just $5 to the game publisher.

Although Ninja Metric's research is done in support of a business and thus not made available for peer review and public consumption, white papers on the company website claim that the company figures that about only 10 percent of players are social whales, but that they influence anywhere from 10 to 40 percent of total spending.[15] The key to creating more social value, according to Williams, is player engagement. That is, players have to interact with each other. "We now have seen social value be higher or lower based on different types of games," he says. "The more social the mechanics, the higher it is."[16]

What kinds of social mechanics in mobile games could be talking about? For one possibility, let's talk about llama topiaries. One day a few years ago when skimming my friends' status updates on Facebook, one particularly flustered post caught my eye. "Attention Facebook friends," it began. "Please for the love of God stop sending me gifts and invites for *Farmville*, *Mafia Wars*, *Vampires*, and whatever other crappy THING you've been playing. DO NOT WANT. Just . . . STOP. GOD."

Those of you who have played casual games with a social bent on Facebook or smartphones can probably sympathize. How many times have you checked your notifications and thought, "Gee, you sent me a . . . virtual goat. Thanks, I guess." Indeed, developers of these social games have gone to great lengths to make "gifting" of imaginary stuff a core element to the gameplay. At *Farmville*'s peak, one in five Facebook users had installed the game.[17] Notification spam got so annoying that *Farmville* played no small part in the Facebook's decision to revamp how game invites and gifting announcements worked, making them less intrusive. But the feature still thrives in all kinds of games and is a major way that they can encourage players to interact with each other—or to "drive consumer engagement," as one of the presenters at the Mobile Games Forum no doubt would say. Just this morning I got a notification from the *Marvel Puzzle Quest* on my phone that one of my friends had sent me some in-game currency for free. Why do people send gifts back and forth like that?

The answer has to do with one of the most powerful habits in social psychology: "reciprocity." When people give you something, you feel the need to give something back; it's that simple. Or possibly if you're like my friend who posted the Facebook status update above, you yell at them. But usually you want to reciprocate. Some evolutionary psychologists think that this is an evolutionary advantage in that it encourages societies to form—and enforce—mutually beneficial norms.[18] Adhering to the norm is seen as a good deed, and others want to return that deed. Breaking the norm is an attack and will earn you a misdeed in return, like shunning or a punch to the neck.

The reciprocity effect is used by marketers and savvy businesspeople all the time. Every year the March of Dimes charity sends me a lovely set of return address labels for use with my Christmas cards. The labels are a gift, but not coincidentally they come in the same envelope as a plea to donate. The message is clear: "Hey. We totally just gave you some free stuff. You should return the favor with a donation." Psychologist Robert Cialdini explained in a 2001 article in *Scientific American* how the Disabled American Veterans organization used this same trick to increase the success rate of their appeals for donations from 18 to 35 percent.[19]

The same technique applies when supermarkets give you free samples of new cheese crackers, or when video game developers give out free T-shirts to trade show attendees. I'm not saying that you'll be mind-controlled and compelled to return the favor by buying the crackers or giving the game a favorable write-up, but you'll at least think about it more than you would have otherwise, and that helps improve the odds over large groups of people. Many organizations—including some gaming websites and magazines—even invoke "no gifts" codes of conduct to guard against the reciprocity effect. The gaming website Polygon.com, for example, has a public ethics statement that says, in part, "Our writers will not accept gifts (including food and drinks) in excess of $50 in value."[20]

But what about *Farmville, Marvel Puzzle Quest, Clash of Clans*, and the many other free-to-play games that rely on reciprocity to drive player engagement? These are free games, right? And most of the gifts are free, too, right? For the most part, yes. But Zynga, the makers of *Farmville* and many similar games, nevertheless wants new players to come in and existing players to stick around. The gifts in these games are useful to their recipients within the game, so seeing a notification that you've received one encourages you to log in to the game and put it to use. And actually just clicking on the link will start new players down the path to installing and playing the game, which increases Zynga's numbers. Then the reciprocity effect encourages you to return the favor by sending a gift back, which creates a cycle of reciprocating fruit plants, livestock, and penguin statues. Even worse is when you realize that if you don't perpetuate the gifting loop, you'll hurt your friends by making them waste in-game money for things they were hoping to get from you as gifts. You heartless monster, you.

This is an effective mechanism for getting people to perpetually log in to these games instead of moving on to something else. There's the notification telling you that you need to log in to reciprocate the gift, and while you're there you might as well play for a while. This is the recipe by which habits are created. You can even send gifts to people who don't play the game yet, encouraging them to pay you back by starting up a game as your neighbor or teammate. Soon, there are farms cropping up everywhere in an unholy amalgamation of psychology and agriculture.

But there's more than one reason why people like to share and show off what they have. Not to put too fine a point on it, but sometimes you just want somebody to be envious of your farm or your settlement or whatever it is you've built. You want them to see what you have and nod in appreciation over how you spelled out a vulgarity through strategic placement of strawberry bushes. This is no less true of games that let you show off other things, such as gear and cosmetic items. Envy, it turns out, is another important mechanism by which player engagement can happen.

GOLD WITH ENVY

The word "envy" usually has negative connotations. I feel envious when you've got something I want and I wish that weren't the case. This probably brings to mind some green-eyed monster sulking and brooding in the corner over how things aren't fair and how one day it will show them, it will show them all. But psychologists studying the nature of envy have identified two varieties that motivate us to reduce that gap in different ways.[21] Malicious envy is when I want to close the gap between us by having the object of envy destroyed or taken away. This will bring you down to my level. Malicious envy usually happens when I think you don't deserve what you have. We're more likely to experience it if the target just got lucky or acquired something through unfair or illegal means. Benign envy, on the other hand, is more aspirational. It happens when you have something I want, but I think that's cool and would rather close the gap by building myself up to your level. This is more likely when I think that you've worked to get what you have or otherwise deserve it.

Malicious envy is usually bad for everyone involved, as it involves frustration and can lead to sabotage and perceptions of unfairness. Players experiencing too much of that emotion might correct things by just not playing the game if they can't or won't recalibrate their comparison targets. But recent research has shown that benign envy and the upward social comparisons that it involves can help us feel better about ourselves and motivate us to improve performance. Seeing another *Clash of Clans* player build up some impressive fortifications may make us green with envy, but it may also make us feel like we should also be capable of doing that and make us more motivated to try. "Comparing yourself to someone better off can give you information on how to succeed," says Simon Laham, a social psychologist at the University of Melbourne and author of the book *The Science of Sin: The Psychology of the Seven Deadlies and Why They Are So Good for You.*[22] "You observe the secrets of others' successes and change your expectations of what's possible to achieve."

Clever game designers encourage this kind of envy all the time. The social game *The Simpsons: Tapped Out*, for example, encourages you to visit the towns of other players every day by giving you experience points and in-game currency every time you do so. And, of course, while visiting you get to see all the interesting and enviable things that the other player has done and bought while you're there. Look at all those buildings. They have a Lard Lad Donut Shop! And a King Toot's Music Shop! Nice. You are rewarded for becoming envious and engaging with other players. This is also the reason why so many people thought it was ridiculous for *The Elder Scrolls IV: Oblivion* to charge players $2.50 to deck their horse out in fancy armor. *Oblivion* is a single-player game—nobody but you was going to see that horse armor, no matter how sweet it was.

Researchers have found that when we make these kinds of upward comparisons, we tend to look for and find similarities between the target and ourselves because we have a bias toward a positive self-image. This not only broadens our perceptions of what is possible for us, but it also nudges us toward thinking more highly of ourselves—if she's like me and she did it, then so can I. It also helps greatly if we can pick out (or assume) similarities on attributes obviously related to performance on the task in question. For example, Niels van de Ven, Marcel Zeelenberg, and Rik Pieters from Tilburg University in The Netherlands did an experiment where they caused different subjects to experience the different kinds of envy.[23] Then they had subjects take the Remote Associates Test (RAT), which measures creativity and intelligence. The RAT presents three words and then asks the test taker to think of a word that connects them. As an example, the correct answer to "Swiss/cake/cottage" would be "cheese." Because "Swiss cheese," "cheesecake," and "cottage cheese." Here's a hard one: "shadow/chart/drop." Give up? The answer is "eye."

The RAT is used in this kind of research because if someone doesn't get the answer to a given question right away, it will usually come if he is motivated to persist in sitting there and thinking about it long enough. What van de Ven and his colleagues found was that making a person envious of a successful person before taking the RAT caused them to persist longer at solving the puzzles relative to those experiencing malicious envy or no envy at all. And it wasn't like they were even envious of the other person's performance on the RAT test; they were just reading a description of the person and his accomplishments. Making upward comparisons to other people tends to make us feel more generally competent by association, which motivates us to try harder on whatever it is we're trying to do. Of course, it helps if the target of the envy is similar to us and doing a task that requires an attribute related to whatever we're trying to do. You may remember that lesson from the chapter on competition and high scores. Other research on envy has found that being envious of a person is more motivating when they are similar to you but not when it seems impossible or impractical to do what they did to get their loot or accolades.[24]

It's not a stretch to think that seeing someone show off the rewards she gained for completing a particularly difficult in-game challenge could make us assume that we could do the same. Because she's essentially just like us and didn't do anything we couldn't. Or, alternatively, we may be more motivated to make in-game purchases to reduce the envy. Other studies by van de Ven, Zeelenberg, and Pieters found that benign envy can even motivate us to pay an "envy premium" for products.[25] Subjects in their study who were made envious of another person's iPhone were willing to pay 64 percent more than a nonenvious control group for a new phone to narrow the gap caused by their gadget envy. This is Dmitri Williams's social value made explicit: People might spend money simply because they are interacting with someone who has something that they envy. Interestingly, another group in the study that experienced malicious envy—that is, they didn't think the person deserved the iPhone and wanted them not to have it—were willing to pay more for a Blackberry phone as a way to simultaneously reduce the envy and differentiate themselves from someone they had looked down on.

So think on all this the next time you look at a rival and want to buy a better outfit for your character or preorder the expansion pack to get a unique weapon. A great deal of effort may have gone into making sure that you see that other player in a very particular light, with the end goal of making you spend more money or play the game longer because you feel a little bit jealous. But then again, if you're having fun and keeping it under control, maybe it's just all part of the experience. Plus you get to make the next person jealous of you.

THINGS TO REMEMBER FROM THIS CHAPTER

- Emotional contagion describes how emotional states can be transmitted from one person to another. It can even happen through social media, though probably not as efficiently.
- Our judgments, opinions, and even perceptions of reality can be influenced by what people around us are reporting. This is known as "social proof." Someone might say that a short line is long if enough other people seem to believe it.
- Social proof can also govern the popularity of products given user ratings. Those given high ratings early on are more likely to keep receiving positive ratings. This is why early reviews are more important than later ones.

- Speaking of which, could you take a moment to give this book a review on your favorite online retailer? That would be awesome. Thank you.
- "Reciprocity" is the impulse we feel to repay favors done for us or gifts given to us. Many social games use this as a way of getting us to spread links and invitations.
- "Benign envy" is an emotion I feel when you have something I want, and I want to build myself to get it, too. This is useful for motivating people to achieve goals and keep playing.
- Being envious can also just make us feel more competent, thanks to the social comparison processes it triggers. We're biased toward making comparisons that do this.

Part 4

The Games Themselves

13

DO WE SHAPE OUR IN-GAME AVATARS OR DO THEY SHAPE US?

"All mortals tend to turn into the things they are pretending to be."

—C. S. Lewis

In one episode of the USA Network's *Burn Notice*, former spy Michael Westen infiltrates a secure facility using a gadget that costs about $2 at your local office supply store. "Like con men, spies know that in the workplace, a clipboard is as good as a skeleton key," Westen tells viewers before using one to walk right into an office setting and steal some important bits of information. For all his tiresome "when you're a spy . . ." platitudes, he's right. Clothes and accessories have power.

But don't just take my word for it because I'm wearing a lab coat and holding a clipboard of my own. Psychologist Leonard Bickman preceded the writers of *Burn Notice* by several decades when he published a study in the *Journal of Applied Social Psychology* showing that someone dressed as a guard was more easily able to get random people on the street to comply with weird requests like picking up a paper bag up or giving a dime to someone else.[1] Amusingly, Bickman had one experimental condition where the requestor was dressed as a milkman, but people tended not to comply with his demands as much. Probably because they were too busy wondering what the heck a milkman was. Another study by different researchers had a man stand at a busy intersection and then flagrantly disobey the "Do Not Cross" signal.[2] Depending on whether he was dressed in a suit or blue-collar clothes, more or fewer people followed the experimenter out into danger. When he wore a suit, 3.5 times more people followed him like he was some kind of jaywalking pied piper.

Human brains are always looking for shortcuts when making judgments, and if you're wearing or carrying something that provides that kind of shortcut it will often be used. Clothes—especially uniforms—are well-established indicators of status, authority, and expertise. Job seekers everywhere know that when you wear a sharp suit, interviewers treat you differently than they do when you stride into the room wearing gym shorts and a tank top. Most of the time, hospital patients listen closely to the advice of people wearing white overcoats, because those people are probably doctors and the guy in the grey coveralls is probably just there to restock the vending machines. One day a man wearing a fireman's hat barged into my office and asked me to scoot back from my desk. I immediately complied, assuming he was doing a fire safety inspection and wanted to look for daisy-chained extension cords or hobo bonfires. It turns out that's exactly what he was doing, and the assumptions I made based on his clothing were correct. They almost always will be, that is, outside of some basic cable spy shows or university psychology labs. But the power of clothing is sometimes much subtler and trickier. Sometimes we are the ones being tricked by our clothes.

Take, for example, a 2012 study by Hajo Adam and Adam Galinsky that invited participants to don one of two garments: either a doctor's lab coat or a white painter's smock.[3] Subjects were then given a task requiring attention to detail. They had to scrutinize sets of nearly identical pictures in order to catalog slight discrepancies between them. You've probably played a similar "spot the difference" game in a puzzle book or magazine you flipped through while waiting to see your dentist. Those wearing the doctor's lab coat performed better on this attention-to-detail task relative to both those wearing the painter's smock or those in a control group who just saw a lab coat draped over a nearby chair. More interesting still is that of the three groups, those wearing artist smocks—a garment associated with creative, free-spirited professions—did worst on the task by finding the fewest discrepancies between the photos.

But by far the most interesting thing about the study I haven't mentioned yet was that both the lab coats and the artist smocks were actually the same exact garment. Both were simply oversized, white coats that subjects put on over their other clothes. The only difference was that one group was told they were wearing lab coats, and the other was told they were wearing artist smocks. Plot twist!

Adam and Galinsky's study clearly demonstrates how making even superficial changes to our appearance can affect our behavior, our attitudes, and even our thoughts. Those in the lab coats had their minds tricked into thinking in a more systematic, detail-oriented manner. In psychology we call this "priming" because experiencing one thought or idea primes associated thoughts and makes them more likely to come to mind. Wearing different clothes and ascribing specific meanings to them made people think they were the kind of person who would do well on a detail-oriented task, and so they did—a concept the researchers called "enclothed cognition."

Let's take things a bit further. What if instead of just putting on a lab coat or a safety helmet, we became taller? Or more beautiful? Or what if we became an ogre? Or some kind of weird plant dude with huge biceps? Because that's not far off from what we do when we select a character to represent us in a video game, and research shows that the appearance of avatars—that is, the in-game representations of ourselves—can affect our thoughts and behaviors just like wearing different clothes can. These effects can even continue after we set down the controller or push away from the keyboard.

I'M A NIGHT ELF WITH PERFECT KNEECAPS AND FIVE RANKS IN "HANDSOME"

Let's be honest up front: It's easy to explain why we choose the avatars we do when it's because of the game's demands. We decide to look like an elf because we want to maximize our wizard character and elves get +3 to Intelligence. Or we're playing a military-themed shooter, so we have no choice but to look like a muscular soldier in combat fatigues. But just as often it's not that simple, or we get choices as to what kind of military elf to look like. There are also virtual playgrounds where we have options for our appearance that aren't constrained by the game's mechanics at all. *The Sims* games and *Dragon Age: Inquisition* give you plenty of freedom in the form of various sliders and settings during character creation. You can control nose breadth, chin depth, eye spacing, ear alignment, lip color, skin tone, forehead slope, hair style, eyebrow arch, and the placement of various facial tattoos, if you like. You want your make-believe gangster avatar to be a shining, faceless being of liquid sunlight that rocks a purple fedora and combat boots? The *Saints Row* games will absolutely let you do that.

Or you could make something closer to what you see in the mirror every morning. The Xbox One game *Kinect Sports Rivals* takes digitizing your likeness further by using the console's camera and motion-tracking software to create your own likeness based on what it sees. The avatar creation process in that game almost seems like science fiction: A player stands in front of his Xbox One and moves his head around so the camera can have a good look. All the time, polygons float and coalesce on the screen to create your likeness in a suitably futuristic way. The "ta-da!" moment when you've provided enough information and the game is ready to reveal its digitized version of your mug is actually pretty dramatic thanks to how accurate the system is. Aside from the fact that the game automatically assigns everyone an athletic physique (it is a sports game, after all), the avatars look pretty much like what the camera sees. They're cartoony in the Xbox One's signature style, but they're generally recognizable, and it's impressive to see what looks quite like you wake-racing, bowling, or playing tennis in the game.

So is creating a video game avatar like having access to instant fashion makeovers whenever you want them and having a supply of all the clipboards you can carry? Does the phenomenon of enclothed cognition apply when we engage with other people through a virtual skin? Does it matter if the avatar looks like us or like someone else? The answer to all these questions is yes, but with some important caveats given the interplay between the technology and our sense of self. To start to understand how, let's look at a new application of an old psychological theory about how appearance affects attitudes and behavior.

I'VE GOT HUGE PECTORAL MUSCLES. GIVE ME 80 PERCENT OF YOUR MONEY

Nick Yee was born in Hong Kong where spent his childhood playing video games before moving to the United States at age 14. He holds a

Ph.D. in communications and spent several years working at video game giant Ubisoft as a research scientist studying how psychology and other social sciences can inform game design before he and his research partner Nic Ducheneaut created their own consulting company. This seems like a weird career for someone with his credentials, but Yee's academic career actually began with video games. While an undergraduate at Haverford College in 1999 and working in the university computer lab, Yee installed a copy of a video game for two older students who were doing their senior projects on personality and game genres. The game was *Everquest*, and though it can't claim to be the first massively multiplayer online game, it's arguably the one whose success made the genre blow up big and that paved the way for games like *World of Warcraft*, *The Elder Scrolls Online*, and *Guild Wars*. When future historians look back on *Everquest*, they will probably regret how much time they spent playing it instead of doing their job as historians.

The two seniors conducting the research were "meh . . ." on *Everquest*, but Yee was fascinated by it both from the perspective of a player and from that of a burgeoning academic. He began working with others at Haverford College to survey *Everquest* fans about how they played the game and interacted with fellow players within the virtual environment. This was in the early days of the World Wide Web when online survey and website technology were in their infancy. Getting information out of people through the Internet required no small amount of ingenuity and hacking together HTML code to create your own websites. Yee did all this and began collecting data online from *Everquest* players about their demographics, their personalities, and their motivations for playing video games.

After graduating, Yee continued the research, creating a website called the Daedalus Project that served as a clearinghouse for his studies and a portal for new participants. After applying to several graduate schools, he landed at Stanford University's Communications program. There he started working with other researchers, such as Jeremy Bailenson, to study virtual reality environments and how the appearance of our in-game avatars affects us. It was in many ways a natural continuation of the research that he had begun through his hacked-together online surveys of *Everquest* players, but now he had access to Stanford's state-of-the-art virtual reality lab, complete with a $30,000 head-mounted display and plenty of open space. And as we'll see, he put them to good use.

Yee and Bailenson's research on how our avatars affect in-game behaviors has its roots in what's called "self-perception theory." This is a watershed concept in social psychology pioneered by physicist-turned-psychologist Daryl Bem during the 1960s. The theory says that in any given situation we think, at some level, about how a third party would view our appearance and behaviors. We then change our own beliefs and attitudes to match this imaginary person's expectations of us. We are concluding that our behavior must be caused by our attitudes, and since attitudes are often easier to change than the reality of our current or past actions, attitudes are what get changed. Though not always. Plenty of other research has shown that if the attitudes or beliefs are onerous enough, people may willfully ignore or downplay their own behavior to reconcile the dissonance. But often it's more mentally efficient to just change our attitudes. For example, someone hurtling themselves out of a perfectly good airplane might think, "I'm skydiving, so I'm the kind of person who seeks out thrills." He's probably right. At least I hope he is, for his sake.

In one clever study of this theory by Fritz Strack and his colleagues, subjects were given a ball-point pen and told to hold it in their mouth in one of two ways.[4] Some were asked to hold it with pursed lips and others were told to hold it between their front teeth, with their lips drawn up and back. As you might guess, the former tricked the subjects into frowning, while the latter got them to smile. When asked to rate the laugh-out-loud value of a cartoon, those who were being made to smile thought it was way funnier than those who were forced to frown. Their own behavior, forced as it was, affected their attitude toward what they were seeing, which in turn made them chuckle at some silly drawing.

This kind of "first behavior then attitude" effect can also be hijacked in much more subtle ways, and in at least one case it was done with the help of naked ladies. University of North Carolina's Stuart Valins hooked male participants up to a monitor that beeped in time with their heart rates while they perused centerfolds from *Playboy* magazine.[5] When the researchers used their control over the machine to covertly fake an accelerated heartbeat, subjects decided that they must have a thing for the particular model they were viewing at the time. First we perceive what we look like or what we're doing, and then we draw conclusions about our attitudes and beliefs. But it turns out that behavior isn't even strictly necessary. Just thinking about how we appear to others can often affect our attitudes, which can circle back to affect our behaviors. Sometimes it's as simple as putting on a black hat instead of a white one.

Mark Frank and Thomas Gilovich showed this effect by studying athletes in the National Football League and the National Hockey League.[6] Specifically, they looked at teams that wore black uniforms versus teams wearing other colors to see if those wearing black—a color typically associated with the wardrobes of the villainous—were guilty of more infractions and associated penalties. Through a series of clever experiments, they were able to untangle the causal chain of events, showing that it wasn't just that referees were biased against players in dark clothing, or even that more rule-breakers were attracted to teams with black jerseys. The researchers even conducted one experiment where they had subjects randomly don either white or black uniforms, then observed that the latter tended to gravitate toward more violent activities when given a list of party games to choose from. Frank and Gilovich argued that these behaviors could be traced back to self-perception theory: I'm wearing black. I'm expected to be aggressive. I'm aggressive. I should pick the party game where I get to shoot someone in the face with a dart gun. Even if that whole chain of thoughts wasn't conscious, the results were there.

Let's return to Nick Yee and his preoccupation with how our in-game avatars affect our behavior. Yee seized on social identity theory and the studies described above in some of his early research and applied it to a totally new context: understanding how people behave depending on what virtual avatars they slip into. Scientists all decked out in their fanciest of pants like to use phrases such as "immersive virtual spaces" and "computer-mediated environments" at times like this, but we're basically talking about video games and virtual reality. In one of his earliest experiments, Yee had subjects don a wicked head-mounted display that let them perceive and move around in a simple virtual environment.[7] The headgear consisted of a large, grey-and-black visor with motion sensors and with a high-resolution display that fit over the user's head so that it could present images directly to each eyeball, not too different from the Oculus Rift headset I discussed in the chapter on immersion. Inside the virtual world Yee's setup created, there was just a virtual room, another virtual person controlled by someone else, and a virtual mirror.

The mirror was important, because it obviously wasn't a real mirror any more than the room was real, so the researcher could use it to show whatever "reflection" of the subjects' avatars he wanted. In fact, Yee randomly showed subjects one of three types of reflections of their assigned avatar: an ugly one, a normal one, or an attractive one. Yee was interested in how this would affect subjects' interactions with the other person in the virtual room. After following directions to inspect their avatars in the mirror, subjects were asked to approach the other avatar in the room and chat with its owner. This avatar was controlled by a research assistant and followed a simple script to keep the conversation going if it slowed down.

The study revealed that how attractive a user's avatar was affected how he or she behaved. Relative to those using avatars that had been repeatedly clubbed with the ugly stick, people assigned attractive avatars stood closer to the other person and disclosed more personal details about themselves. Then, in a follow-up study using the same setup, Yee found that people using taller avatars were more assertive and confident when they engaged in a simple negotiation exercise with another person where they either accepted or rejected ultimatums to split a pot of money between them.[8] Generally speaking, people with prettier and taller avatars were more confident and outgoing than those poor saps saddled with virtual representations that were ugly and stumpy—which is exactly what often happens in the real world to taller and prettier people.[9] And like in the real world, we first make an observation about our avatar, then we infer something about our character, then we continue to act according to our perceived expectations.

Yee and Bailenson named this special application of self-perception theory the "Proteus effect" after the Greek god who could change his physical form at will. The Proteus effect holds that avatars are not just ornaments. Avatars alter the identity of the people who use them because players make inferences about what attitudes are expected of them based on their appearance, then are more likely to alter their attitudes and behavior to match.

Various other research has built on and extended this concept. For example, one study by Christopher Klimmt at Hanover University and his colleagues found that after playing a *Call of Duty* game, players were more likely to associate words like "me" or "myself" with words like "soldier" or "pistol," but people who played a *Need for Speed* game associated themselves more with words like "racing" or "driver." [10] Bailenson and his colleagues have done research to show that after playing a game where they inhabited the body of a superhero, subjects were more likely to engage in helpful behavior, such as cleaning up a mess that the experimenter pretended to make. [11] And flipping back to the dark side of all this, Bailenson and other colleagues even showed that female gamers could be made to think more about their body image and even become more accepting of rape myths (e.g., "victims of rape share responsibility for their attack if they drink or flirt") when required to control an avatar that wore more sexually provocative clothing. [12]

It's important to reiterate that the Proteus effect works by bringing in our own expectations about how one is expected to behave based on appearance. Sometimes this can reveal a great deal about players and the biases that they bring to a game. For example, *The Proteus Paradox*, Nick Yee's book that represents the culmination of all his research into the topic, describes a study on gender-bending and healing in *World of Warcraft*. [13] Yee was curious if stereotypes held up about women playing support classes because of their supposedly more helpful nature and their proclivity to nurse others in need. As I said: stereotype. To do this, he used third-party modifications for the game, which allowed him to track how much female players stepped into the role of using magic and other remedies to heal other players. Yee found nothing—female players, regardless of avatars used, were no more likely to want to play medic than were male players. But here's the interesting part: The sex of the player was unrelated to healing behaviors, but the sex of the avatar was strongly related. That is, when either male or female players used a female avatar, they fulfilled the stereotype of a nurturing woman more often. Not everyone, but more people than you would expect from random chance alone. This is because, Yee argues, it's hard to leave our real-life biases behind, and players of both sexes were nudged toward behaving in ways in line with what they perceived as those expectations even if they didn't accept the stereotype themselves.

Think about what this means the next time you are playing a game, especially one where you have the freedom to choose your appearance. Depending on the circumstances, you think what others expect, given your avatar, may subtly influence how you actually behave. And another person with a different worldview may behave a completely different way but for the same reason. Of course, self-perception theory and the Proteus effect don't indicate that games control your mind and make you dance like a puppet—unless you're trying to duplicate your avatar's awesome moves in *Just Dance* or *Dance Dance Revolution*, I suppose. The requirements of the game will marshal the strongest influence on our behavior—if we have to be aggressive or diplomatic or evasive to win, we will. But the virtual skin we have to slip (or squeeze) into can subtly affect us and nudge our actions one way or another. And don't think this has gone unnoticed by the folks in the marketing department.

OH, LOOK, YOUR MASTER CHIEF IS "DOING THE DEW." YOU THIRSTY?

The Nintendo Wii and Wii U aren't the only gaming consoles known for making use of avatars within the interface of the system itself. The Xbox 360 and Xbox One consoles from Microsoft also use cheerful avatars to greet you and signal your activity to your friends. Given this, many people make their avatars look like them at least in some superficial way. So imagine one day that you're poking around in the Xbox One dashboard when you notice that your avatar in that system interface is holding up a "Cassina" soft drink and grinning like some kind of moron. Do you think you would be more likely to remember that brand and pick some up next time you're at the market? Research by Sun Joo Ahn and Jeremy Bailenson suggests that you would.[14] In their study, the researchers digitally altered photographs of people to show them holding up fictitious brands of soda. Other photos showed just a soft drink bottle and a demand to "Drink Cassina!"—identical to the others except for the picture of the subject holding the bottle. Even though every one of the study participants obviously knew the photo was doctored (they had not, after all, posed for any such picture), they tended to express a slight preference for the fake brand, simply because they had seen a representation of themselves holding it. In a second experiment, Ahn and Bailenson actually had subjects enter a virtual reality environment where their avatar wore a T-shirt advertising one of the fictitious brands. Lo and behold, subjects once again showed preferences for fictitious Nanaco or Fentora brand soft drinks when their avatar sported a shirt with the corresponding logo. Think this is outlandish? It's not. Microsoft's gaming consoles already sell or give away branded clothing and accessories for your Xbox avatar to wear. Maybe next time you're at the mall you'll be more likely to notice the brand of hats or T-shirts that you saw your avatar wearing the day before. The marketers hope so.

Other researchers have found similar results when they showed people pictures of themselves in a certain brand of clothing. One study by Rachel Bailey, Kevin Wise, and Paul Bolls at the University of Missouri in Columbia looked at how kids reacted to advertisements for candy and junk food that were thinly disguised as Web games.[15] This interested them because a 2006 study by the Kaiser Family Foundation found that 73 percent of the snack food websites it examined featured some kind of advertising-based game.[16] Kids might be invited, for example, to play a Whack-a-Mole knockoff where they frantically click on "Nestle Push-up Frozen Treats" that are popping up on a field. Baily, Wise, and Bolls found that if these "advergames" allowed players to customize their in-game avatars, they were more excited by the game, they remembered the junk food brands better, and they said that they enjoyed the game more.

What's truly disconcerting is that the other avatar, agent, or image doesn't even have to look exactly like us for this effect to work. Even if a person in a picture looks only a little like us, researchers have discovered that we tend to treat it more favorably and pay more attention to it. Bailenson and his colleagues once did an experiment where they showed pictures of political candidates George W. Bush and John Kerry right before their showdown in the 2004 U.S. presidential election.[17] Subjects were asked to give their opinions about each candidate while looking at the photos. For some of the voters, though, Bailenson and his team had used software to subtly morph the photos of Bush or Kerry so that they shared similarities of facial structure with the voter. Nothing extreme, just a nudge on this slider and a tweak on that value, like a player creating an avatar in *The Sims*. Relative to those looking at photos of candidates that had been morphed to look like someone else, people who saw pictures of candidates whose faces looked more similar to their own were more likely to say they would support that candidate, provided they weren't already hard-line partisan supporters of one candidate or another. It even worked when the voter whose face was being morphed with the male politicians was a woman —or vice versa in the case of a follow-up study featuring then Senator Hillary Clinton. In a separate study,[18] Bailenson and many of the same researchers showed that people are more receptive to an argument or proposal if the virtual agent making it has been programmed to emulate facial expressions and head movements idiosyncratic to that person. In both this and the study of presidential candidates, subjects failed to notice what was going on. Imagine a game using the Xbox's Kinect, the PlayStation 4 Camera, or your computer's webcam to slightly alter a digital spokesperson so that it shares the slope of your nose, the shape of your jaw, and the width of your cheekbones. Thirsty for a refreshing Cassina brand soft drink yet?

NOW, CALMLY PLAY WITH THIS VIRTUAL BUCKET OF SPIDERS . . .

Findings on the effects of avatars on player behavior aren't all of the "OMG, they could be controlling your minds!" variety, though. For example, psychiatrists have long used mental visualization as a technique for treating phobias and social disorders. Someone deathly afraid of turnips, for example, can be coaxed into imagining herself sitting at a farmer's market near a bin of the horrifying root vegetables. With repetitions of that mental exercise, the patient gets more and more acclimated to the stimulus and is better able to deal with it. The @HiWeAreSpiders Twitter account has embraced this concept in an attempt to help people with their arachnophobia through friendly tweets from spiders across the Web, often including pictures. The account's tweets often end with "Hugs! ::)," and its description states, "Hi! We are spiders. We are very misunderstood . . . Look up." Through this kind of imaginary exposure to smiling spiders perched on keyboards, a person can eventually seize control of her fears. It's the same principle as self-perception theory: I'm exchanging tweets with spiders, therefore I'm the kind of person who isn't afraid of tech-savvy spiders. It's okay to go back into the shower.

Along those same lines, a body of work around what's called "social learning theory" has shown that we can be encouraged adopt new, beneficial behaviors by watching others perform them, and the more similar the other person is to us the more likely it is to work. Researcher

Seung-A Annie Jin at Boston College's Communication Department did a series of experiments with Nintendo Wii avatars and the fitness game *Wii Fit*—a title not unlike the *Kinect Sports Rivals* game mentioned earlier in this chapter.[19] Appropriately enough, an avatar on the Nintendo Wii console (and the subsequent Wii U) is referred to as a "Mii." This creates awkward references to one's "Wii U Mii," which is extremely difficult to say with a straight face. Jin, being a scientist, forged ahead through this silliness and found that players who were able to create a Mii that approximated their ideal body shapes generally felt more connected to that avatar and felt that they were more capable of effecting changes in that little virtual dude's behavior. This is a fancy way of saying that the exercise game felt more interactive and immersive. This linkage was strongest, in fact, when there was a big discrepancy between participants' perceptions of their ideal and actual selves.

Jesse Fox and Jeremy Bailenson conducted another study in which they outfitted participants with a head-mounted display and a set of controls that let them navigate a simple virtual environment.[20] Some people then saw avatars with photorealistic images of their faces attached, but others saw either no avatars or avatars with an unfamiliar face. Everybody was told about the importance of physical activity, asked to practice some simple exercises, and then invited to keep exercising for as long as they wanted. Through a series of experiments based on this setup, Fox and Bailenson found that when people saw avatars that looked like them mirroring the exercises, they tended to exercise longer. This was even truer when they saw the avatar slim down in the process of working out. When asked later, people who saw their face on exercise-happy avatars even reported hitting the gym after they were dismissed and sent home.

I don't mean to make you have a panic attack while adjusting the hair style of your next in-game avatar, but keep in mind that to the degree that a game allows you to customize your avatar's appearance, your choice not only says something about you, but it can also unconsciously affect how you behave on both sides of the screen. But should you be similarly worried about seeing your avatar commit violence? That's perhaps the most common question asked about the overlap between psychology and video games, so we turn to it in the next chapter.

THINGS TO REMEMBER FROM THIS CHAPTER

- "Enclothed cognition" is a theory about how the clothes we wear affect our thoughts and assumptions about what we can do. This can extend to video game avatars, especially when we can customize them.
- We tend to behave how we think others expect us to behave based on our appearance in a virtual world. This is called the "Proteus effect" and it is a specific application of "self-perception" theory to video games and virtual worlds.
- Seeing representations of ourselves doing things can affect our behavior and attitudes. For example, we may like products more if we see a representation of ourselves using them.
- This affect can happen even if the avatar looks only a little like us.
- This phenomenon can also be used to our benefit, such as with therapy and exercise programs.

14

WHY DO WE LIKE VIOLENT GAMES SO MUCH? AND SHOULD WE BE WORRIED THAT WE DO?

"I like video games, but they're really violent. I'd like to play a video game where you help the people who were shot in all the other games. It'd be called *Really Busy Hospital*."

—Dmitri Martin, comedian

I once murdered dozens of innocent people in a Moscow airport. Well, in a video game. The "No Russian" mission in Activision's *Call of Duty: Modern Warfare 2* gets its title from the warning given by the game's villain right before the shooting starts. Vladimir Makarov is a radical Russian revolutionary who wants to commit mass murder and then pin it on U.S. and NATO forces in order to foment civil unrest. Thus he warns his men to speak only English and no Russian right as the mission starts. And just to make it that much more dramatic, my avatar at that point in the game was a CIA spy placed in the extremely difficult position of maintaining his cover during the slaughter. I needed to play along or I'd be found out and killed. As the level started, Makarov's crew and I began a slow walk through the Zakhaev International Airport and opened fire. Travelers, airport staff, and tourists screamed, pleaded for their lives, and tried to protect family members from the impassive gunmen. Their efforts were futile. I remember thinking that the cold, steady nature of the executions in this game were strongly reminiscent of stories about the Columbine High School shooting that had happened about 10 years before in real life.

And there I was, participating in it. Technically, I didn't actually have to shoot anyone to complete the No Russian mission. Turning your guns on Makarov or his goons results in instant mission failure, but you can just watch the violence without otherwise participating if you want. Or if that's too much, the mission can be skipped entirely. The game presents you with that option both in the process of starting a new game and at any point during the No Russian mission. What's more, there are no points, achievements, trophies, weapon unlocks, or alternate endings to be missed if you skip it. But as I said, I played through the whole level and so did (I assume) millions of other gamers who bought *Modern Warfare 2*. I still felt complicit in the virtual murders in that I had to allow them to happen, and the whole experience felt more violent and criminal than blasting cyberdemons, aliens, or even human soldiers in an opposing army.

I'm not the only one who has arched an eyebrow at increasing levels of violence and gunplay in video games over the last 30 years. The study of how psychology and video games interact is frequently dominated by the question of whether video games cause violence outside of the game. On multiple occasions I've been approached by talk show hosts or members of the press who want to quiz me on how much violent games were responsible for a school shooting, stabbing, or similar tragedy. I usually decline because it's such a loaded question and the person often wants me to support a particular viewpoint regardless of the details of the case in question. The United States, in particular, has a long history of these moral panics, during which real or imaginary woes are claimed to be the result of comic books, popular music, movies, tabletop role-playing games, television, or even pulp fiction novels. It was inevitable that video games would get their turn.

Many outlets in the mainstream media certainly agree. In 2013, the *Journal of Communication* published an analysis of how the "violence in media topic" was described by 540 articles from the 25 highest-circulating newspapers in the United States over the last 30 years.[1] According to the researchers, 53 percent of the pieces suggested that consuming violent media increases violent behavior, but only 9 percent told readers that there was no such relationship. (The balance of the stories, 38%, were neutral on the topic or said that the relationship was unknown.) Politicians and groups advocating for the welfare of children also frequently champion the idea that violent games cause violent behavior. Without firsthand experience to temper them, these kinds of stories and public relations campaigns become entrenched in people's beliefs though psychological mechanisms, such as the "familiarity bias." That is, we tend to think things are true if they are made easier to remember through dramatization and repetition. One survey found that older Americans (age 65 or older) who never or rarely played video games were six times more likely to believe that violent games cause violent behavior.[2]

Naturally, this annoys many gamers. Those of us who enjoy first-person shooters and other violent games aren't keen on being labeled as murderers-in-training or burgeoning sociopaths just because we occasionally use virtual guns to spray fictional bullets around a pretend Moscow airport. Some studies have found that those who identify themselves as gamers are much more likely to be skeptical of—or even hostile toward—scientific research suggesting that violent games have negative effects.[3] As I described in the chapter on fanboys, one experiment even found that when subjects were told that they were participating in a study on video game violence, those who considered themselves gamers were more likely to try to sabotage the results of a word-completion task by suppressing responses that suggested aggressive thoughts.[4] Those participants who did not see themselves as gamers didn't try to appear less prone to violent thoughts, nor did the gamers when the purpose of the experiment was described in terms unrelated to the effects of video game violence.

What do psychologists find when they carefully study the issue in an unbiased, controlled way? Do all those mainstream media stories report a causal link because that's what the evidence clearly shows? Are all those gamers justified in rolling their eyes and claiming that it's nothing but another moral panic? If so much ink has been spilled and so many pixels have been lit up over the topic, surely we can look to science for a clear answer, right? Unfortunately, no. Sorry. As we will see, views on the topic still vary widely among psychologists, even though they are usually (but not always) free of bombastic language and moral outrage. Conclusions on both sides of the debate are so weighed down by caveats and limitations that academic discussion on the effects of video game violence frequently turns into a discussion about the merits of the methods used in the research itself and not the larger questions that spawned it.

Thus it seems only natural to start our discussion with the story of a kid gleefully beating the living daylights out of a clown.

SOCIAL LEARNING AND AGGRESSIVE SCRIPTS: THE CASE AGAINST VIOLENT GAMES

In 1961, Albert Bandura conducted one of the most important experiments in the history of social psychology.[5] Over the course of the study, 72 children from Stanford University's nursery school were brought individually into a room, seated in a corner, and told to play with some stamps and stickers. Meanwhile, in plain view of the child, an adult went to another of the room's corners. Waiting for him or her in that corner were some other toys, including a five-foot-tall "Bobo doll." This was an inflatable doll decorated to look like a clown but with a rounded, weighted base that would return it to an upright position if knocked over. While the child looked on, the adult proceeded to abuse the Bobo doll as if reenacting a Quentin Tarantino film. They punched it, kicked it, and even clubbed it with a hammer. This must have seemed supremely weird to the watching child, but then again when you're only four years old the vast majority of things you encounter in a given day can probably be categorized as "weird." So they just watched, presumably with a "well, would you look at that" expression on their faces.

In the second phase of the experiment, the researcher took the child into another room where he or she was invited to play with some more appealing toys, such as a fire engine, a jet fighter, or a dress-up doll. The kids were told to play with what they liked, but once they had picked out a favorite toy, the experimenter stepped in, took the toy away, and said something along the lines of, "NO. This one's not for the likes of you. Give it here." The purpose of this was to anger the child a little, because guess what he or she saw when taken into yet another room a moment later? That's right: the Bobo doll. The researchers were interested in how much these slightly annoyed children would imitate the aggressive behavior toward the doll that they had seen displayed by the confederate a few minutes earlier. And sure enough, relative to a control group that had only observed the experimenter ignore the doll, the kids were far more likely to administer a Bobo beatdown.

Bandura's experiment was important because it bucked the then prevalent idea that humans learned only through directly experiencing punishments or rewards. It showed that we are also capable of learning new behaviors and forming new beliefs based on what we see others do and observing what happens to them as a result. Though Bandura's experiment wasn't without flaws and limitations, this idea of "social cognitive learning" took off and generated much additional study and refinement. It is the root of today's most studied models of how violent video games teach people to be aggressive and violent in real life.

For example, the General Aggression Model (GAM) is the social cognitive learning model cited most often when studying the effects of video game violence.[6] It offers predictions about both short-term and long-term exposure to video game violence by pulling together several theories about how people learn, develop, and process information in their environments. The GAM starts by acknowledging that both personal factors (e.g., how short-tempered I am by nature) and situational factors (e.g., the fact that someone is yelling at me) affect our internal mental state at any given moment. The GAM goes on to say that situational factors like playing violent games can activate knowledge structures—networks of related concepts—that are related to violence. Examples of nodes in these knowledge structures include concepts as simple as "knife" or "hurt." Activating one of these nodes by thinking about it can then cascade to other associated nodes, such as "knife" leading to "stab" through mental associations. Playing violent games can also activate other important drivers of our internal state, such as emotions (e.g., anger or frustration) and physiological responses (e.g., rapid heartbeat or tense muscles). These emotions and physiological states can then drive each other in a cycle. And there is evidence that these internal states can also activate thoughts or ideas in our associative memory. In general, this sideways activation of one thought or behavior by activating a related thought or behavior is known as "psychological priming." Though, curiously, the GAM authors don't generally use this term.

But here's the most important part: According to the GAM, activation of associative memory structures also triggers mental scripts through similarly associated links. Scripts are what they sound like: sets of instructions that govern not only how we are supposed to react to a situation but also what we pay attention to and how we deal with ambiguous information. We could have a script for insulting someone, or a script for attacking someone, or a script for calming someone down. And like the child watching the Bobo doll getting pummeled, we can acquire these scripts and form associations with knowledge structures through observation. The more strongly situational inputs seen with playing violent games activate knowledge structures tied to such scripts, the more likely that those scripts are to become salient and govern our appraisal of what a situation is like and how we should behave in it.

So according to the GAM, playing a violent game (e.g., *Mortal Kombat*) activates knowledge structures consisting of concepts associated with what we are seeing, doing, and feeling (e.g., hurting, punching, getting angry), which then activate associated scripts (e.g., hey, you, let's fight!). This is even more likely with naturally aggressive people or people who are physically agitated.

So that's the short-term effects of violent video games. What about long-term effects? According to the GAM, when those scripts are repeatedly accessed and practiced, they become habitual and automatic. We are then more likely to go to them instead of other, nonviolent scripts when faced with real-life situations that activate the same knowledge structures. This is especially likely to be true in ambiguous or novel situations where competing, nonaggressive scripts are not activated. If a violent script is activated more strongly than a nonviolent one, someone is going to be punched and rude things will be said about his mother. Proponents of the GAM even argue that over time this cycle of script activation and subsequent behavior creates changes in our personality and choice of social interactions, making it more likely that we will find ourselves in situations where aggression seems like the right response. Games, in essence, put us in the habit of using aggressive actions to deal with a wide variety of situations, even if we're not consciously aware of it. As such, they are viewed as a risk factor for violent behavior on par with poverty or coming from a dysfunctional family.[7]

There is some empirical support for the GAM, or at least parts of it. Many experiments seeking to test it have compared subjects who play violent games with others who play nonviolent games. They usually look at how easily players of violent games access violent thoughts, which seems like something that would happen when those aggression-related knowledge structures are activated. For example, in 2004, Craig Anderson, one of the primary architects of the GAM, had some subjects play either a nonviolent game (the adventure game *Myst* or the pinball game *3-D Ultra Pinball*) or a violent game (the fighting game *Street Fighter II* or the first-person shooter *Marathon 2*).[8] After they were done, the experimenter had all subjects perform an exercise where they completed a word by adding a missing letter. They would, for example, look at "EXPLO_E" and be asked to fill in the blank with a letter to make a word. Those who had just played *Street Fighter II* were more likely to come up with "EXPLODE" in this example, but those playing *Myst* were more likely to come up with "EXPLORE." This, the researchers argued, was evidence that violent thoughts and knowledge structures were primed by playing games and more quickly accessed than with nonviolent games. Similar claims have been made by having subjects make up endings to ambiguous story stems, with the result that those playing violent games came up with endings involving more aggression and harm, even though there was no reason to do so.[9]

Other studies have looked beyond mental states to actual behaviors. One of the most popular tools for doing this is the Taylor Competitive Reaction Time Test, where subjects are led to believe that they are blasting someone in another room with bursts of unpleasant noise. In reality, there is never a recipient of the awful noise, but the subjects don't know that. The original version of the test actually had subjects use painful electric shocks instead of unpleasant but ultimately harmless white noise, but apparently we aren't allowed to do that kind of thing anymore. Thanks, ethics! Studies using this test in the context of violent video games would have one group play a violent game, then compare the length and intensity of the noise blasts they dole out to the blasts given by a control group or a group that played a nonviolent game.[10] Other studies have operationalized aggressive behavior as how much hot sauce a person uses while preparing a dish for someone who supposedly hates spicy food,[11] or how much someone sabotages another person's chances for winning prizes in a lottery.[12]

It's also interesting to note that these studies might have attained more pronounced results if they had used games that were as violent as those found in many homes. Internal review boards at universities would almost surely prevent research that would expose children (or adults for that matter) to truly gruesome scenes like those found in some games. No research study I know of had kids control the on-screen actions to immolate innocent civilians with white phosphorus (à la *Spec Ops: The Line*) or torture someone by pulling out his teeth with pliers (à la *Grand Theft Auto V*). What's more, many of the studies don't even use children as subjects; they frequently use college students out of convenience. So in a way they're usually not even dealing with the group of people who are allegedly at risk or doing research with the particular games causing the most concern.

But there's more to it than violent behavior. It's also worth noting that the GAM would predict prosocial behavior instead of violent behavior under the right circumstances. Some research has shown that people are more likely to act prosocially after playing a game that requires cooperative or helping behaviors. One study, for example, showed that shooting zombies while defending a teammate results in more prosocial thoughts than shooting the same foes with the same weapons for no other reason than sport.[13] Another pair of researchers had subjects play the puzzle game *Lemmings* where players guide a band of creatures to safety across dangerous terrain. Relative to people who played violent games, these subjects were more likely to help other people in real life by picking up dropped pencils, volunteering for additional research, or even interceding on behalf of a young woman who was apparently being harassed by an ex-boyfriend.[14] Rather than being an argument against the idea that video games cause violence, these results bolster the GAM, since prosocial knowledge scripts are being activated according to the same mechanisms as violent ones. In fact, Craig Anderson, perhaps the biggest proponent of the GAM, has recently begun to refer to it as the General Learning Model (GLM) to reflect this wider view.[15]

On top of these individual studies (and many others), Anderson and seven of his colleagues published a meta-analysis on the effects of violent video games in a 2010 issue of the prestigious *Psychological Bulletin*. In it, they combined findings from decades' worth of studies on the topic and used complicated statistical techniques to see what the data said when taken in aggregate. Their conclusion was that the data definitely prove that there's a link. Playing violent video games, the authors say, represents a significant risk factor for increased aggressive behavior, angry thoughts, and decreased empathy for others.[16] They seemed pretty sure about this, even with the caveats that there are dozens of potential causes for violent behavior and that violent video game play represented only a small to moderate risk by itself. "We believe that the debates can and should finally move beyond the simple question of whether violent video game play is a causal risk factor for aggressive behavior," the authors write in the article's conclusion. "The scientific literature has effectively and clearly shown the answer to be 'yes.'"[17]

Case closed, right? Well, not so fast. The conclusions of this 2010 meta-analysis and the correctness of the GAM are far from universal among psychologists studying the topic. I've only presented one side so far, and in 2010 arguments from that side failed to impress one particularly important group of old men and women clad in flowing black robes and imperious expressions. No, they weren't all powerful wizards, but you're close. They were Supreme Court justices. Oh, and the guy who played Conan the Barbarian was involved, too, so it's a pretty cool story.

THE CASE AGAINST THE CASE AGAINST VIOLENT GAMES

In 2005, California assemblyman (later state senator) Leland Yee wrote and proposed California Law AB 1179, which would make it illegal to sell violent video games to anyone under 18. Prior to his career in politics, Yee was a child psychologist (note that Leland Yee is a different person from Nick Yee, whom I discussed earlier in this book). Like many in his field, he was concerned about the violence he saw in modern video games, and he strongly believed in the research showing a link between virtual and real-world violence. The language in Yee's bill went a little further, though, claiming that such games cause harm to players, including actual damage to the brains of children. Governor Schwarzenegger (that's the Conan the Barbarian guy, among other things) signed the bill into law later that year, setting up businesses that sold violent games to minors for a fine of $1,000 per infraction. One must also assume that the bill allowed Schwarzenegger himself to storm into the retail establishment and break the offending clerk in half, thereby reducing the amount of violence in the world.

Or it would have if the law had gone into effect. Like similar legislation previously attempted in other states, Yee's law was immediately challenged on legal grounds. The Entertainment Software Association and the Video Software Dealers Association sued the state of California to stop implementation of the law. Lower courts consistently ruled against California, saying that the weight of scientific evidence was insufficient to justify a restriction on free speech in the form of video game sales. Schwarzenegger doggedly appealed the case up through the court system until the Supreme Court of the United States agreed to consider it. And so, in late 2010, the nine Supreme Court justices pondered exactly how bewildered the framers of the U.S. Constitution would have been if they had sat down to a few matches of *Mortal Kombat*. I'm not kidding. According to court transcripts, at one point Justice Alito quipped that the real question before them was "what James Madison thought about video games."

Ultimately, the Supreme Court ruled that the law was unconstitutional and could not be put into effect. The case was decided mainly on the grounds of free speech, with the majority of justices deciding that games—including violent ones—were a form of speech and that there were insufficient grounds for the government to stymie their sale. But it's important to realize that the Court could have ruled differently had they been convinced that there was a dire need to protect children from the perils of playing violent games. It has done that kind of thing before with pornography, for example. The fact that the Court scrutinized the research and found it unconvincing is telling. The majority Court opinion, written by Justice Antonin Scalia, stated:

> The State's evidence is not compelling. California relies primarily on the research of Dr. Anderson and a few other research psychologists whose studies purport to show a connection between exposure to violent video games and harmful effects on children. These studies have been rejected by every court to consider them, and with good reason: They do not prove that violent video games *cause* minors to *act* aggressively.[18] [emphasis in the original]

Scalia goes on to quote the Entertainment Merchant's Association to drive the point home: "Nearly all of the research is based on correlation, not evidence of causation, and most of the studies suffer from significant, admitted flaws in methodology."[19]

What are these flaws that the Supreme Court majority opinion refers to? Several of them had been repeatedly pointed out by skeptics and critics in the course of commenting on the Supreme Court case, but they had been around for years before.[20] Such skeptics persist in these criticisms despite how much the "yes, there's a link" crowd claims that the debate should be over, so let's review some of them.

One of the biggest criticisms relates to the measures of aggressive and violent behavior used in laboratory studies. Forcing someone to listen to unpleasant noise, dumping hot sauce on his food, or making it more difficult for her to win a lottery are poor proxies for punching someone in his stupid face or even yelling at someone with the intent to cause distress and fear. This is particularly true when an authority figure is standing there telling you that you are absolutely allowed to use whatever amount of white noise or hot sauce you like. Real-world violence has consequences and is the result of multiple factors. Experiments using noise blasts don't usually test the effects of violent games on real violence outside the laboratory. There are many factors that may cause or inhibit real-life violence, and the U.S. Supreme Court felt that the lab studies cited for arguments against video game violence lacked what psychologists call "external validity." That is, their results don't generalize well to real-life situations.

Other measures of the effects of violent games through priming of memory structures and scripts don't exactly draw a clear picture in bold lines, either. Granted, several studies show that having someone play a violent game can make them more likely to think of "SHOOT" when they see "SHO_T." Or to pick out violence-related words more quickly when viewing a jumble of letters. Or to come up with violent ends to incomplete stories with ambiguous beginnings. That part of the GAM seems to have some support. But it's not much different from mental priming in general. Priming of associative structures is a well-understood psychological phenomenon that makes certain ideas more salient and influential in the short term by tricking people into thinking about them. Having someone complete word puzzles that include "elderly," "bingo," and "wrinkle" can make them walk more slowly on their way out of the research lab.[21] But this depends on the nature of the person and what cognitive structures they've built up between their ears. One experiment showed that some people could be primed for aggression-related thoughts by seeing a hunting rifle, but the effect disappeared when the subjects were avid hunters, for whom that particular type of gun had different associations.[22] Though I suppose from the deer's point of view the difference doesn't amount to much. In any case, priming tends to be fragile and doesn't last long. It alone doesn't seem like a sturdy hook on which to hang an argument about the long-term effects of violent games on mental health, personality, and society.

Even if these long-term effects of games are supposed to be on account of repeated use of aggression-related scripts, as the GAM predicts, that's something that's very difficult to test. Indeed, little research on the topic of violent games has tracked people over time and looked at the long-term effects of violent games in what scientists call "longitudinal studies." What longitudinal studies there are have mixed or weak results. Craig Anderson conducted a meta-analysis just on longitudinal studies and found a moderate relationship between violent games and real-life aggression over time.[23] But when competing causes of violent behavior (e.g., prior aggression or even just being a male) were taken into account, the effects disappeared. Again, real-life violence is a tree with many roots, and many critics argue that we don't know enough about how big a risk factor exposure to violent games is relative to other risks, such as living in poverty, being from a dysfunctional family, having access to weapons, or suffering from mental illness.[24]

Some researchers have also claimed that the meta-analyses showing a link between games and violence are more likely to include experiments that support a link than those that don't. This isn't necessarily intentional, but it might rather come from the open secret in academia that studies are more likely to be published if they find an interesting result than if they find nothing. And if a study isn't published, it's much less likely to be found and included in a meta-analysis. This is a phenomenon known as "publication bias" or the "file drawer problem," in reference to how studies may be tossed in file drawers and forgotten if they don't yield expected or interesting results.[25] Whatever the reason for the bias, if a meta-analysis only has studies finding a link as its inputs, it will of course also spit out a link in its output.

Another criticism of existing research on violent video games has to do with the games used in the studies. For example, one 2004 study found that those who played a violent game had more aggressive thoughts and moods than those who played a nonviolent one.[26] But in the nonviolent game, *Glider Pro 4*, subjects used just two keyboard keys to guide a paper airplane through a simple, 2D environment. The violent game, *Marathon 2*, is a standard first-person shooter where subjects used a mouse and 20 keys to navigate through a complex, 3D environment. One game had much more complex controls than the other, which represents an alternative explanation for the results.

Andrew Przybylski and his colleagues explored this problem in a series of studies where they made players feel frustrated and incompetent while playing the puzzle game *Tetris*.[27] Some subjects had to play with nonintuitive and difficult-to-master controls, and others played a version of the game that made it harder by, for example, giving the player a 2 x 2 block when what she really needed at that moment was a 1 x 4 block to complete a row. All throughout the seven experiments, the researchers included measures of control mastery, feelings of competence, and aggressive thoughts. The short version of the results is that video games could make people feel aggressive and think violent thoughts simply by thwarting their sense of competence, either through tricky controls or game difficulty. This was true even in the absence of violent imagery. The implication is that efforts to simplify and standardize experimental designs have led researchers to do an inadequate job at avoiding such alternative explanations for postgame aggression.

So who is right? Is playing violent games a significant risk factor for violent behavior in real life? As much as this might annoy you to hear if you're a gamer, I don't think we know for sure. The research clearly shows that exposure to violent games (or media of any kind) can increase the accessibility of violent thoughts through priming. So I would believe you if you said you and your brother sometimes came to blows while playing *Street Fighter*. Priming is an established psychological phenomenon, even if the strength of its effects is sometimes overstated. But the long- or medium-term effects of video game violence are not equally well understood or researched, for all the reasons described above. The kind of research needed to answer that question is very difficult to do, and there have been few attempts. I think it's safe to say that anyone uttering the phrase "murder simulator" can safely be ignored, but outside of such extreme claims the data are mixed or simply unknown.

But in a way, it doesn't matter. Violent games are here to stay simply because they are considered a form of free speech and many people— normal, well-adjusted people like you and me—like at least some of them. So maybe an equally important question is, "Why this is so?" Why do violent games sell so well, especially shooters like *Call of Duty*, *Halo*, and *Gears of War?* It's a question worth spending some time on in the rest of this chapter.

PSYCHOLOGICAL NEEDS AND VIOLENCE: WHY WE LIKE SHOOTING STUFF IN VIDEO GAMES

I brought up self-determination theory (SDT) in the chapter on quests and goals, but some researchers believe that it also has much to tell us about why violent shooters are popular. To review, SDT says that people are motivated to play a particular video game based on how well it satisfies three basic psychological needs: competence, autonomy, and relatedness. Competence deals with a sense of control, mastery, and feeling like you're making things happen the way you want. A well-designed difficulty curve makes us feel an ever-increasing sense of competence, as does appropriate matchmaking in multiplayer games. Games high in autonomy give you the opportunity to make many meaningful decisions about what goals to pursue and how to pursue them. Finally, relatedness is concerned with a feeling that you matter to other players and that you have meaningful social interactions with them.

These needs certainly aren't unique to shooters, but one could argue that many of the qualities inherent to virtual gunplay create well-worn paths to satisfying these needs. Violent shooters like those in the *Call of Duty* series provide immediate and unambiguous feedback about skill mastery and performance. You see your opponents take damage, and winning a particularly tough firefight or perching at the top of scoreboard is a simple and powerful indication of your competence. Scott Rigby, a researcher who also works at Immerersyve, Inc., where he consults with game developers on these kinds of issues, told me, "I'll often put up a slide with a great screenshot of a headshot, and it always elicits smiles. The smiles here aren't because everyone is sadistic —they are because this is a moment of mastery satisfaction that all gamers can relate to. The blood may not be the value component, but really is just a traditional way dense informational feedback on mastery is provided."[28] In other words, gamers don't love gore any more than race car drivers have a fetish for checkered flags.

What about autonomy? Combat-oriented games offer plenty of that, too. Rigby notes that when you look at what distinguishes the top-selling first-person shooter titles from other shooters, blockbusters tend to satisfy more than one of SDT's basic needs at once. Great shooters like those in the *Call of Duty* franchise will not only satisfy competence needs, but they will also provide solid satisfaction of autonomy needs. Just think about all the weapons and powers to choose from in a *Bioshock* game, the nine different classes to play in *Team Fortress 2*, or the many paths you can approach an enemy encounter in a *Halo* map.

And, of course, multiplayer shooters are built around the concept of relatedness, with the most popular modes putting players on teams to boost a sense of teamwork, opposition to a common foe, and a feeling that their actions affect the success of their teammates. "There's social status in being, say, a great sniper in a multiplayer game, and gaining recognition as an asset to your team," says Cheryl Olson, author of the book about video game violence *Grand Theft Childhood*.[29] And it can even happen in a well-crafted single-player game.

So given all this, how important is the "violent" part of "violent shooters?" Could it be that it's not the violence per se, but the satisfaction of competence, autonomy, and relatedness that matter? When the first-person shooter *Bioshock Infinite* came out in 2013, reviewers and fans frequently cited it as an example of how video games were evolving to lean more heavily on complex narratives, social commentary, and philosophy. And yet in *Bioshock Infinite* the player spends the majority of his or her time shooting, stabbing, zapping, and blowing stuff up. For all its other lofty aspirations, it's still a violent shooter. Ken Levine, creative director on the game, said in an interview with National Public Radio's *All Things Considered* that he was often asked if he could have made *Bioshock Infinite* equally successful without all the violence. [30] It was an interesting question, Levine said, but he didn't think he could make a game like that.

Or could he? Andrew Przybylski, Richard Ryan, and C. Scott Rigby concocted a series of experiments that Levine may be interested in hearing about.[31] The researchers wanted to disentangle the violence of a game from its ability to satisfy our desires for competence and autonomy. In one study, they modified *Half-Life 2* so that some participants played a violent and bloody game replete with firearms and death. Other people played a nonviolent version with the same mechanics and map, but it was framed as a game of tag where opponents were gently teleported to a penalty box when highlighted with an in-game tool. The results? Both versions equally satisfied those basic psychological needs of competence and autonomy, which predicted how satisfied people were with the game and how much they wanted to play more of it. The researchers concluded that it's not the violence per se that made the game enjoyable, but the degree to which the games met players' desires for competence and autonomy. Interviews of adolescents done by Lawrence Kutner and Cheryl Olson for the book *Grand Theft Childhood* yielded a similar insight that violent video games were neat and all, but what the kids really liked was the challenge, action, and options that came with it. The violence is just there. [32]

All this argues that shooters aren't so popular simply because they let you kill stuff real good. They're also the product of straightforward design choices that tend to meet basic psychological needs. These needs range from letting us dabble in forbidden or otherwise impossible situations in order to chip away at stress, anxiety, or frustration, to letting us scratch psychological itches related to choosing what to do and being able to do it well.

The caveat, though, seems to be that this doesn't have to be so. "Themes of war and combat themselves have always had value in communicating personal victory over challenge," said Rigby when I asked him why military shooters are so popular. [33] "So we believe combat themes will always be a favorite for developers and players. Our hope, though, is that by understanding the underlying motivational psychology, developers would also be empowered to not feel chained to blood and violence as their only option."

Or, you know, you could just enjoy a good shooter. It's up to you, but I think you'll be okay either way.

THINGS TO REMEMBER FROM THIS CHAPTER

- The evidence from research on violent video games is not as clear-cut and definitive as people on the extremes of either side would have you believe.
- "Social learning theory" describes how we can learn new behavioral scripts and internalize action/reward pairings simply by watching other people beat the daylights out of a clown.

- The General Aggression Model (GAM) holds that in addition to personal and situational factors, our aggression can be triggered by cascades of associations between violent acts and thoughts. This can prime violent scripts that lay out how to interpret and react to a given situation.
- GAM also predicts prosocial behaviors through the same mechanisms.
- Critics of the "yes, there's a link" research argue that the behavioral measures of "violence" used in most research are unimpressive and far removed from actual, real-world violence.
- The "file drawer problem" (also called "publication bias") refers to the fact that studies finding no relationship when one is expected are unlikely to be published or included in meta-analysis. This is another criticism against the "yes, there's a link" camp.
- There are also often uncontrolled-for, alternative explanations for video game violence research. These are called "confounds." That the complexity of game controls might cause frustration and violent thoughts is one example.
- Violent shooters are appealing, in part, because they often do a good job of satisfying self-determination theory's needs of competence, autonomy, and relatedness. Some research suggests that this is irrespective of the violent content.

15

DO VIDEO GAMES MAKE YOU SMARTER?

"Chess is a mere amusement of a very inferior character, which robs the mind of valuable time that might be devoted to nobler acquirements."

—from an article in an 1859 issue of *Scientific American*[1]

Despite what the uncredited person above wrote in *Scientific American* more than 150 years ago, if you ask random strangers what game really smart people play, most of them will say chess. Chances were there were chess clubs in your school where the brainy and nerdy excelled, and we've all seen Hollywood use the game as a trope for letting the audience know that an on-screen character is a deep thinker. A chessboard in the background of a shot is better shorthand than anything else for "hey, this person is smart." And if the filmmakers really want to dial it up to 11, they will show the character playing speed chess where moves have to be made under time pressure. Or they'll show him or her attending to multiple chess games at once, perhaps on a park bench against experienced players. Or multiple speed chess!

To be fair, chess has earned its reputation. The rule set is relatively simple, but anyone who has competed against an accomplished player or even a challenging computer program knows that winning a game requires very complex mental acrobatics and thinking ahead about how to counter any number of possible upcoming moves. In his book about the work of mathematical genius John von Neumann, author William Poundstone explains how one could, at least theoretically, create a table of all possible chess strategies, showing the pairings of every set of possible moves and countermoves for Player A with every possible set of moves and countermoves for Player B.[2] Each cell in that table would describe an outcome of that pairing of moves and countermoves: White wins in 64 moves, draw in 104 moves, black wins in 88 moves, and so on. But the theoretical possibility of such a complete description of all possible games is somewhat lost beside the fact that such a table printed in compact, 10-point font would be so large as to span several galaxies. Or slightly bigger if you use the old trick of adding 1.5-inch margins to the paper.

And yet chess has got nothing on the complexity of *StarCraft*.

Real-time strategy games like those in the *StarCraft* series have competitive modes where players manage armies and economies from an overhead perspective in order to conquer their opponents. Games are played on maps that contain natural resources like minerals and gas. Those resources are collected and used to build and upgrade a base full of buildings. Those buildings produce a wide array of military units that are sent out to scout for and battle with the enemy. Some units are more or less powerful against other units—imagine a sophisticated version of rock/paper/scissors but with better graphics and more objects in play. Many more objects, because *StarCraft* games have three different factions a player can choose from, each of which has dozens of possible units and structures. Memorizing all those units and being able to recall how they each interact is no small feat of long-term and working memory. Plus deciding on the composition of one's army requires logical reasoning and problem-solving: A player's choice of what buildings and units to build should be informed by what her opponent is doing. Thus effective scouting and information-gathering are as important to the game as martial might and resource management.

In addition to all this, wars in *StarCraft* and games like it are often fought on multiple fronts requiring multitasking and the splintering of one's attention. Most matches involve expanding to a second or even third base of operations in order to pull in the far-flung resources needed for a win. And unlike a chessboard, the map in *StarCraft*—its game board, if you will—is too large to see or interact with all in one view. Players have only limited information on what's going on at any given moment. Successful players have to click around all over the map in order to issue commands, activate units' abilities, queue up production, and keep resource collection going. Accomplished *StarCraft* players can switch their attention around and click their mouse buttons fast enough to perform at least 400 different actions per minute. That's almost seven actions every single second, and some elite players are even faster. Most casual players would probably only be able to do one-eighth of that on a good day.[3]

It's all mind-bogglingly complex. Even if you had several galaxies on which to write a table of strategies and counterstrategies, it wouldn't be enough since everything happens in real time, and, unlike in games of chess, a *StarCraft* player only has partial information about what her opponent is doing at any given moment. Yet people obviously play the game all the time. It's massively popular in the competitive gaming scene, especially in Korea where teams of players live and train together in dormitory-like houses full of computers and bunk beds. It is literally their job to play the game all day and to watch recordings of past games so that they can compete in professional matches where only those with the experience and mental fortitude needed to master the game can come out on top.

So *StarCraft* players must be smarter than other people, right? Or, put another way, smarter people tend to make better *StarCraft* players, right? Researchers have actually tried to answer these questions. In 2013, neuroscientists in Korea subjected the brains of 23 professional *StarCraft* players to an MRI in order to study the structure of their brains.[4] The brain is a malleable and shapeable organ that will respond with tiny but detectable physical growth with use of specific areas. The Korean researchers found that the thickness of certain areas of elite players' brains was correlated with tenure as a professional player. The longer a subject had been playing *StarCraft* and the better his win rate, the more thickness he had in areas of his brain known to be associated with attention shifting, inhibition of impulses, and executive functions like decision-making. Playing the game, the authors argue, literally made their brains bigger. This is similar to London taxi cab drivers, who must prepare for a grueling gauntlet of tests known colloquially as "The Knowledge" by memorizing thousands of different routes through London streets. Research shows that the brain regions associated with spatial representations of environments are larger in London taxi drivers than in the general population.[5]

Another group of researchers from the University of California, San Diego, analyzed recordings of 2,015 *StarCraft* games and considered the relationships between measures of action speed (that "actions per minute" metric mentioned earlier) and how far apart on the map actions were on average.[6] The researchers argued that this latter statistic served as a measure of how players were able to manage the cognitively demanding task of divvying up and allocating attention on the fly. If a player has a group of Hydralisks burrow near an enemy base in one action, then upgrades a Spawning Pool back in his base with the next action, then orders an Overlord to scout a potential expansion locale clear across the map, he is displaying what the authors describe as superior "spatial variance of action." It's a hallmark of an efficient and powerful brain, and indeed the researchers found that displays of this cognitive ability predicted whether or not a player won or lost any given game. Of course, correlation does not signify causation. People with naturally excellent attention-allocation skills may be drawn to games like *StarCraft* because they find that they're good at them. Or smarter people might just naturally be attracted to complicated, mentally demanding games like *StarCraft* or chess. I'll address this point a little further on.

So, given all this, should you think that playing *StarCraft* makes you smarter? Is it only real-time strategy games? What about simulation games like *Civilization*? Or puzzle games like *Bejeweled* or *Peggle*? Heck, what about shooters like those in the *Call of Duty* series? Can those make you smarter? The answer is a definitive "well, maybe. It depends." Some researchers (and more than a few marketing professionals) certainly believe that even simple games can make you smarter. Or at the very least, they can help train specific cognitive abilities like memory, concentration, and problem-solving. These "brain-training" games can be found on the Web, cell phones, or even dedicated gaming platforms like the Nintendo 3DS. But do they work? Let's find out.

BRAIN TRAINING: IT'S LEG DAY AT YOUR BRAIN'S GYM

My history with brain-training games started in 2006 with the Stroop Test mini game in *Brain Age* for the Nintendo DS. The Stroop Test measures your brain's ability to reconcile discrepancies between the meaning of a written word for a color (say, "blue") and the color font the word is written in. The *Brain Age* mini game version challenges you to read the word out loud as fast as you can into the Nintendo DS's microphone without making errors. It's much harder than it sounds not to mentally stumble over the word "green" when it's written with yellow letters, but the fact that the Nintendo DS's microphone didn't understand my voice very well made it even harder. This led my family to wonder why I was sitting in front of a Christmas tree and screaming, "Blue. Blue! BLUE, DAMMIT!," into a little machine. The game would use my performance on the Stroop Test and a few other mini games to calculate my "brain age," which was the age at which my brain was functioning. My brain age usually put me on par with your typical 110-year-old since my pronunciation of the world "blue" is apparently some kind of impenetrable nonsense to the people at Nintendo. But the idea was that with daily play I could improve my brain age and sharpen my wits until I had the mind of a 20-year-old.

Since then, there have been many sequels to *Brain Age* and a host of Web- and app-based services designed to exercise your brain in order to make it work better. They go by mashed-up names that invoke both brain power and physical fitness: Lumosity, Jungle Memory, Cognifit, and Cogmed. You can subscribe to one of these services on its website, for example, and tell it what kinds of cognitive abilities you'd like to improve. You may want to improve working memory, learn to focus your attention better, or increase the speed at which you process information. The site will then assign you a training regimen where you are expected to log in regularly and play several little mini games. These aren't games along the lines of *League of Legends* or *Grand Theft Auto*. They're usually more like little memory, matching, and math games that you might think are more appropriate for children. In one game you may press buttons to tell whether or not a shape is the same as or different from a shape flashed on the screen for a second. Or in another you need to quickly flip train tracks around in order to guide a parade of little trains to their color-coded station houses.

The games may sound rudimentary and silly, but these services typically try to make sure you understand that science was involved by using phrases like "neuroscience" and "brain plasticity" and "shut up, we know what we're talking about here." Like with the elite *StarCraft* players in Korea and the taxi cab drivers in London, the general argument is that the human brain is malleable and parts of it can be improved through repeated use. Play a lot of memory games, for example, and you will get better at holding phone numbers or shopping lists in your head. Practice allocating and reallocating your attention and you will be able to drive more safely and manage more base expansions in *StarCraft*. Skills like these are particularly important to our more senior citizens, who see their cognitive abilities dull and decline with age. So obviously the people writing the marketing material at these brain-training companies say this kind of brain training works, but what does the science say?

Well, it says a lot of things, because once again the body of research doesn't yet draw a clear picture of such a relatively new subject. But it's safe to say that many leading neuroscientists are skeptical at best. In late 2014, the Stanford Center on Longevity and the Berlin Max Planck Institute for Human Development gathered a crowd of such experts to draft a consensus on the efficacy of brain-training games.[7] The statement, which the Stanford Center on Longevity's website surrounds with pictures of silver-haired gentlemen staring blankly at laptops, objects to claims that brain-training games combat mental decline and Alzheimer's disease. "There is little evidence," says the statement, "that playing brain games improves underlying broad cognitive abilities, or that it enables one to better navigate a complex realm of everyday life." It also warns the reader not to confuse getting better at a highly specific skill with broad improvements that cross multiple skills or broad concepts. Improvement on a specific set of brain-training games is not the same as getting smarter, these experts agree. In all, more than 70 academics and other experts gave their public endorsement to the statement. This skepticism is similar to what many other specific studies have also found. A 2013 meta-analysis, for example, combined data from many different sources and found that working memory training wasn't effective outside of short-term gains that were specific to the games in question.[8]

Other studies are more optimistic, however. A group of researchers from the University of California in San Francisco did a study where they trained healthy, mentally able adults between 60 and 85 years of age with a video game.[9] The game, *NeuroRacer*, had been specially designed by some of the authors to help bolster working memory and the ability to screen out visual distractions and focus attention on what's important. It challenges players to keep a little car in place while it drives along a road. Players must simultaneously respond to signs and prompts to press specific controller buttons. If I had designed the game, I would have tasked players with keeping a rolling death machine centered on the postapocalyptic highway while using separate buttons to periodically fire missiles at roving road bandits. But I guess the researchers wanted to keep their version simple. Relative to a control group, those who played *NeuroRacer* for 12 hours over the course of a month scored better on subsequent measures of multitasking abilities, sustained attention, and working memory (that is, retaining information in short-term memory). These improvements were still present six months later.

Another study of the effects of brain-training games on older adults had subjects use a specific tool called the Posit Science Brain Fitness Program.[10] Not only did the subjects get better at the particular tasks that were part of the program (which is to be expected), but these improvements also reportedly generalized to larger contexts. For example, subjects increased their auditory processing speed by 131 percent and saw improvements in working memory that put them on par with people 10 years younger. When the subjects were asked to self-report about the quality of their lives, they claimed to be able to remember things better, though it's wise to be somewhat skeptical of potentially biased self-reports.

So I think the science has not yet provided a definitive answer as to what kinds of brain-training games work, if any of them work at all. One common theme throughout the literature, though, is that there is no evidence to substantiate broad claims of things like games making players "smarter" or "more intelligent." And there is certainly no evidence that they can prevent or cure diseases and mental conditions like Alzheimer's or dementia brought on by advanced age. Instead, if there's anything to these games and the surrounding training programs, it probably has more to do with developing very specific skills and not broader concepts—things like learning to screen out visual clutter while paying attention to a particular object in view, or remembering the sequence of shapes as they're presented.

When you take a step back and start to consider cognitive skills at this specific level, the question of whether video games can develop certain cognitive skills gets much clearer. In fact, there is a growing body of research that shows video games can help people improve a variety of skills related to perception, attention, and visual acuity. But despite everything I've said about real-time strategy games like *Star-Craft*, this research focuses on action games. Specifically, it focuses on first-person shooters like those in the *Call of Duty, Halo, and Battlefield* franchises. These often vilified games might be doing us far more good than we realize.

THE BENEFITS OF ACTION GAMES AND FIRST-PERSON SHOOTERS

You know what country we haven't mentioned yet? France. I should talk a bit about France. Specifically, I should mention that Daphne Bavelier, an accomplished researcher currently in the University of Rochester's Cognitive Neuroscience department, was born there. At one point the young Bavelier decided she wanted to spend some time abroad, so she came to the United States to spend a semester studying there. Decades later, she's still there, so I guess this story is actually going to be more about the United States than France after all. Sorry. Anyway, the trip turned into a long-term stay, and Bavelier became quite an accomplished academic. She stayed in the United States to earn a Ph.D. in brain and cognitive science from MIT and eventually ended up at the University of Rochester in the state of New York where she has authored more than 20 publications on first-person shooters and other action games. But instead of focusing on the violence inherent in these games, she and her colleagues have looked at how playing action games can improve our cognitive abilities.

According to an interview Bavelier gave to MedGadget.com,[11] she started her time at Rochester doing research on visual attention and the fields of view in deaf people. An undergraduate lab technician named Shawn Green helped her design a task to be used in a study of how much information deaf people can extract from their peripheral vision based on just a brief glance at a scene. But when Green went to pilot the software used in the task in order to make sure everything was working, he grabbed a convenient sample of people who were always hanging around the computer lab anyway: members of an on-campus video game club. Green was surprised when every one of them completely aced the task, scoring 100 percent. Whoops. That's usually a sure signal that something is amiss. But rather than shake their fists, throw out their data, and start over with a different sample, Bavelier and Green recognized this accident for what it was: a big clue that people who play video games may be better at certain cognitive tasks than most other people. Thus was born a research program that even today continues to buck the traditional view that action games are mindless activities that ruin your eyesight, make you dumb, and shorten your attention span. In fact, Bavelier and her team have discovered that the opposite of all these things is true.

Think about the kinds of visual and mental skills required by the last first-person shooter you played. You have to hold a representation of the 3D environment in your head and use a 2D computer screen to find your way through it. You have to scan the environment for threats and distinguish, for example, between a pile of debris and another player at the end of a long hallway. Then, once you've spotted another player, you may have to perceive and use fine details to decide what class he is, if he sees you, what he's doing, and if he is on your team or not. The same goes for auditory cues like gunfire, footsteps, opening doors, and the sounds of special abilities being activated. This all happens constantly, rapidly, and while you're dividing your attention between various parts of the screen. Might playing a pile of action games exercise parts of your brain like a muscle and make you better at these cognitive tasks?

Bavelier, Green, and their colleagues believe so. Most of the research they do continues to deal with action games and their effects on the brains of players. They have found, for example, that action gamers have better vision than others. These gamers can measure the fine detail in a scene better than can other people. The "crowding test," for example, challenges subjects to squint and identify a small letter on a large white space. People with poor eyesight have trouble with this, which means they have trouble reading small print on a page or a prescription bottle. Green and Bavelier showed that people who play action games need less help in identifying the details about such small text, relative to those who don't play action games.[12] They found that this is even true if one is only using her periphery vision and that action gamers process information from their periphery vision better than others.[13]

Action gamers are also less likely to miss something as a result of depleted mental resources when it crosses their visual path. This ability is usually assessed with what's called the "attentional blink paradigm." Subjects are asked to watch a stream of black letters and signal when they see a white letter show up. After they see the white letter, the stream continues and they're supposed to signal a second time if they see the letter X. Vigilantly watching for and identifying the white letter in a stream of black saps attentional resources that need time to regenerate, so people miss the letter X more often when it comes directly on the heels of the white text. But less so for action gamers, who seem to have developed a surfeit of needed mental resources.[14]

Other research has found that attention is a mental tool generally wielded more effectively by action gamers. Those who play lots of action games can split their attention better than nongamers or those who play other kinds of games, allowing them to track more objects of attention. In a typical test of this ability, an experimenter sits a subject down in front of a computer screen and shows him a mess of moving circles. Some of the circles are blue, but most of them are yellow, and all of them are moving around randomly. The subject is given the heads-up that all the blue circles are going to turn yellow and become indistinguishable from all the others, but that he is to keep track of them nonetheless. At the end of the trial, the experimenter will highlight a random circle, and the subject will need to say whether it started out as blue or yellow. This is easy if there are only one or two blue circles to begin with. An average person can handle tracking four circles before their attentional system collapses in a pile of failure. But those who play a lot of action games? They can typically handle tracking up to six circles.[15] And presumably they could headshot every one of them.

Green, Bavelier, and the other researchers on these experiments argue that this ability is related to a superior visual working memory, meaning that action gamers develop the ability to hold more visual information in short-term memory.[16] A study by a different group of researchers examined this question directly, training subjects on *Call of Duty: Black Ops* and *Call of Duty: Modern Warfare* for 30 hours over 30 days.[17] These freshly minted action gamers then completed a task where they saw a set of colored blocks on a gray background, then saw the scene disappear and a new set of blocks reappear. Or maybe it was the same set of colored blocks as before; the subjects' task was to hold the first set of blocks in working visual memory, then report on whether the second set was different or the same. Relative to people who played a nonaction game (*The Sims*) for 30 hours, those who played the first-person shooters were more accurate, reflecting a more efficient visual working memory.

And it's not just that action gamers can take in information better. Some researchers argue that they make quicker and more accurate use of it once it's in their brains. In one study, Green, Bavelier, and their colleague Alexandre Pouget had some subjects play 50 hours of action games, though presumably not in a row.[18] They then showed them a screen full of dots that at first glance appeared to be moving erratically, but which were, over time, making more moves in one direction than others. So given enough time, one could see that the dots were eventually going to migrate to either the left or right side of the screen. The subjects' task was to report which side the dots were destined for, and to do so as quickly as possible based on as little observation as they could. Relative to nongamers, those who played just 50 hours of action games arrived at their conclusions 25 percent faster and with no reduction in accuracy. The feat was also replicated using headphones and repetitions of sounds that "moved" from both ears to either the left or right ear. The authors argue that action gamers develop a heightened sensitivity to the world around them and make more efficient use of their sensory evidence to form judgments about what's going on.

Finally, some research has shown that action gamers are better at imaging what objects and environments would look like if they were rotated in 3D space. This skill is typically called by the impressive name of "spatial cognition," and it's something plenty of data show that boys typically excel at more than girls.[19] One group of researchers at the University of Toronto wondered if they could close this gap by having girls and women play more action games. To find out, they had a group of subjects, both male and female, play 10 hours of the first-person shooter *Medal of Honor: Pacific Assault* over a span of 2 weeks. Before and after the training, subjects took tests that measured their ability to recognize what complex, 3D shapes (think *Tetris* blocks gone mad) would look like if rotated in space. Relative to a control group that played no games, these subjects got better at the 3D shape-rotation test. What's more, the women in the sample of gamers benefited more than the men. This is in line with other research showing relationships between spatial cognition and exposure to computers and video games among male and female college students.[20] Men, who as a group are better at spatial cognition, tend to have more experience with games that demand that skill.

Keep in mind that in all these studies the researchers weren't just comparing people who happened to play a lot of action games with those who didn't. Doing so could expose the research to what's called a "selection bias." That is, it might be that people with more impressive eyesight or who had more skill at focusing their attention end up discovering and playing more action games. Probably because those features make them better players than half-blind nitwits who couldn't pay attention to a blank wall if they pressed their nose up against it. It's like how playing basketball at the professional level doesn't make you taller; taller people just tend to be better at basketball than shorter people. Instead, these experiments randomly assigned people to experimental groups and had them play action games (or not) for just 40 or 50 hours over the course of several days before finding measurable changes in mental abilities.

Bavelier, Green, and others doing research in this program argue that playing action games—and only action games—creates changes in the brain that make these new skills possible. Furthermore, they argue that these skills can generalize to other important areas of life. Being able to pick out an object that doesn't contrast very well from its gray background, for example, means that you can drive more safely in a thick fog. Being able to read small text means being able to read prescription bottles more accurately. Being able to split up and constantly reallocate attention means that you can pick out dangers from a crowded scene while cycling down a sidewalk.

In fact, some researchers think that distinguishing between skills in a video game and specific cognitive skills is beside the point. "I'll argue that cognitive skills are not a proxy of video game skill, but perhaps they are video game skill," said Nicholas Bowman of West Virginia University's Department of Communications when I asked him about the relationship between cognitive skills and video game skill.[21] "Video games are cognitive challenges, which require cognitive skills." Bowman and his colleagues conducted some research of their own about what effect an audience would have on playing the competitive shooter *Quake III Arena*, but he wanted to know if more skilled players were affected in the same way as novices.[22] To find out, the researchers administered separate measures of targeting ability, hand–eye coordination, 2D mental-rotation ability, and 3D mental-rotation ability (essentially the same spatial cognition ability as described earlier). They found that scores on these tests were better conceptualizations of skill in the video game than actual game scores, and that they related to other things, as you would predict—an idea psychologists call "construct validity." Navigating through a 3D space isn't a testament to your spatial cognition, Bowman says. It is a direct measurement of your spatial cognition.

Though I couldn't find any research on the question, I think you could make the same argument about other kinds of mental skills and other kinds of video games. Doing well in word-completion games like *Scrabble* or *Words with Friends* isn't just something that correlates with your verbal intelligence, it's a direct expression of it. And logical reasoning clearly comes in to play when deciding on a technology upgrade path during a game of *Civilization* or laying out an urban infrastructure in *SimCity*. Perhaps someday research will follow that tests these ideas. Psychology graduate students forgoing their dissertation for just one more turn in a video game take note: Here's how you combine your two passions and graduate on time.

So what's the final verdict on the questions raised by this chapter's title? Do games make you smarter? Are gamers more intelligent than nongamers? Well, not in the sense that you or the people around you use the word "intelligence." And certainly not in the way that psychologists use it in a technical sense. Definitions of intelligence or general mental ability vary among experts, but they generally refer to a much more global concept related to verbal ability, mathematical skill, logical reasoning, learning, and problem-solving. There has not been any research to show that playing video games of any kind will make you brainier in such broad, all-encompassing ways. And it won't give you the brain of a 20-year-old at age 70.

The research on the effects of games on this idea of intelligence isn't there, but it does appear that dedicated gamers as a group score higher on certain mental abilities: visual acuity, speed of processing, hand–eye coordination, multitasking, controlling and focusing our attention, and generally sharper perception of the world around us. These are important mental skills that predict success in all aspects of not only play but also work and study.

That's got to count for something, smarty pants.

THINGS TO REMEMBER FROM THIS CHAPTER

- Many video games are far more demanding of our cognitive skills and resources than people realize.
- There is some evidence that playing these games increases the size of certain parts of players' brains.
- The marketing claims of most brain-training software and games are overstated and experts are generally skeptical. There's no evidence that they will reverse brain aging or treat the symptoms of diseases like Alzheimer's or dementia.
- There are some studies, however, showing that specially designed games can bolster specific skills, such as working memory and reallocation of attention.
- Another body of research has shown that we can benefit from playing action games like first-person shooters. These benefits largely relate to visual skills, such as visual acuity, use of peripheral vision, efficient allocation of visual attention, making quick and accurate use of visual (and auditory) information to draw conclusions, and quickly spotting things amid clutter.
- The cognitive benefits of video games tend to be more specific and refined than would be suggested by broad terms such as "smarter" or "intelligence."

Conclusion

WHERE DO PSYCHOLOGY AND VIDEO GAMES GO FROM HERE?

I hope I've convinced you that psychology is important to video games, because I'm almost out of space. But assuming you weren't just sitting by the pool pretending to read this book in order to impress someone, you've seen how the application of established and emerging psychological principles can help you understand why players do what they do, why game designers make the decisions they do, how game marketers get you to buy things, and what effects games have on the people who play them.

Part 1 of the book focused on players and player behavior, both good and bad. On the bad side, we explored how anonymity and deindividuation combine to create toxic player behavior, and under what circumstances players will outright cheat. Plus we looked at how the drivers of what seems like innocent fanboyism can also fuel the grim business of harassing women and relative newcomers to the video game scene. But it's not all bad. You also learned how with the right tweaks the same quirks of human psychology can make people helpful instead of toxic, honest instead of devious, and welcoming instead of antagonistic. You also learned about the benefit of nostalgia and why one need not be so cynical about it, even if you do see good old games through a rose-tinted display. All of these things—toxic behavior, fanboyism, cheating, nostalgia—are products of how a game's mechanics and social systems come together in the minds of different players, and details matter. Sometimes the details aren't under your control, nor are the ways that other players incorporate them into their ideas about what behavior is acceptable or desired. But the intersection of games, players, and psychology isn't completely unpredictable. Keep that in mind the next time you have a good or bad experience and use it to help craft better ones for you and your fellow players.

Part 2 looked at the psychology behind common game design principles in an effort to understand why designers rely on them to motivate players. People play to chase high scores and prove themselves to be better than their rivals. You saw how information about your performance can be framed, sliced, and diced in order to compel you to try just one more time to beat a high score or do something a little more impressive than your friends. But games have come a long way since the scoreboards on coin-operated games. Many modern games entice us to keep playing by dangling specific types of rewards, making us feel like we're accomplishing something important, and letting us watch numbers inch up over time. The psychology of goal setting, achievement, and motivation were brought to bear on explaining why this works so well and why we will do things that honestly aren't that much fun. Other games keep us playing by occasionally rewarding us with increasingly awesome loot, so we also applied old lessons about rewards and reward schedules to understand why loot-based games are so compelling (and why they sometimes are not). Finally, sometimes you stay in a game world because it feels so real and it's so amazing to explore, so we learned about what new and old tools game designers and hardware designers can use to build immersive worlds that we want to spend time in for their own sake.

In part 3 we looked at the business of parting you from your money and how psychology can forewarn and forearm you—to an extent. Lessons from behavioral economics and consumer psychology were applied to digital distribution, free-to-play games, in-app purchases, subscriptions, and the ways that games get players to market and sell to each other. These are old tricks that have been studied by psychologists for decades, but they're still applicable to the new ways that games are being sold and marketed. You should know the tricks now, and I hope you'll recognize them the next time you encounter them in the wild so that you can spend money on your own terms. Buying stuff can be great. I'll probably buy something later today and really enjoy it. But understanding why you're buying and not being nudged into making unintended purchases is also pretty great.

Finally, part 4 looked at the way that video games affect us. Do they make us violent? Probably not. But the way we perceive our avatars—and more importantly the way that others perceive them—can make us more confident, helpful, or friendly. And games frequently have other benefits, such as teaching us new skills, polishing existing skills, and making us more cognitively flexible. Games are pretty awesome. But they're not always as wonderful as some people might want you to believe. The truth comes down somewhere in the middle, as it often does. Again, it all depends on the details of the game and the intricacies of the social situations that they put us in or remind us of.

So psychology matters to games. It's for this reason that I wish its methods, theories, and models were more frequently utilized in the gaming industry. Psychology should be a part of every curriculum at schools and universities aiming to teach people how to make games, and video games should be used as a context to illustrate lessons in every psychology class. I will grudgingly admit that topics like coding, art, animation, music, and sound design are probably more central to making video games than is psychology. But understanding the mental roots of behavior is still an important part of game design. You need to know the basics of motivation, rewards, social dynamics, cognition, habit formation, emotions, attention, decision-making, perception, and more in order to build a gaming system that will interact with the minds of your players in the way you want. Any given game designer may know what makes a game fun for her, but, as they say in scientific circles, a sample of one is bad statistics. You have to understand people in general. So here's my advice to game designers: Read more books about psychology, invite psychologists to your conferences, listen to lectures by social scientists, hire psychologists as consultants, and read academic articles whenever you can. Maybe make the hero of your next game a really handsome psychologist. And give me huge pectoral muscles.

I also wish more psychologists were working in the games industry, because they have such great opportunities to make games and gaming communities so much better. Psychologists can help game designers and community managers understand everything I described in this book, and people with the rigorous academic training that comes with an advanced degree in psychology also know how to do science in this context. They know how to scour the scientific literature to see what other people have discovered and how to apply it to their specific game-design problems and goals. They understand experimental design, statistics, probability, peer review, generalizability of results, and other scientific concepts. More importantly, they value these things over gut instincts, anecdotes, institutionalized habits, and personal experience that can all be tainted by cognitive biases. Training in these things matters.

Speaking of personal experience, it's my general perception based on one-on-one conversations and what I read online that some psychologists do work in the games industry, but they are often limited to roles in user-experience testing and data mining because they are "the numbers guy" or "the stats jockey." Having and using these skills is obviously great, but I suggest that psychologists also get more involved with actual issues of game design, prototyping, community management, and play-testing. Game design should be informed by psychology from the beginning, and the scientific methods that trained psychologists know should be employed to prototype, test, and tweak things for the better. Some companies, such as Riot Games, Valve, Ubisoft, Epic Games, and others, are already doing this and seeing the rewards. I just wish they would share more of their research with the scientific community. Come on people, publish!

On the topic of publication, it's great to see so many academics in universities and other educational institution doing research that focuses on video games. People who grew up playing video games are settling in to these positions. They're turning their minds to questions about psychology and video games that not only interest them, but that are also becoming increasingly important to society given gaming's popularity. Better yet, research by these academics is being held to high standards and published in prestigious journals. It's great when this happens in journals such as *Computers in Human Behavior* that cater to research about video games, but it's even better to see video game research published in venerable, top-tier, and more widely read journals, such as *Journal of Applied Psychology*, *Psychological Bulletin*, or *Journal of Personality and Social Psychology*. Quality research on the psychology of video games is happening and will continue to happen. It's just another sign of how important and widespread the hobby is becoming in every corner of culture.

I look forward to seeing academic research move away from the current hot topics of violence in games, educational games, and video game addiction. For sure, these are important topics, and for sure they're on the minds of enough people to help when applying for funding or getting papers published. I get that. But there are also so many additional questions that need to be answered. How do avatar-customization options affect engagement with a game? Can psychological priming be used to make people more civil and cooperative in a multiplayer game? Do game systems that encourage focused thought and involvement help create a sense of spatial presence? What other cognitive skills can different types of games improve? By what mechanisms does player engagement generate more playing and more spending in the social networks that connect players? How do game difficulty and the timing of a sales pitch affect in-app purchases? In this book I frequently took results from studies outside of video games and argued why they should apply to people playing games. Anonymity and deindividuation online is one example, and decoupling the pain of payment through prepaying in game currencies is another. I think I'm on firm ground in doing this, but the graduate students and assistant professors of today need to think carefully about the generalizability of this research to video games and then do experiments to see what's what. So do the psychologists working inside the industry, for that matter.

So there's more to do and more to see. I look forward to it. To help keep track of this brave new world, I've set up a website—www.psychologyofgames.com—where you can go to learn more about the topic and to act as an ongoing complement to this book. You should go check it out a few seconds from now when you're done with this book. Because there's still so much more to learn about psychology and so many ways to use it both to make games awesome and to enjoy playing them more. Let's get to it.

NOTES

INTRODUCTION

1. Apple, "App Store Rings in 2015 with New Records," Apple press release, January 8, 2015, http://www.apple.com/pr/library/2015/01/08App-Store-Rings-in-2015-with-New-Records.html (accessed May 11, 2015).

2. James Brightman, "GTA V Exceeds $1 Billion in Only 3 Days," *GamesIndustry International* (blog), September 20, 2013, http://www.gamesindustry.biz/articles/2013-09-20-gta-v-exceeds-USD1-billion-in-only-3-days (accessed April 24, 2014).

3. Wybe Schutte, "Infographic: The US Games Market," Newzoo, December 12, 2013, http://www.newzoo.com/infographics/infographic-the-us-games-market/ (accessed April 24, 2014).

4. King, "Candy Crush Saga Celebrates One Year Anniversary and Half a Billion Downloads," King press release, November 15, 2013, http://company.king.com/news-and-media/ (accessed April 24, 2014).

5. April Fehling, "Museums Give Video Games Bonus Life, but the Next Level Awaits," *All Tech Considered* (blog), December 23, 2013, http://www.npr.org/blogs/alltechconsidered/2013/12/22/255843345/museums-give-video-games-bonus-life-but-the-next-level-awaits/ (accessed April 24, 2014).

6. Rachel Kowert, Ruth Festl, and Thorsten Quandt, "Unpopular, Overweight, and Socially Inept: Reconsidering the Stereotype of Online Gamers," *Cyberpsychology, Behavior, and Social Networking* 17, no. 3 (2014): 141–46.

I. WHY DO PERFECTLY NORMAL PEOPLE BECOME RAVING LUNATICS ONLINE?

1. Jeffrey Lin, "Enhancing Sportsmanship in Online Games," lecture given at the 2014 Game Developers Conference, San Francisco, March 19, 2014.

2. John Gaudiosi, "How Riot Games Created the Most Popular Game in the World," *Fortune Tech Technology* (blog), July 10, 2013, http://tech.fortune.cnn.com/2013/07/10/how-riot-games-created-the-most-popular-game-in-the-world/ (accessed April 14, 2014).

3. "Worlds 2014 by the Numbers," Riot Games, December 1, 2014. http://www.riotgames.com/articles/20141201/1628/worlds-2014-numbers (accessed January 7, 2015).

4. Patrick Dorsey, "'League of Legends' Ratings Top NBA Finals, World Series Clinchers," ESPN, December 3, 2014, http://espn.go.com/espn/story/_/page/instawesome-leagueoflegends-141201/league-legends-championships-watched-more-people-nba-finals-world-series-clinchers/ (accessed January 7, 2015).

5. Mike Williams, "Talking Shop: Riot Games' Lead Designer of Social Systems," *GamesIndustry International*, May 15, 2013, http://www.gamesindustry.biz/articles/2013-05-15-talking-shop-riot-games-lead-designer-of-social-systems/ (accessed April 15, 2014).

6. Jeffrey Lin, personal communication with the author, January 6, 2015.

7. Jeffrey Kuznekoff and Lindsey Rose, "Communication in Multiplayer Gaming: Examining Player Responses to Gender Cues," *New Media & Society* 15, no. 4 (2012): 541–56, doi:10.1177/1461444812458271.

8. Tom Postmes and Russell Spears, "Deindividuation and Antinormative Behavior: A Meta-Analysis," *Psychological Bulletin* 123, no. 3 (1998): 238–59, doi: 10.1037/0033-2909.123.3.238.

9. Mike Fahey, "Blizzard Scraps Plans to Display Real Names in Forums," *Kotaku* (blog), July 9, 2010, http://kotaku.com/5583405/blizzard-scraps-plans-to-display-real-names-in-forums/ (accessed July 17, 2014).

10. Edward Diener, Scott C. Fraser, Arthur L. Beaman, and Roger T. Kelem, "Effects of Deindividuation Variables on Stealing among Halloween Trick-or-Treaters," *Journal of Personality and Social Psychology* 33, no. 2 (1976): 178–83, doi: 10.1037/0022-3514.33.2.178.

11. Postmes and Spears, "Deindividuation and Antinormative Behavior."

12. Joseph Walther, "Computer-Mediated Communication: Impersonal, Interpersonal, and Hyperpersonal Interaction," *Communication Research* 23, no. 1 (1996): 3–43.

13. Philip Zimbardo, *The Lucifer Effect: Understanding How Good People Turn Evil* (New York: Random House, 2007).

14. Robert Johnson and Leslie L. Downing, "Deindividuation and Valence of Cues: Effects on Prosocial and Antisocial Behavior," *Journal of Personality and Social Psychology* 37, no. 9 (1979): 1532–39, doi: 10.1037/0022-3514.37.9.1532.

15. Jeffrey Lin, "The Science behind Shaping Behavior in Online Games," lecture given at the 2013 Game Developers Conference, San Francisco, March 27, 2013.

16. Lin, "Enhancing Sportsmanship in Online Games."

17. Kathleen D. Vohs, Nicole L. Mead, and Miranda R. Goode, "The Psychological Consequences of Money," *Science* 314, no. 5802 (2006): 1154–56, doi: 10.1126/science.1132491.

18. Lin, "Enhancing Sportsmanship in Online Games."

19. Jeffrey Lin, personal communication with the author, January 5, 2015.

2. WHY DO PEOPLE CHEAT, HACK, AND PEEK AT STRATEGY GUIDES?

1. "Drug-Free Sport Is Utopia," BBC News, November 24, 2008, http://news.bbc.co.uk/sport2/hi/olympic_games/7747181.stm (accessed March 11, 2015).

2. For example, see De Paoli and Aphra Kerr, "'We Will Always Be One Step ahead of Them': A Case Study on the Economy of Cheating in MMORPGs," *Journal of Virtual Worlds Research* 2, no. 4 (2010).

3. Nina Mazar, On Amir, and Dan Ariely, "The Dishonesty of Honest People: A Theory of Self-Concept Maintenance," *Journal of Marketing Research* 45, no. 6 (2008), doi: 10.1509/jmkr.45.6.633.

4. Agata Blachnio and Malgorzata Weremko, "Academic Cheating Is Contagious: The Influence of the Presence of Others on Honesty. A Study Report," *International Journal of Applied Psychology* 1, no. 1 (2011), doi: 10.5923/j.ijap.20110101.02.

5. Jeremy Blackburn et al., "Branded with a Scarlet 'C': Cheaters in a Gaming Social Network," in *Proceedings of the 21st International Conference on World Wide Web*, April 16–20, 2012, 81–90 (Lyon, France: International World Wide Web Conference Committee).

6. "VACBanned Statistics," VACBanned.com, http://vacbanned.com/view/statistics (accessed May 9, 2014).

7. Blackburn et al., "Branded With a Scarlet 'C,'" 81.

8. Jamie Madigan, "The Psychology of Video Games: Why We Do What We Do with Friends (and Screw That Other Guy)," lecture given at the 2010 Login Conference, Seattle, Washington, May 14, 2010.

9. Stephen Totilo, "Lessons of the Mario Kart Cheaters," *Kotaku* (blog), May 17, 2010, http://kotaku.com/5541043/lessons-of-the-mario-kart-cheaters (accessed May 9, 2014).

10. Francesca Gino, Shahar Ayal, and Dan Ariely, "Contagion and Differentiation in Unethical Behavior: The Effect of One Bad Apple on the Barrel," *Psychological Science* 20, no. 3 (2009): 393–98, doi: 10.1111/j.1467-9280.2009.02306.x.

11. Ibid., 396.

12. Daniel Kahneman, "Prospect Theory," in *Thinking, Fast and Slow* (New York: Farrar, Straus and Giroux, 2011), 278–88.

13. Nico Van Yperen, Melvyn Hamstra, and Marloes Van Der Klauw, "To Win, or Not to Lose, at Any Cost: The Impact of Achievement Goals on Cheating," *British Journal of Management* 22 (2011), doi: 10.1111/j.1467-8551.2010.00702.x.

14. Christopher Bryan, Gabrielle Adams, and Benoît Monin, "When Cheating Would Make You a Cheater: Implicating the Self Prevents Unethical Behavior," *Journal of Experimental Psychology: General* 142, no. 4 (2012), doi: 10.1037/a0030655.

15. Mazar, Amir, and Ariely, "Dishonesty of Honest People."

16. Dan Ariely, "Testing the Simple Model of Rational Crime (SMORC)," in *The (Honest) Truth a bout Dishonesty: How We Lie to Everyone — Especially Ourselves* (New York: Harper, 2012), 11–29.

17. Lisa Shu, Nina Mazar, Francesca Gino, Dan Ariely, and Max Bazerman, "Signing at the Beginning Makes Ethics Salient and Decreases Dishonest Self-Reports in Comparison to Signing at the End," in *Proceedings of the National Academy of Sciences* 109, no. 38 (2012): 15197–200.

18. Mazar and Ariely, "Dishonesty of Honest People."

19. For example, see Mia Consalvo, *Cheating: Gaining Advantage in Video-games* (Cambridge, MA: MIT Press, 2009).

3. WHY ARE FANBOYS AND FANGIRLS SO READY FOR A FIGHT?

1. "Joss Whedon Red Carpet Interview for Much Ado about Nothing," YouTube video, 2:39, posted by "Click Online," February 24, 2013, https://www.youtube.com/watch?v=4Bwf9RQMMfg.

2. "Science Friction: Star Wars and Doctor Who Fans Come to Blows over Autographs," *The Guardian*, May 16, 2013, http://www.theguardian.com/uk/2013/may/15/university-norwich-star-wars-club-fight (accessed December 24, 2014).

3. Paul Tassi, *Fanboy Wars: The Fight for the Future of Video Games* (Forbes Media, 2014).

4. For example, Paul Tassi, "Microsoft Stumbles through Xbox One Announcement," *Forbes*, May 21, 2013, http://www.forbes.com/sites/insertcoin/2013/05/21/microsoft-stumbles-through-xbox-one-announcement-shows-little-answers-less/ (accessed March 13, 2015).

5. William Usher, "Xbone Nickname Is Disrespectful to Xbox One, Says Major Nelson," Cinemablend, September 8, 2013, http://www.cinemablend.com/games/Xbone-Nickname-Disrespectful-Xbox-One-Says-Major-Nelson-58934.html (accessed March 13, 2015).

6. Tom Phillips, "Microsoft's PR Blunders Caused Sony to Re-write E3 PlayStation 4 Script," Eurogamer, July 7, 2014, http://www.eurogamer.net/articles/2014-07-09-microsofts-pr-blunders-caused-sony-to-re-write-e3-playstation-4-script (accessed March 13, 2015).

7. Don Mattrick, "Your Feedback Matters—Update on Xbox One," Xbox.com, June 19, 2013, http://news.xbox.com/2013/06/update (accessed March 13, 2015).

8. Scott Lowe, "Xbox One No Longer Requires Kinect to Function," IGN.com, August 12, 2013, http://www.ign.com/articles/2013/08/12/xbox-one-no-longer-requires-kinect-to-function (accessed March 13, 2015).

9. Phil Spencer, "Delivering More Choices for Fans," Xbox.com, May 13, 2014, http://news.xbox.com/2014/05/xbox-delivering-more-choices (accessed March 13, 2015).

10. Brian Crecente, "Plague of Game Dev Harassment Erodes Industry, Spurs Support Groups," Polygon, August 15, 2013, http://www.polygon.com/2013/8/15/4622252/plague-of-game-dev-harassment-erodes-industry-spurs-support-groups (accessed March 13, 2015).

11. Robert Knox and James Inkster, "Postdecision Dissonance at Post Time," *Journal of Personality and Social Psychology* 8, no. 4, (1968), doi: 10.1037/h0025528.

12. Edith Greene, "Whodunit? Memory for Evidence in Text," *American Journal of Psychology* 94, no. 3 (1981), doi: 10.2307/1422258.

13. Mara Mather, Eldar Shafir, and Marcia Johnson, "Misremembrance of Options Past: Source Monitoring and Choice," *Psychological Science* 11, no. 2 (2000), doi: 10.1111/1467-9280.00228.

14. Muzafer Sherif, *Intergroup Conflict and Cooperation: The Robbers Cave Experiment* (Toronto: York University, 1961).

15. Ibid., 98.

16. Scott Reid and Michael Hogg, "Uncertainty Reduction, Self-Enhancement, and Ingroup Identification," *Personality and Social Psychology Bulletin* 31 no. 6 (2005), 804–17, doi:10.1177/0146167204271708.

17. Henri Tajfel, "Experiments in Intergroup Discrimination," *Scientific American* 223, no. 5 (1970), doi: 10.1038/scientificamerican1170-96.

18. Entertainment Software Association, *2014 Essential Facts about the Computer and Video Game Industry*, 3, http://www.theesa.com/wp-content/uploads/2014/10/ESA_EF_2014.pdf.

19. Amy O'Leary, "In Virtual Play, Sex Harassment Is All Too Real," *New York Times*, August 1, 2012, http://www.nytimes.com/2012/08/02/us/sexual-harassment-in-online-gaming-stirs-anger.html (accessed December 30, 2014).

20. Colin Campbell, "Sarkeesian Driven Out of Home by Online Abuse and Death Threats," Polygon, August 27, 2014, http://www.polygon.com/2014/8/27/6075679/sarkeesian-driven-out-of-home-by-online-abuse-and-death-threats (accessed September 18, 2014).

21. Soraya McDonald, "Feminist Video Game Critic Anita Sarkeesian Cancels Utah Lecture after Threat," *Washington Post*, October 15, 2014, http://www.washingtonpost.com/news/morning-mix/wp/2014/10/15/gamergate-feminist-video-game-critic-anita-sarkeesian-cancels-utah-lecture-after-threat-citing-police-inability-to-prevent-concealed-weapons-at-event/ (accessed December 30, 2014).

22. Caitlin Dewey, "The Only Guide to Gamergate You Will Ever Need to Read," *Washington Post*, October 14, 2014, http://www.washingtonpost.com/news/the-intersect/wp/2014/10/14/the-only-guide-to-gamergate-you-will-ever-need-to-read/ (accessed December 30, 2014).

23. Samuel McClure et al., "Neural Correlates of Behavioral Preference for Culturally Familiar Drinks," *Neuron* 44, no. 2 (2004), doi: 10.1016/j.neuron.2004.09.019.

24. Russell Belk, "Possessions and the Extended Self," *Journal of Consumer Research* 15, no. 2 (1988), doi: 10.1086/209154.

25. Rohini Ahluwalia, Robert Burnkrant, and H. Rao Unnava, "Consumer Response to Negative Publicity: The Moderating Role of Commitment," *Journal of Marketing Research* 37, no. 2 (2000), doi: 10.1509/jmkr.37.2.203.18734.

26. Peter Nauroth et al., "Gamers against Science: The Case of the Violent Video Games Debate," *European Journal of Social Psychology* 44, no. 2 (2014), doi:10.1002/ejsp.1998.

27. Jens Bender, Tobias Rothmund, and Mario Gollwitzer, "Biased Estimation of Violent Video Game Effects on Aggression: Contributing Factors and Boundary Conditions," *Societies* 3, no. 4 (2013), doi:10.3390/soc3040383.

28. Jennifer Escalas and James Bettman. "You Are What They Eat: The Influence of Reference Groups on Consumers Connections to Brands," *Journal of Consumer Psychology* 13, no. 3 (2003), doi: 10.1207/S15327663JCP1303_14.

29. McGregor, Ian, Reeshma Haji, and So-Jin Kang, "Can Ingroup Affirmation Relieve
Outgroup Derogation?" *Journal of Experimental Social Psychology* 44, no. 5
(2008): 1395–1401,doi:10.1016/j.jesp.2008.06.001.

4. WHY DO WE GET NOSTALGIC ABOUT GOOD OLD GAMES?

1. Tim Wildschut et al., "Nostalgia: Content, Triggers, Functions," *Journal of Personality and Social Psychology* 91, no. 5 (2006), doi:10.1037/0022-3514.91.5.975.

2. Erica Hepper et al., "Pancultural Nostalgia: Prototypical Conceptions across Cultures," *Emotion* 14, no. 4 (2014), doi:10.1037/a0036790.

3. Ibid.

4. Wildschut et al., "Nostalgia."

5. Ibid.

6. Katherine Loveland, Dirk Smeesters, and Naomi Mandel, "Still Preoccupied with 1995: The Need to Belong and Preference for Nostalgic Products," *Journal of Consumer Research* 37, no. 3 (2010), doi: 10.1086/653043.

7. Robert Schindler and Morris Holbrook, "Nostalgia for Early Experience as a Determinant of Consumer Preferences," *Psychology and Marketing* 20, no. 4 (2003), doi: 10.1002/mar.10074.

8. Wing-Yee Cheung et al., "Back to the Future: Nostalgia Increases Optimism," *Personality and Social Psychology Bulletin* 39, no. 11 (2013), doi: 10.1177/0146167213499187.

9. Dan Ariely, "Paying More for Less," in *The Upside of Irrationality: The Unexpected Benefits of Defying Logic at Work and at Home.* (New York: Harper, 2010).

10. Daniel Kahneman, Jack L. Knetsch, and Richard H. Thaler, "Experimental Tests of the Endowment Effect and the Coase Theorem," *Journal of Political Economy* 98, no. 6 (1990), doi: 10.1086/261737.

11. Paul Bloom, "Irreplaceable," in *How Pleasure Works: The New Science of Why We Like What We Like* (New York: W. W. Norton, 2010), 91–115.

12. Ibid., 109.

13. David McRaney, "The Self-Enhancement Bias," in *You Are Now Less Dumb: How to Conquer Mob Mentality, How to Buy Happiness, and All the Other Ways to Outsmart Yourself* (New York: Gotham, 2013), 249–74.

14. Daniel Gilbert and Jane E. J. Ebert, "Decisions and Revisions: The Affective Forecasting of Changeable Outcomes," *Journal of Personality and Social Psychology* 82, no. 4 (2002), doi: 10.1037/0022-3514.82.4.503.

15. Jason Leboe and Tamara Ansons, "On Misattributing Good Remembering to a Happy Past: An Investigation into the Cognitive Roots of Nostalgia," *Emotion* 6, no. 4 (2006), doi: 10.1037/1528-3542.6.4.596.

16. Entertainment Software Association, *2014 Essential Facts about the Computer and Video Game Industry*, 2014, http://www.theesa.com/wp-content/uploads/2014/10/ESA_EF_2014.pdf.

5. HOW DO GAMES GET US TO KEEP SCORE AND COMPETE?

1. Leon Festinger, "A Theory of Social Comparison Processes," *Human Relations* 7, no. 2 (1954): 117–40, doi:10.1177/001872675400700202.

2. George Goethals and John Darley, "Social Comparison Theory: An Attributional Approach," in *Social Comparison Processes: Theoretical and Empirical Perspectives*, eds. Jerry Suls and Richard Miller (Washington, D.C.: Hemisphere, 1977), 259–78, doi: 10.4324/9781410615749.

3. René Martin, Jerry Suls, and Ladd Wheeler, "Ability Evaluation by Proxy: Role of Maximal Performance and Related Attributes in Social Comparison," *Journal of Personality and Social Psychology* 82, no. 5 (2002), doi:10.1037//0022-3514.82.5.781.

4. Ladd Wheeler, Richard Koestner, and Robert E. Driver, "Related Attributes in the Choice of Comparison Others: It's There, but It Isn't All There Is," *Journal of Experimental Social Psychology* 18, no. 6 (1982) doi:10.1016/0022-1031(82)90068-3.

5. Ladd Wheeler, "Motivation as a Determinant of Upward Comparison," *Journal of Experimental Social Psychology* 1 (1966), doi:10.1016/0022-1031(66)90062-X.

6. Herbert Marsh and Kit-Tai Hau, "Big-Fish–Little-Pond Effect on Academic Self-Concept: A Cross-Cultural (26-Country) Test of the Negative Effects of Academically Selective Schools," *American Psychologist* 58, no. 5 (2003), doi: 10.1037/0003-066X.58.5.364.

7. For a detailed discussion of the little fish, big pond effect in the context of academics, see Malcom Gladwell, *David and Goliath: Underdogs, Misfits, and the Art of Battling Giants* (New York: Little, Brown, 2013).

8. Ethan Zell and Mark Alicke, "The Local Dominance Effect in Self-Evaluation: Evidence and Explanations," *Personality and Social Psychology Review* 14, no. 4 (2010), doi:10.1177/1088868310366144.

9. Victoria Husted Medvec, Scott Madey, and Thomas Gilovich, "When Less Is More: Counterfactual Thinking and Satisfaction among Olympic Medalists," *Journal of Personality and Social Psychology* 69, no. 4 (1995), doi:10.1037/0022-3514.69.4.603.

10. Stephen Garcia, Avishalom Tor, and Richard Gonzalez, "Ranks and Rivals: A Theory of Competition," *Personality & Social Psychology Bulletin* 32, no. 7 (2006), doi:10.1177/0146167206287640.

11. Devin Pope and Maurice Schweitzer, "Is Tiger Woods Loss Averse? Persistent Bias in the Face of Experience, Competition, and High Stakes," *American Economic Review* 101, no. 1 (2011), doi:10.1257/aer.101.1.129.

12. Justin Kruger and David Dunning, "Unskilled and Unaware of It: How Difficulties in Recognizing One's Own Incompetence Lead to Inflated Self-Assessments," *Journal of Personality and Social Psychology* 77, no. 6 (1999), doi:10.1037/0022-3514.77.6.1121.

6. HOW DO GAMES GET US TO GRIND, COMPLETE SIDE QUESTS, AND CHASE ACHIEVEMENTS?

1. Christos Reid, personal communication with the author, March 26, 2014.

2. Ibid.

3. Richard Bartle, "Hearts, Clubs, Diamonds, Spades: Players Who Suit MUDS," http://mud.co.uk/richard/hcds.htm (accessed July 11, 2014).

4. Nick Yee, "Motivations for Play in Online Games," *Cyberpsychology & Behavior* 9, no. 6 (2006), doi:10.1089/cpb.2006.9.772.

5. Nick Yee, Nicolas Ducheneaut, and Les Nelson, "Online Gaming Motivations Scale: Development and Validation," in *Proceedings of the SIGCHI Conference on Human Factors in Computing Systems* (2012), 2803–6, doi:10.1145/2207676.2208681.

6. Andrew Przybylski, Scott Rigby, and Richard Ryan, "A Motivational Model of Video Game Engagement," *Review of General Psychology* 14, no. 2 (2010), doi:10.1037/a0019440.

7. Richard Ryan and Edward Deci, "Self-Determination Theory and the Facilitation of Intrinsic Motivation, Social Development, and Well-Being," *American Psychologist* 55, no. 1 (2000), doi:10.1037/0003-066X.55.1.68.

8. Richard Ryan, Scott Rigby, and Andrew Przybylski, "The Motivational Pull of Video Games: A Self-Determination Theory Approach," *Motivation and Emotion* 30, no. 4 (2006), doi:10.1007/s11031-006-9051-8.

9. Scott Rigby and Richard Ryan, *Glued to Games: How Video Games Draw Us In and Hold Us Spellbound* (Santa Barbara, CA: Praeger, 2011).

10. Edwin Locke, "Motivation through Conscious Goal Setting," *Applied and Preventive Psychology* 5, no. 2 (1996), doi:10.1016/S0962-1849(96)80005-9.

11. Roy Baumeister and Kathleen Vohs, "Self-Regulation, Ego Depletion, and Motivation," *Social and Personality Psychology Compass* 1, no. 1 (2007), doi:10.1111/j.1751-9004.2007.00001.x.

12. Ting Yan et al., "Should I Stay or Should I Go: The Effects of Progress Feedback, Promised Task Duration, and Length of Questionnaire on Completing Web Surveys," *International Journal of Public Opinion Research* 23, no. 2 (2010), doi:10.1093/ijpor/edq046.

13. Bulma Zeigarnik, "On Finished and Unfinished Tasks," in *A Source Book of Gestalt Psychology*, ed. W. D. Ellis (New York: Harcourt Brace, 1938), 300–14.

14. Joseph Nunes and Xavier Dreze, "The Endowed Progress Effect: How Artificial Advancement Increases Effort," *Journal of Consumer Research* 32 (2006), doi:10.1086/500480.

15. Rigby and Ryan, *Glued to Games*.

16. Ryan, Rigby, and Przybylski, "Motivational Pull of Video Games."

17. Sharon Brehm, *Psychological Reactance: A Theory of Freedom and Control* (New York: Academic, 1981).

18. Jack Brehm, *A Theory of Psychological Reactance* (New York: Academic, 1966).

19. Michael Mazis, "Antipollution Measures and Psychological Reactance Theory: A Field Experiment," *Journal of Personality and Social Psychology* 31, no. 4 (1975), doi:10.1037/h0077075.

20. Jiwoong Shin and Dan Ariely, "Keeping Doors Open: The Effect of Unavailability on Incentives to Keep Options Viable," *Management Science* 50, no. 5 (2004), doi:10.1287/mnsc.1030.0148.

21. Przybylski, Rigby, and Ryan, "Motivational Model of Video Game Engagement."

22. Dan Ariely and Michael Norton, "Conceptual Consumption," *Annual Review of Psychology* 60 (2009), doi:10.1146/annu-rev.psych.60.110707.163536.

23. Ran Kivetz and Anat Keinan, "Repenting Hyperopia: An Analysis of Self-Control Regrets," *Journal of Consumer Research* 33, no. 2 (2006), doi:10.1086/506308.

7. HOW DO DEVELOPERS KEEP US SO EXCITED ABOUT NEW LOOT?

1. David Wong, "5 Creepy Ways Video Games Are Trying to Get You Addicted," Cracked.com, March 8, 2010, http://www.cracked.com/arti-

cle_18461_5-creepy-ways-video-games-are-trying-to-get-you-addicted.html (accessed January 1, 2015).

2. Rick Martin, "Japan's Consumer Affairs Agency Deems 'Kompu Gacha' Sales a Violation of Law," Games in Asia, May 7, 2012, https:// www.techinasia.com/japanese-consumer-affairs-agency-kompu-gacha/ (accessed January 1, 2015).

3. See just about any textbook on the subject, such as Raymond Miltenberger, *Behavior Modification: Principles and Procedures*, 5th ed. (Belmont, CA: Cengage Learning, 2011).

4. James Olds and Peter Milner, "Positive Reinforcement Produced by Electrical Stimulation of Septal Area and Other Regions of Rat Brain," *Journal of Comparative and Physiological Psychology* 47, no. 6 (1954), doi:10.1037/h0058775.

5. Wolfram Schultz, Peter Dayan, and P. Read Montague, "A Neural Substrate of Prediction and Reward," *Science* 275 (1997), doi:10.1126/science.275.5306.1593.

6. For an overview of the research done by Schultz and his colleagues as it relates to the brain's prediction system, see Jonah Lehrer, "The Predictions of Dopamine," in *How We Decide* (New York: Houghton Mifflin Harcourt, 2009), 28–56.

7. For example, see Wolfram Schultz, Paul Apicella, and Tomas Ljungberg, "Responses of Monkey Dopamine Neurons to Reward and Conditioned Stimuli during Successive Steps of Learning a Delayed Response Task," *Journal of Neuroscience* 13, no. 3 (1993).

8. Stefan Klein, *The Science of Happiness: How Our Brains Make Us Happy—and What We Can Do to Get Happier* (New York: Marlowe & Company, 2006).

9. Nick Yee, *The Proteus Paradox: How Online Games and Virtual Worlds Change Us—and How They Don't* (New Haven, CT: Yale University Press, 2013).

10. "Diablo III Auction House Update," YouTube video, 2:03, posted by "Diablo," September 17, 2013, https://www.youtube.com/watch?v=ijCgKciMIE4.

8. HOW DO GAMES MAKE US FEEL IMMERSED IN IMAGINARY WORLDS?

1. Andrew Przybylski, Scott Rigby, and Richard Ryan, "A Motivational Model of Video Game Engagement," *Review of General Psychology* 14, no. 2 (2010), doi:10.1037/a0019440.

2. Werner Wirth et al., "The Development of Video Game Enjoyment in a Role-Playing Game," *Cyberpsychology, Behavior, and Social Networking* 16, no. 4 (2013), doi:10.1089/cyber.2012.0159.

3. Seung-A Annie Jin, "'I Feel Present. Therefore, I Experience Flow': A Structural Equation Modeling Approach to Flow and Presence in Video Games," *Journal of Broadcasting & Electronic Media* 55, no. 1 (2011), doi:10.1080/08838151.2011.546248.

4. Przybylski, Rigby, and Ryan, "Motivational Model of Video Game Engagement."

5. Michael Abrash, "What VR Could, Should, and Almost Certainly Will Be within Two Years," YouTube video, 27:56, posted by "Steamworks Development," February 11, 2014, https://www.youtube.com/watch?v=G-2dQoeqV-Vo.

6. Farhad Manjoo, "If You Like Immersion, You'll Love This Reality," *New York Times*, April 02, 2014, http://www.nytimes.com/2014/04/03/technology/personaltech/virtual-reality-perfect-for-an-immersive-society.html.

7. Matthias Hofer et al., "Structural Equation Modeling of Spatial Presence: The Influence of Cognitive Processes and Traits," *Media Psychology* 15, no. 4 (2012), doi:10.1080/15213269.2012.723118.

8. Peter Rubin, "The Inside Story of Oculus Rift and How Virtual Reality Became Reality," *Wired*, May 20, 2014, http://www.wired.com/2014/05/oculus-rift-4/ (accessed March 18, 2015).

9. Ibid.

10. Victor Luckerson, "Facebook Buying Oculus Virtual-Reality Company for $2 Billion," *Time*, March 25, 2014, http://time.com/37842/facebook-oculus-rift/ (accessed March 18, 2015).

11. Tao Lin, et al., "Exploring the Effects of Display Characteristics on Presence and Emotional Responses of Game Players," *International Journal of Technology and Human Interaction* 9, no. 1 (2013), doi:10.4018/jthi.2013010104.

12. Abrash, "What VR Could, Should, and Almost Certainly Will Be."

13. Werner Wirth, et al., "A Process Model of the Formation of Spatial Presence Experiences," *Media Psychology* 9, no. 3 (2007), doi:10.1080/15213260701283079.

14. Paul Skalski, et al., "Mapping the Road to Fun: Natural Video Game Controllers, Presence, and Game Enjoyment," *New Media & Society* 13, no. 2 (2010), doi:10.1177/1461444810370949.

15. The Mike Abrash YouTube video cited in note 5, above, includes some great illustrations of these illusions. Also see Scott Murray, Huseyin Boyaci, and Daniel Kersten, "The Representation of Perceived Angular Size in Human

Primary Visual Cortex," *Nature Neuroscience* 9, no. 3 (2006), doi:10.1038/nn1641.

16. Wirth et al., "Process Model."

17. Steve Gaynor, interview with author, September 25, 2013.

18. Werner Wirth, Matthias Hofer, and Holger Schramm, "The Role of Emotional Involvement and Trait Absorption in the Formation of Spatial Presence," *Media Psychology* 15, no. 1 (2012), doi:10.1080/15213269.2011.648536.

9. WHY DO WE GO CRAZY FOR DIGITAL GAME SALES?

1. Brendan Sinclair, "The Gamification of Buying Games," *GamesIndustry.biz* (blog), May 20, 2014, http://www.gamesindustry.biz/articles/2014-05-20-the-gamification-of-buying-games (accessed August 9, 2014).

2. Jeff Macke, "Ron Johnson's JCPenney: Anatomy of a Retail Failure," *Yahoo Finance* (blog), April 9, 2013, http://finance.yahoo.com/blogs/breakout/ron-johnson-jcpenney-anatomy-retail-failure-114635276.html (accessed August 19, 2014).

3. Steve Denning, "J.C.Penney: Was Ron Johnson's Strategy Wrong?" *Forbes*, April 9, 2013, http://www.forbes.com/sites/stevedenning/2013/04/09/j-c-penney-was-ron-johnsons-strategy-wrong/ (accessed December 27, 2014).

4. Macke, "Ron Johnson's JCPenney."

5. "Industry Facts," Entertainment Software Association, http://www.theesa.com (accessed May 8, 2015).

6. Stephen Worchel, Jerry Lee, and Akanbi Adewole, "Effects of Supply and Demand on Ratings of Object Value," *Journal of Personality and Social Psychology* 32, no. 5 (1975), doi:10.1037/0022-3514.32.5.906.

7. Michael Mazis, "Antipollution Measures and Psychological Reactance Theory: A Field Experiment," *Journal of Personality and Social Psychology* 31, no. 4 (1975), doi:10.1037/h0077075.

8. Christopher Hsee, "Less Is Better: When Low-Value Options Are Valued More Highly Than High-Value Options," *Journal of Behavioral Decision Making* 11 (1998), doi:10.1002/(SICI)1099-0771(199806)11:2 107::AID-BDM292 3.0.CO;2-Y.

9. Ibid.

10. Robert Cialdini, *Influence: Science and Practice* (Boston: Pearson, 2009).

11. For example, Joseph Nunes, "The Endowed Progress Effect: How Artificial Advancement Increases Effort," *Journal of Consumer Research* 32 (2006), doi:10.1086/500480.

12. Amos Tversky and Daniel Kahneman, "Judgment under Uncertainty: Heuristics and Biases," *Science* 185 (1974), doi:10.1126/science.185.4157.1124.

13. Daniel Kahneman, *Thinking, Fast and Slow* (New York: Farrar, Straus, and Giroux, 2011).

14. Ibid.

15. Dan Ariely, George Loewenstein, and Drazen Prelec, "'Coherent Arbitrariness': Stable Demand Curves without Stable Preferences," *Quarterly Journal of Economics* 118, no. 1 (2003), doi: 10.1162/00335530360535153.

16. William Poundstone, *Priceless: The Myth of Fair Value (and How to Take Advantage of It)* (New York: Hill and Wang, 2010).

10. HOW DO GAMES AND APPS GET YOU WITH IN-GAME PURCHASES?

1. Chris Anderson, *Free: The Future of a Radical Price* (New York: Hyperion, 2009).

2. Ian Bogost, "Making a Mockery: Ruminations on *Cow Clicker*," lecture given at the 2010 Game Developer's Conference, San Francisco, March 9, 2010, http://www.gdcvault.com/play/1013828/Making-a-Mockery-Ruminations-on.

3. "Apple Inc. Will Provide Full Consumer Refunds of at Least $32.5 Million to Settle FTC Complaint It Charged for Kids' In-App Purchases without Parental Consent," Federal Trade Commission, January 15, 2014, http://www.ftc.gov/news-events/press-releases/2014/01/apple-inc-will-provide-full-consumer-refunds-least-325-million (accessed January 2, 2015).

4. Dan Pearson, "Report: Mobile to Become Gaming's Biggest Market by 2015," *GamesIndustry.biz* (blog), October 22, 2014, http://www.gamesindustry.biz/articles/2014-10-22-report-mobile-to-become-gamings-biggest-market-by-2015 (accessed January 2, 2015).

5. Peter Warman, "In Q1, 'Candy Crush' Outgrosses All Nintendo Games Combined," [a]list daily, May 28, 2014, http://www.alistdaily.com/news/in-q1-candy-crush-outgrosses-all-nintendo-games-combined (accessed November 4, 2014).

6. Colin Campbell, "Analysis: Mobile Games Explosion Comes with a Price," Polygon, May 9, 2014, http://www.polygon.com/2014/5/9/5692510/mobile-games-market-analysis-candy-crush-clash-of-clans (accessed November 5, 2014).

7. Matt Bai, "Master of His Virtual Domain," *New York Times*, December 21, 2013, http://www.nytimes.com/2013/12/22/technology/master-of-his-virtual-domain.html (accessed November 4, 2014).

8. "Gartner Says Less Than 0.01 Percent of Consumer Mobile Apps Will Be Considered a Financial Success by Their Developers through 2018," Gartner, accessed November 4, 2014, http://www.gartner.com/newsroom/id/2648515 (January 13, 2014).

9. Kristina Shampanier, Nina Mazar, and Dan Ariely, "Zero as a Special Price: The True Value of Free Products," *Marketing Science* 26 no. 6 (2007), doi:10.1287/mksc.1060.0254.

10. Ibid.

11. "Free Museums: Visits More Than Double," *BBC News*, December 1, 2011, http://www.bbc.com/news/uk-15979878 (accessed January 3, 2015).

12. Adriana Jakovcevic et al., "Charges for Plastic Bags: Motivational and Behavioral Effects," *Journal of Environmental Psychology* 40 (2014), doi:10.1016/j.jenvp.2014.09.004.

13. Mark Brown, "Will Gamers Pay Real Money, Just to Benefit Other Players?" Pocket Gamer, October 13, 2014, http://www.pocketgamer.co.uk/r/iPhone/Smarter Than You/feature.asp?c=62180 (accessed March 16, 2015).

14. Ibid.

15. Bas Verplanken and Astrid Herabadi, "Individual Differences in Impulse Buying Tendency: Feeling and No Thinking," *European Journal of Personality* 83 (2001), doi: 10.1002/per.423.

16. John Mowen and Nancy Spears, "Understanding Compulsive Buying among College Students: A Hierarchical Approach," *Journal of Consumer Psychology* 8, no. 4 (1999), doi:10.1207/s15327663jcp0804_03.

17. Alishia Williams and Jessica Grisham, "Impulsivity, Emotion Regulation, and Mindful Attentional Focus in Compulsive Buying," *Cognitive Therapy & Research* 36 (2012), doi:10.1007/s10608-011-9384-9.

18. Roy Baumeister and John Tierney, *Willpower: Rediscovering the Greatest Human Strength* (New York: Penguin, 2011).

19. Mark Muraven, Dianne Tice, and Roy Baumeister, "Self-Control as a Limited Resource: Regulatory Depletion Patterns," *Journal of Personality and Social Psychology* 74, no 3 (1998), doi:10.1037//0022-3514.74.3.774.

20. Ibid.

21. Baba Shiv and Alexander Fedorikhin, "Heart and Mind in Conflict: The Interplay of Affect and Cognition in Consumer Decision Making," *Journal of Consumer Research* 26 (1999), doi:10.1086/209563.

22. Kathleen Vohs, Roy Baumeister, and Dianne Tice, "Self-Regulation: Goals, Consumption, Choices," in *Handbook of Consumer Psychology*, eds.

Curtis Haugtvedt, Paul Herr, and Frank Kardes (New York: Lawrence Erlbaum, 2006), 349–66.

23. Kathleen Vohs and Ronald Faber, "Spent Resources: Self-Regulatory Resource Availability Affects Impulse Buying," *Journal of Consumer Research* 33, no. 4 (2007), doi:10.1086/510228.

24. Dean Spears, "Economic Decision-Making in Poverty Depletes Behavioral Control," *BE Journal of Economic Analysis & Policy* 15 (2010), doi:10.2202/1935-1682.2973.

25. Shiv and Fedorikhin, "Heart and Mind in Conflict."

26. Kathleen Vohs et al., "Making Choices Impairs Subsequent Self-Control: A Limited-Resource Account of Decision Making, Self-Regulation, and Active Initiative," *Journal of Personality and Social Psychology* 94, no. 5 (2008), doi:10.1037/0022-3514.94.5.883.

27. Vohs and Faber, "Spent Resources."

28. Nick Yee and Nicholas Ducheneaut, "High-Value Monetizers—Debunking Assumptions Using Personality Psychology," lecture given at the 2014 Game Developer's Conference, San Francisco, March 17, 2014.

29. Elizabeth Hirschman, "Differences in Consumer Purchase Behavior by Credit Card Payment System," *Journal of Consumer Research* 6 no. 1 (1979), doi:10.1086/208748.

30. Drazen Prelec and Duncan Simester, "Always Leave Home without It: A Further Investigation of the Credit-Card Effect on Willingness to Pay," *Marketing Letters* 12, no. 1 (2001), doi:10.1023/A:1008196717017.

31. Drazen Prelec and George Lowenstein, "The Red and the Black: Mental Accounting of Savings and Debt," *Marketing Science* 17, no. 1 (1998), doi:10.1287/mksc.17.1.4.

32. Dilip Soman, "The Effect of Payment Transparency on Consumption: Quasi-Experiments from the Field," *Marketing Letters* 14, no. 3 (2003), doi:10.1023/A:1027444717586.

33. Priya Raghubir and Joydeep Srivastava, "Monopoly Money: The Effect of Payment Coupling and Form on Spending Behavior," *Journal of Experimental Psychology Applied* 14, no. 3 (2008), doi:10.1037/1076-898X.14.3.213.

34. Hirschman, "Differences in Consumer Purchase Behavior."

35. Dilip Soman, "Effects of Payment Mechanism on Spending Behavior: The Role of Rehearsal and Immediacy of Payments," *Journal of Consumer Research* 27 (2001), doi:10.1086/319621.

11. HOW DO GAMES KEEP PLAYERS PAYING?

1. Jeff Gerstmann, "Deal of a Lifetime?" Giant Bomb, January 22, 2010, http://www.giantbomb.com/articles/deal-of-a-lifetime/1100-1839/ (accessed January 6, 2015).

2. Justin Olivetti, "The Game Archaeologist Discovers the Island of Kesmai." Massively, March 16, 2013, http://massively.joystiq.com/2012/03/06/the-game-archaeologist-discovers-the-island-of-kesmai/ (accessed January 6, 2015).

3. Prices taken from each game's entry on Wikipedia.org.

4. Brigitte Madrian and Dennis Shea, "The Power of Suggestion: Inertia in 401(k) Participation and Savings Behavior," *Quarterly Journal of Economics* 116, no. 4 (2001), doi:10.1162/003355301753265543.

5. Eric Johnson and Daniel Goldstein, "Do Defaults Save Lives?" *Science* 302 (2003), doi:10.1126/science.1091721.

6. Christopher Anderson, "The Psychology of Doing Nothing: Forms of Decision Avoidance Result from Reason and Emotion," *Psychological Bulletin* 129 no. 1 (2003), doi:10.1037/0033-2909.129.1.139.

7. Stephen Fleming, Charlotte Thomas, and Raymond Dolan, "Overcoming Status Quo Bias in the Human Brain," in *Proceedings of the National Academy of Sciences of the United States of America* 107, no. 13 (2010): 6005–9, doi:10.1073/pnas.0910380107.

8. David Lazarus, "Talk Isn't Cheap? For Cellphone Users, Not Talking Is Costly Too," *Los Angeles Times*, March 8, 2009, http://articles.latimes.com/2009/mar/08/business/fi-lazarus8 (accessed January 5, 2015).

9. Donald Kridel, Dale Lehman, and Dennis Weisman, "Option Value, Telecommunications Demand, and Policy," *Information Economics and Policy* 5, no. 2 (1993), doi:10.1016/0167-6245(93)90018-C.

10. Anja Lambrecht and Bernd Skiera, "Paying Too Much and Being Happy about It: Existence, Causes, and Consequences of Tariff-Choice Biases," *Journal of Marketing Research* 43 (2006), doi:10.1509/jmkr.43.2.212.

11. Drazen Prelec and George Lowenstein, "The Red and the Black: Mental Accounting of Savings and Debt," *Marketing Science* 17, no. 1 (1998), doi:10.1287/mksc.17.1.4.

12. Amos Tversky and Daniel Kahneman, "Advances in Prospect Theory: Cumulative Representation of Uncertainty," *Journal of Risk and Uncertainty* 5, no. 4 (1992), doi:10.1007/BF00122574.

13. Jeff Gerstmann, "Deal of a Lifetime?"

12. HOW DO GAMES GET PLAYERS TO MARKET TO EACH OTHER?

1. Adam Kramer, Jamie Guillory, and Jeffrey Hancock, "Experimental Evidence of Massive-Scale Emotional Contagion through Social Networks," *Proceedings of the National Academy of Sciences of the United States of America* 111, no. 24 (2014), doi:10.1073/pnas.1320040111.

2. James Fowler and Nicholas Christakis, "Dynamic Spread of Happiness in a Large Social Network: Longitudinal Analysis over 20 Years in the Framingham Heart Study," *British Medical Journal (Clinical Research Ed.)* 337, no. a2338, (2008), doi:10.1136/bmj.a2338.

3. Mary Howes, Jack Hokanson, and David Loewenstein, "Induction of Depressive Affect after Prolonged Exposure to a Mildly Depressed Individual," *Journal of Personality and Social Psychology* 49, no. 4 (1985), doi:10.1037/0022-3514.49.4.1110.

4. Kramer, Guillory, and Hancock, "Experimental Evidence."

5. Gregory McNeal, "Facebook Manipulated User News Feeds to Create Emotional Responses," *Forbes*, June 28, 2014, http://www.forbes.com/sites/gregorymcneal/2014/06/28/facebook-manipulated-user-news-feeds-to-create-emotional-contagion/ (accessed November 23, 2014).

6. Soloman Asch, "Studies of Independence and Conformity: A Minority of One against a Unanimous Majority," *Psychological Monographs: General and Applied* 70, no. 9 (1956), doi:10.1037/h0093718.

7. Metacritic, "Duke Nukem Forever (PC)," http://www.metacritic.com/game/pc/duke-nukem-forever (accessed March 18, 2015).

8. Ben Kuchera, "*Duke Nukem*'s PR Threatens to Punish Sites That Run Negative Reviews," *Ars Technica*, June 15, 2011, http://arstechnica.com/gaming/2011/06/duke-nukems-pr-threatens-to-punish-sites-that-run-negative-reviews/ (accessed November 23, 2014).

9. Daniel Emery, "Duke Nukem PR Firm Dropped following Online Review Row," *BBC News*, June 16, 2011, http://www.bbc.co.uk/news/technology-13795782 (accessed March 18, 2015).

10. Matthew Salganik, Peter Dodds, and Duncan Watts, "Experimental Study of Inequality and Unpredictability in an Artificial Cultural Market," *Science* 311 (2006), doi:10.1126/science.1121066.

11. William Usher, "Shadow of Mordor Review Contract Causes Ruckus in the Gaming Industry," CinemaBlend.com, http://www.cinemablend.com/games/Shadow-Mordor-Review-Contract-Causes-Ruckus-Gaming-Industry-67801.html (accessed November 23, 2014).

12. Jim Sterling, "Shadiness of Mordor," *The Escapist*, October 6, 2014, http://www.escapistmagazine.com/videos/view/jimquisition/9782-Shadow-of-Mordors-Promotion-Deals-with-Plaid-Social (accessed November 23, 2014).

13. "Former Maxis Man: Spore DRM Is a Screw Up," Sprong, September 8, 2008, http://spong.com/article/16171/Former-Maxis-Man-Spore-DRM-is-a-Screw-Up (accessed November 23, 2014).

14. See http://www.ninjametrics.com/social-whales.

15. See http://www.ninjametrics.com/ninja-metrics-content-library-white-papers-ebooks-infographics-and-more.

16. Dmitri Williams, personal communication with the author, November 14, 2014.

17. Pete Cashmore, "FarmVille Surpasses 80 Million Users," *Mashable*, February 20, 2010, http://mashable.com/2010/02/20/farmville-80-million-users/ (accessed January 7, 2015).

18. Matt Ridley, *The Origins of Virtue: Human Instincts and the Evolution of Cooperation* (New York: Viking Penguin, 1997).

19. Robert Cialdini, "The Science of Persuasion," *Scientific American* 284, no. 2, (2004), doi:10.1038/scientificamerican0201-76.

20. "Ethics Statement," Polygon, http://www.polygon.com/pages/ethics-statement (accessed January 7, 2015).

21. Niels van de Ven, Marcel Zeelenberg, and Rik Pieters, "Leveling Up and Down: The Experiences of Benign and Malicious Envy," *Emotion* 9, no. 3 (2009), doi:10.1037/a0015669.

22. Simon Laham, personal communication with the author, November 4, 2014.

23. Niels van de Ven, Marcel Zeelenberg, and Rik Pieters, "Why Envy Outperforms Admiration," *Personality & Social Psychology Bulletin* 37, no. 6 (2011), doi:10.1177/0146167211400421.

24. Peter Salovey and Judith Rodin, "Some Antecedents and Consequences of Social-Comparison Jealousy," *Journal of Personality and Social Psychology* 47, no. 4 (1984), doi:10.1037/0022-3514.47.4.780.

25. Niels van de Ven, Marcel Zeelenberg, and Rik Pieters, "The Envy Premium in Product Evaluation," *Journal of Consumer Research* 37, no. 6 (2011), doi:10.1086/657239.

13. DO WE SHAPE OUR IN-GAME AVATARS OR DO THEY SHAPE US?

1. Leonard Bickman, "The Social Power of a Uniform," *Journal of Applied Social Psychology* 4, no. 1 (1974), doi:10.1111/j.1559-1816.1974.tb02599.x.

2. Monroe Lefkowitz, Robert Blake, and Jane Srygley Mouton, "Status Factors in Pedestrian Violation of Traffic Signals," *Journal of Abnormal and Social Psychology* 51, no. 3 (1955), doi:10.1037/h0042000.

3. Hajo Adam and Adam Galinsky, "Enclothed Cognition," *Journal of Experimental Social Psychology* 48, no. 4 (2012), doi:10.1016/j.jesp.2012.02.008.

4. Fritz Strack, Leonard Martin, and Sabine Stepper, "Inhibiting and Facilitating Conditions of the Human Smile: A Nonobtrusive Test of the Facial Feedback Hypothesis," *Journal of Personality and Social Psychology* 54, no. 5 (1988), doi:10.1037/0022-3514.54.5.768.

5. Stuart Valins, "Emotionality and Information Concerning Internal Reactions," *Journal of Personality and Social Psychology* 6, no. 4 (1967), doi:10.1037/h0024842.

6. Mark Frank and Thomas Gilovich, "The Dark Side of Self- and Social Perception: Black Uniforms and Aggression in Professional Sports," *Journal of Personality and Social Psychology* 54, no. 1 (1988), doi:10.1037/0022-3514.54.1.74.

7. Nick Yee, Jeremy Bailenson, and Nicolas Ducheneaut, "The Proteus Effect: Implications of Transformed Digital Self-Representation on Online and Offline Behavior," *Communication Research* 36, no. 2, (2009), doi:10.1177/0093650208330254.

8. Ibid.

9. For a review of this phenomenon, see Alice Eagjy et al., "What Is Beautiful Is Good, but . . . : A Meta-Analytic Review of Research on the Physical Attractiveness Stereotype," *Psychological Bulletin* 110, no. 1 (1991), doi:10.1037/0033-2909.110.1.109.

10. Christoph Klimmt et al., "Identification with Video Game Characters as Automatic Shift of Self-Perceptions," *Media Psychology* 13, no. 4 (2010), doi:10.1080/15213269.2010.524911.

11. Robin Rosenberg, Shawnee L. Baughman, and Jeremy N. Bailenson, "Virtual Superheroes: Using Superpowers in Virtual Reality to Encourage Prosocial Behavior," *PloS One* 8, no. 1 (2013), doi:10.1371/journal.pone.0055003.

12. Jesse Fox, Jeremy N. Bailenson, and Liz Tricase, "The Embodiment of Sexualized Virtual Selves: The Proteus Effect and Experiences of Self-Objectification via Avatars," *Computers in Human Behavior* 29, no. 3 (2013), doi:10.1016/j.chb.2012.12.027.

13. Nick Yee, "The Locker Room Utopia," in *The Proteus Paradox: How Online Games and Virtual Worlds Change Us—and How They Don't* (New Haven, CT: Yale University Press, 2014), 96–114.

14. Sun Joo Ahn and Jeremy Bailenson, "Self-Endorsing versus Other-Endorsing in Virtual Environments," *Journal of Advertising* 40, no. 2 (2011), doi: 10.2753/JOA0091-3367400207.

15. Rachel Bailey, Kevin Wise, and Paul Bolls, "How Avatar Customizability Affects Children's Arousal and Subjective Presence during Junk Food Spon-

sored Online Video Games," *CyberPsychology & Behavior* 12, no. 3 (2009), doi: 10.1089/cpb.2008.0292.

16. Henry J. Kaiser Family Foundation, "It's Child's Play: Advergaming and the Online Marketing of Food to Children—Report," http://kff.org/other/its-childs-play-advergaming-and-the-online-2/ (accessed April 22, 2014).

17. Jeremy Bailenson, Nick Yee, and Nathan Collins, "Facial Similarity between Voters and Candidates Causes Influence," *Public Opinion Quarterly* 72, no. 5 (2009), doi: 10.1093/poq/nfn064.

18. Jeremy Bailenson et al., "Detecting Digital Chameleons," *Computers in Human Behavior* 24, no. 1 (2008), doi: 10.1016/j.chb.2007.01.015.

19. Seung-A Annie Jin, "Avatars Mirroring the Actual Self versus Projecting the Ideal Self: The Effects of Self-Priming on Interactivity and Immersion in an Exergame, Wii Fit," *Cyberpsychology & Behavior* 12, no. 6 (2009), doi:10.1089/cpb.2009.0130.

20. Jesse Fox and Jeremy N. Bailenson, "Virtual Self-Modeling: The Effects of Vicarious Reinforcement and Identification on Exercise Behaviors," *Media Psychology* 12, no. 1 (2010), doi: 10.1080/15213260802669474.

14. WHY DO WE LIKE VIOLENT GAMES SO MUCH? AND SHOULD WE BE WORRIED THAT WE DO?

1. Nicole Martins et al., "A Content Analysis of Print News Coverage of Media Violence and Aggression Research," *Journal of Communication* 63, no. 6 (2013), doi:10.1111/jcom.12052.

2. Andrew Przybylski, "Who Believes Electronic Games Cause Real World Aggression?" *Cyberpsychology, Behavior, and Social Networking* 17, no. 4 (2014), doi:10.1089/cyber.2013.0245.

3. Peter Nauroth et al., "Gamers against Science: The Case of the Violent Video Games Debate," *European Journal of Social Psychology* 44, no. 2 (2014), doi:10.1002/ejsp.1998.

4. Jens Bender, Tobias Rothmund, and Mario Gollwitzer, "Biased Estimation of Violent Video Game Effects on Aggression: Contributing Factors and Boundary Conditions," *Societies* 3, no. 4 (2013), doi:10.3390/soc3040383.

5. Albert Bandura, Dorothea Ross, and Sheila A. Ross, "Transmission of Aggression through Imitation of Aggressive Models," *Journal of Abnormal and Social Psychology* 63, no. 3 (1961), doi:10.1037/h0045925.

6. For a detailed description of the general aggression model, see Craig Anderson, Douglas Gentile, and Katherine Buckley, *Violent Video Game Effects on Children and Adolescents: Theory, Research, and Public Policy* (Oxford: Oxford University Press, 2007).

7. Craig Anderson et al., "Violent Video Game Effects on Aggression, Empathy, and Prosocial Behavior in Eastern and Western Countries: A Meta-Analytic Review," *Psychological Bulletin* 136, no. 2 (2010), doi:10.1037/a0018251.

8. Craig Anderson et al., "Violent Video Games: Specific Effects of Violent Content on Aggressive Thoughts and Behavior," *Advances in Experimental Social Psychology* 36, no. 1 (2004), doi:10.1016/S0065-2601(04)36004-1.

9. Brad Bushman and Craig A. Anderson, "Violent Video Games and Hostile Expectations: A Test of the General Aggression Model," *Personality and Social Psychology Bulletin* 28, no. 12 (2002), doi:10.1177/014616702237649.

10. Craig Anderson and Karen E. Dill, "Video Games and Aggressive Thoughts, Feelings, and Behavior in the Laboratory and in Life," *Journal of Personality and Social Psychology* 78, no. 4 (2000), doi:10.1037//O022-3514.78.4.772.

11. Paul Adachi and Teena Willoughby, "The Effect of Video Game Competition and Violence on Aggressive Behavior: Which Characteristic Has the Greatest Influence?" *Psychology of Violence* 1, no. 4 (2011), doi:10.1037/a0024908.

12. Douglas Gentile et al., "The Effects of Prosocial Video Games on Prosocial Behaviors: International Evidence from Correlational, Longitudinal, and Experimental Studies," *Personality & Social Psychology Bulletin* 35, no. 6 (2009), doi:10.1177/0146167209333045.

13. Seth Gitter et al., "Virtually Justifiable Homicide: The Effects of Prosocial Contexts on the Link between Violent Video Games, Aggression, and Prosocial and Hostile Cognition," *Aggressive Behavior* 39, no. 5 (2013), doi:10.1002/ab.21487.

14. Tobias Greitemeyer and Silvia Osswald, "Effects of Prosocial Video Games on Prosocial Behavior," *Journal of Personality and Social Psychology* 98, no. 2 (2010), doi:10.1037/a0016997.

15. Katherine Buckley and Craig Anderson, "A Theoretical Model of the Effects and Consequences of Playing Video Games," in *Playing Video Games: Motives, Responses, and Consequences*, eds. Peter Vorderer and Jennings Bryant (Mahwah, NJ: Lawrence Erlbaum, 2006), 363–78.

16. Brad Bushman, Hannah Rothstein, and Craig Anderson, "Much Ado about Something: Violent Video Game Effects and a School of Red Herring: Reply to Ferguson and Kilburn (2010)," *Psychological Bulletin* 136, no. 2 (2010), doi:10.1037/a0018718.

17. Anderson et al., "Violent Video Game Effects on Aggression," 171.

18. *Brown v. Entertainment Merchants Association*, 564 U.S. (2011).

19. Ibid.

20. For a much more detailed review of the Supreme Court case and associated criticisms of the related research, see Christopher Ferguson, "Violent Video Games and the Supreme Court: Lessons for the Scientific Community in the Wake of *Brown v. Entertainment Merchants Association*," *American Psychologist* 68, no. 2 (2011), doi:10.1037/a0030597.

21. John Bargh, Mark Chen, and Lara Burrows, "Automaticity of Social Behavior: Direct Effects of Trait Construct and Stereotype-Activation on Action," *Journal of Personality and Social Psychology* 71, no. 2 (1996), doi:10.1037/0022-3514.71.2.230.

22. Bruce Bartholow et al., "Interactive Effects of Life Experience and Situational Cues on Aggression: The Weapons Priming Effect in Hunters and Nonhunters," *Journal of Experimental Social Psychology* 41, no. 1 (2005), doi:10.1016/j.jesp.2004.05.005.

23. Craig Anderson et al., "Longitudinal Effects of Violent Video Games on Aggression in Japan and the United States," *Pediatrics* 122, no. 5 (2008), doi:10.1542/peds.2008-1425.

24. Christopher Ferguson, Claudia San Miguel, and Richard Hartley, "A Multivariate Analysis of Youth Violence and Aggression: The Influence of Family, Peers, Depression, and Media Violence," *Journal of Pediatrics* 155, no. 6 (2009), doi:10.1016/j.jpeds.2009.06.021.

25. Christopher Ferguson and John Kilburn. "Much Ado about Nothing: The Misestimation and Overinterpretation of Violent Video Game Effects in Eastern and Western Nations: Comment on Anderson et al. (2010)," *Psychological Bulletin* 136, no. 2 (2010), doi:10.1037/a0018566.

26. Craig Anderson et al., "Violent Video Games: Specific Effects of Violent Content on Aggressive Thoughts and Behavior," *Advances in Experimental Social Psychology* 36, no. 1 (2004), doi:10.1016/S0065-2601(04)36004-1.

27. Andrew Przybylski et al., "Competence-Impeding Electronic Games and Players' Aggressive Feelings, Thoughts, and Behaviors," *Journal of Personality and Social Psychology* 106, no. 3 (2014), doi:10.1037/a0034820.

28. Scott Rigby, personal communication with the author, July 8, 2010.

29. Cheryl Olson, personal communication with the author, July 12, 2010.

30. NPR Staff. "Modern Video Games Go Beyond 'Jumping on Blocks,'" *All Tech Considered* (blog), June 28, 2014, http://www.npr.org/blogs/alltechconsidered/2014/06/28/326437835/modern-video-games-go-beyond-jumping-on-blocks (accessed July 10, 2014).

31. Andrew Przybylski, Richard Ryan, and Scott Rigby, "The Motivating Role of Violence in Video Games," *Personality & Social Psychology Bulletin* 35, no. 2 (2009), doi:10.1177/0146167208327216.

32. Lawrence Kutner and Cheryl Olson, "Why Kids Play Violent Games," in *Grand Theft Childhood: The Surprising Truth about Violent Video Games and What Parents Can Do* (New York: Simon & Schuster, 2008).

33. Scott Rigby, personal communication with the author, July 8, 2010.

15. DO VIDEO GAMES MAKE YOU SMARTER?

1. "Chess Playing Excitement," *Scientific American*, July 2, 1859, 9.

2. William Poundstone, *Prisoner's Dilemma* (New York: Random House, 1992).

3. Yannick Lejacq, "How Fast Is Fast? Some Pro Gamers Make 10 Moves per Second," *NBC News*, October 24, 2013.

4. Gi Jung Hyun et al., "Increased Cortical Thickness in Professional On-line Gamers," *Psychiatry Investigation* 10, no. 4 (2013), doi:10.4306/pi.2013.10.4.388.

5. Eleanor Maguire et al., "Navigation-Related Structural Change in the Hippocampi of Taxi Drivers," *Proceedings of the National Academy of Sciences of the United States of America* 97, no. 8 (2000), doi:10.1073/pnas.070039597.

6. Joshua Lewis, Atrick Trinh, and David Kirsh, "A Corpus Analysis of Strategy Video Game Play in *StarCraft: Brood War*," in *Proceedings of the 33rd Annual Conference of the Cognitive Science Society* (2011).

7. "A Consensus on the Brain Training Industry from the Scientific Community," Stanford Center on Longevity, October 20, 2014, http://longevity3.stanford.edu/blog/2014/10/15/the-consensus-on-the-brain-training-industry-from-the-scientific-community-2/ (accessed December 23, 2014).

8. Monica Melby-Lervåg and Charles Hulme, "Is Working Memory Training Effective? A Meta-Analytic Review," *Developmental Psychology* 49, no. 2 (2013), doi:10.1037/a0028228.

9. J. A. Anguera et al., "Video Game Training Enhances Cognitive Control in Older Adults," *Nature* 501 (2013), doi:10.1038/nature12486.

10. Glenn Smith et al., "A Cognitive Training Program Based on Principles of Brain Plasticity: Results from the Improvement in Memory with Plasticity-Based Adaptive Cognitive Training (IMPACT) Study," *Journal of the American Geriatrics Society* 57, no. 4 (2009), doi:10.1111/j.1532-5415.2008.02167.x.

11. Ravi Parikh, "Your (Smarter) Brain on Video Games: Interview with Daphne Bavelier, Ph.D.," MedGadget, December 13, 2013, http://www.medgadget.com/2012/12/your-smarter-brain-on-video-games-interview-with-daphne-bavelier-ph-d.html (accessed December 23, 2014).

12. Shawn Green and Daphne Bavelier, "Action-Video-Game Experience Alters the Spatial Resolution of Vision," *Psychological Science* 18 (2007), doi:10.1111/j.1467-9280.2007.01853.x.

13. Shawn Green and Daphne Bavelier, "Effect of Action Video Games on Spatial Distribution of Visuospatial Attention," *Journal of Experimental Psychology* 32, no. 6 (2006), doi: 10.1037/0096-1523.32.6.1465.

14. R. L. Achtman, Shawn Green, and Daphne Bavelier, "Video Games as a Tool to Train Visual Skills," *Restorative Neurology and Neuroscience* 26, no. 4-5 (2008), doi: 10.1037/0893-164X.19.4.414.

15. Shawn Green and Daphne Bavelier, "Enumeration versus Multiple Object Tracking: The Case of Action Video Game Players," *Cognition* 101, no. 1 (2006), doi:10.1016/j.cognition.2005.10.004.

16. Ibid.

17. Kara Blacker et al., "Effects of Action Video Game Training on Visual Working Memory," *Journal of Experimental Psychology: Human Perception and Performance* 40 no. 5 (2014), doi 10.1037/a0037556.

18. Shawn Green, Alexandre Pouget, and Daphne Bavelier, "Improved Probabilistic Inference as a General Learning Mechanism with Action Video Games," *Current Biology* 20, no. 17 (2010), doi:10.1016/j.cub.2010.07.040.

19. Daniel Voyer, Susan Voyer, and M. Phillip Bryden, "Magnitude of Sex Differences in Spatial Abilities: A Meta-Analysis and Consideration of Critical Variables," *Psychological Bulletin* 117, no. 2 (1995), doi: 10.1037/0033-2909.117.2.250.

20. Melissa Terlecki and Nora Newcombe, "How Important Is the Digital Divide? The Relation of Computer and Videogame Usage to Gender Differences in Mental Rotation Ability," *Sex Roles* 53, no. 5-6 (2005), doi:10.1007/s11199-005-6765-0.

21. Nicholas Bowman, personal communication with the author, February 10, 2014.

22. Nicholas Bowman et al., "Facilitating Game Play: How Others Affect Performance at and Enjoyment of Video Games," *Media Psychology* 16, no. 1 (2013), doi:10.1080/15213269.2012.742360.

BIBLIOGRAPHY

Achtman, R. L., Shawn Green, and Daphne Bavelier. "Video Games as a Tool to Train Visual Skills." *Restorative Neurology and Neuroscience* 26, no. 4-5 (2008): 435–36, doi: 10.1037/0893-164X.19.4.414.

Adachi, Paul, and Teena Willoughby. "The Effect of Video Game Competition and Violence on Aggressive Behavior: Which Characteristic Has the Greatest Influence?" *Psychology of Violence* 1, no. 4 (2011): 259–74, doi:10.1037/a0024908.

Adam, Hajo, and Adam Galinsky. "Enclothed Cognition." *Journal of Experimental Social Psychology* 48, no. 4 (2012): 918–25, doi:10.1016/j.jesp.2012.02.008.

Ahluwalia, Rohini , Robert Burnkrant, and H. Rao Unnava. "Consumer Response to Negative Publicity: The Moderating Role of Commitment." *Journal of Marketing Research* 37, no. 2 (2000): 203–14, doi: 10.1509/jmkr.37.2.203.18734.

Ahn, Sun Joo, and Jeremy Bailenson. "Self-Endorsing versus Other-Endorsing in Virtual Environments." *Journal of Advertising* 40, no. 2 (2011): 93–106.

Anderson, Christopher. *Free: The Future of a Radical Price*. (New York: Hyperion, 2009).

———. "The Psychology of Doing Nothing: Forms of Decision Avoidance Result from Reason and Emotion." *Psychological Bulletin* 129 no. 1 (2003): 139–67, doi:10.1037/0033-2909.129.1.139.

Anderson, Craig, Nicholas Carnagey, Arlin Benjamin, Janie Eubanks, and Jeffery Valentine. "Violent Video Games: Specific Effects of Violent Content on Aggressive Thoughts and Behavior." *Advances in Experimental Social Psychology* 36, no. 1 (2004): 199–249, doi:10.1016/S0065-2601(04)36004-1.

Anderson, Craig, and Karen Dill. "Video Games and Aggressive Thoughts, Feelings, and Behavior in the Laboratory and in Life." *Journal of Personality and Social Psychology* 78, no. 4 (2000): 772–90, doi:10.1037//0022-3514.78.4.772.

Anderson, Craig, Douglas Gentile, and Katherine Buckley. *Violent Video Game Effects on Children and Adolescents: Theory, Research, and Public Policy*. Oxford: Oxford University Press, 2007.

Anderson, Craig, Akira Sakamoto, Douglas Gentile, Nobuko Ihori, Akiko Shibuya, Shintaro Yukawa, Mayumi Naito, and Kumiko Kobayashi. "Longitudinal Effects of Violent Video Games on Aggression in Japan and the United States." *Pediatrics* 122, no. 5 (2008): 1067–72, doi:10.1542/peds.2008-1425.

Anderson, Craig, Akiko Shibuya, Nobuko Ihori, Edward Swing, Brad Bushman, Akira Sakamoto, Hannah R. Rothstein, and Muniba Saleem. "Violent Video Game Effects on Aggression, Empathy, and Prosocial Behavior in Eastern and Western Countries: A Meta-Analytic Review." *Psychological Bulletin* 136, no. 2 (2010): 151–73, doi:10.1037/a0018251.

Anguera, J. A., J. Boccanfuso, J. L. Rintoul, O. Al-Hashimi, F. Faraji, J. Janowich, E. Kong, Y. Larraburo, C. Rolle, E. Johnston, and A. Gazzaley. "Video Game Training Enhances Cognitive Control in Older Adults." *Nature* 501 (2013): 97–101, doi:10.1038/nature12486.

Ariely, Dan. "Paying More for Less." In *The Upside of Irrationality: The Unexpected Benefits of Defying Logic at Work and at Home*, 17–52. New York: Harper, 2010.

———. "Testing the Simple Model of Rational Crime (SMORC)." In *The (Honest) Truth About Dishonesty: How We Lie to Everyone—Especially Ourselves*, 11–29. New York: Harper, 2012.

Ariely, Dan, George Loewenstein, and Drazen Prelec. "'Coherent Arbitrariness': Stable Demand Curves without Stable Preferences." *Quarterly Journal of Economics* 118, no. 1 (2003): 1996–97.

Ariely, Dan, and Michael I. Norton. "Conceptual Consumption." *Annual Review of Psychology* 60 (2009): 475–99, doi:10.1146/annurev.psych.60.110707.163536.

Asch, Soloman. "Studies of Independence and Conformity: A Minority of One against a Unanimous Majority." *Psychological Monographs: General and Applied* 70, no. 9 (1956): 1–70, doi:10.1037/h0093718.

Bailenson, Jeremy, Nick Yee, and Nathan Collins. "Facial Similarity between Voters and Candidates Causes Influence." *Public Opinion Quarterly* 72, no. 5 (2009): 935–61.

Bailenson, Jeremy, Nick Yee, Kayur Patel, and Andrew C. Beall. "Detecting Digital Chameleons." *Computers in Human Behavior* 24, no. 1 (2008): 66–87.

Bailey, Rachel, Kevin Wise, and Paul Bolls. "How Avatar Customizability Affects Children's Arousal and Subjective Presence during Junk Food Sponsored Online Video Games." *CyberPsychology & Behavior* 12, no. 3 (2009): 277–83.

Bandura, Albert, Dorothea Ross, and Sheila A. Ross. "Transmission of Aggression through Imitation of Aggressive Models." *Journal of Abnormal and Social Psychology* 63, no. 3 (1961): 575–82, doi:10.1037/h0045925.

Bargh, J. A., M. Chen, and L. Burrows. "Automaticity of Social Behavior: Direct Effects of Trait Construct and Stereotype-Activation on Action." *Journal of Personality and Social Psychology* 71, no. 2 (1996): 230–44, doi:10.1037/0022-3514.71.2.230.

Bartholow, Bruce D., Craig A. Anderson, Nicholas L. Carnagey, and Arlin J. Benjamin. "Interactive Effects of Life Experience and Situational Cues on Aggression: The Weapons Priming Effect in Hunters and Nonhunters." *Journal of Experimental Social Psychology* 41, no. 1 (2005): 48–60, doi:10.1016/j.jesp.2004.05.005.

Baumeister, Roy, and John Tierney. *Willpower: Rediscovering the Greatest Human Strength*. New York: Penguin, 2011.

Belk, Russell W. "Possessions and the Extended Self." *Journal of Consumer Research* 15, no. 2 (1988): 139, doi: 10.1086/209154.

Bender, Jens, Tobias Rothmund, and Mario Gollwitzer. "Biased Estimation of Violent Video Game Effects on Aggression: Contributing Factors and Boundary Conditions." *Societies* 3, no. 4 (2013): 383–98, doi:10.3390/soc3040383.

Bickman, Leonard. "The Social Power of a Uniform." *Journal of Applied Social Psychology* 4, no. 1 (1974): 47–61, doi:10.1111/j.1559-1816.1974.tb02599.x.

Blachnio, Agata, and Malgorzata Weremko. "Academic Cheating Is Contagious: The Influence of the Presence of Others on Honesty. A Study Report." *International Journal of Applied Psychology* 1, no. 1 (2011): 14–19, doi: 10.5923/j.ijap.20110101.02.

Blackburn, Jeremy, Ramanuja Simha, Nicolas Kourtellis, Xiango Zuo, Mateir Ripeanu, John Skvoretz, and Adriana Iamnitchi. "Branded with a Scarlet 'C': Cheaters in a Gaming Social Network." In *Proceedings of the 21st International Conference on World Wide Web*, April 16–20, 2012, 81–90. Lyon, France: International World Wide Web Conference Committee.

Blacker, Kara J., Kim M. Curby, Elizabeth Klobusicky, and Jason M Chein. "Effects of Action Video Game Training on Visual Working Memory." *Journal of Experimental Psychology: Human Perception and Performance* 40, no. 5 (2014): 1992–2004.

Bloom, Paul. "Irreplaceable." In *How Pleasure Works: The New Science of Why We Like What We Like*, 91–115. New York: W. W. Norton, 2010.

Bowman, Nicholas, Rene Weber, Ron Tamborini, and John Sherry. "Facilitating Game Play: How Others Affect Performance at and Enjoyment of Video Games." *Media Psychology* 16, no. 1 (2013): 39–64, doi:10.1080/15213269.2012.742360.

Brehm, Jack. *A Theory of Psychological Reactance*. New York: Academic, 1966.

Brehm, Sharon. *Psychological Reactance: A Theory of Freedom and Control*. New York: Academic, 1981.

Brown v . Entertainment Merchants Association, 564 U.S. (2011).

Bryan, Christopher, Gabrielle Adams, and Benoît Monin. "When Cheating Would Make You a Cheater: Implicating the Self Prevents Unethical Behavior." *Journal of Experimental Psychology: General* 142, no. 4 (2012): 1001–5, doi: 10.1037/a0030655.

Buckley, Katherine E., and Craig A. Anderson. "A Theoretical Model of the Effects and Consequences of Playing Video Games." In *Playing Video Games: Motives, Responses, and Consequences*, edited by Peter Vorderer and Jennings Bryant, 363–78. Mahwah, NJ: Lawrence Erlbaum, 2006.

Bushman, Brad J., and Craig A. Anderson. "Violent Video Games and Hostile Expectations: A Test of the General Aggression Model." *Personality and Social Psychology Bulletin* 28, no. 12 (2002): 1679–86, doi:10.1177/014616702237649.

Bushman, Brad J., Hannah R. Rothstein, and Craig A. Anderson. "Much Ado about Something: Violent Video Game Effects and a School of Red Herring: Reply to Ferguson and Kilburn (2010)." *Psychological Bulletin* 136, no. 2 (2010): 182–87, doi:10.1037/a0018718.

Cheung, Wing-Yee, Tim Wildschut, Constantine Sedikides, Erica Hepper, Jamie Arndt, and Ad Vingerhoets. "Back to the Future: Nostalgia Increases Optimism." *Personality and Social Psychology Bulletin* 39, no. 11 (2013): 1484–96, doi: 10.1177/0146167213499187.

Cialdini, Robert. *Influence: Science and Practice*. Boston: Pearson, 2013.

———. "The Science of Persuasion." *Scientific American* 284, no. 2, (2004): 76–81, doi:10.1038/scientificamerican0201-76.

Consalvo, Mia. *Cheating: Gaining Advantage in Videogames*. Cambridge, MA: MIT Press, 2007.

De Paoli, Stefano, and Aphra Kerr. "'We Will Always Be One Step ahead of Them': A Case Study on the Economy of Cheating in MMORPGs." *Journal of Virtual Worlds Research* 2 no. 4 (2009): 3–25, doi: http://dx.doi.org/10.4101/jvwr.v2i4.865.

Diener, Edward, Scott C. Fraser, Arthur L. Beaman, and Roger T. Kelem. "Effects of Deindividuation Variables on Stealing among Halloween Trick-or-Treaters." *Journal of Personality and Social Psychology* 33, no. 2 (1976): 178–83, doi: 10.1037/0022-3514.33.2.178.

Eagjy, Alice, Richard D. Ashmore, Mona G. Makhijani, and Laura C. Longo. "What Is Beautiful Is Good, but . . .: A Meta-Anatytic Review of Research on the Physical Attractiveness Stereotype." *Psychological Bulletin* 110, no. 1 (1991): 109–28, doi:10.1037/0033-2909.110.1.109.

Entertainment Software Association. *2014 Essential Facts about the Computer and Video Game Industry*. http://www.theesa.com/wp-content/uploads/2014/10/ESA_EF_2014.pdf.

Escalas, Jennifer, and James Bettman. "You Are What They Eat: The Influence of Reference Groups on Consumers Connections to Brands." *Journal of Consumer Psychology* 13, no. 3 (2003): 339–48, doi: 10.1207/S15327663JCP1303_14.

Ferguson, Christopher J. "Violent Video Games and the Supreme Court: Lessons for the Scientific Community in the Wake of *Brown v. Entertainment Merchants Association*." *American Psychologist* 68, no. 2 (2011): 57–74, doi:10.1037/a0030597.

Ferguson, Christopher J. and John Kilburn. "Much Ado about Nothing: The Misestimation and Overinterpretation of Violent Video Game Effects in Eastern and Western Nations: Comment on Anderson et al. (2010)." *Psychological Bulletin* 136, no. 2 (2010): 174–78; discussion 182–87, doi:10.1037/a0018566.

Ferguson, Christopher J., Claudia San Miguel, and Richard D. Hartley. "A Multivariate Analysis of Youth Violence and Aggression: The Influence of Family, Peers, Depression, and Media Violence." *Journal of Pediatrics* 155, no. 6 (2009): 904–8.e3, doi:10.1016/j.jpeds.2009.06.021.

Festinger, L. "A Theory of Social Comparison Processes." *Human Relations* 7, no. 2 (1954): 117–40, doi:10.1177/001872675400700202.

Fleming, Stephen M., Charlotte L. Thomas, and Raymond J. Dolan. "Overcoming Status Quo Bias in the Human Brain." In *Proceedings of the National Academy of Sciences of the United States of America* 107 (2010): 6005–9, doi:10.1073/pnas.0910380107.

Fowler, James H., and Nicholas A. Christakis. "Dynamic Spread of Happiness in a Large Social Network: Longitudinal Analysis over 20 Years in the Framingham Heart Study." *British Medical Journal* 337 (2008): 337:a2338, doi:10.1136/bmj.a2338.

Fox, Jesse, and Jeremy N. Bailenson. "Virtual Self-Modeling: The Effects of Vicarious Reinforcement and Identification on Exercise Behaviors." *Media Psychology* 12, no. 1 (2010): 1–25.

Fox, Jesse, Jeremy N. Bailenson, and Liz Tricase. "The Embodiment of Sexualized Virtual Selves: The Proteus Effect and Experiences of Self-Objectification via Avatars." *Computers in Human Behavior* 29, no. 3 (2013): 930–38, doi:10.1016/j.chb.2012.12.027.

Frank, Mark, and Thomas Gilovich. "The Dark Side of Self- and Social Perception: Black Uniforms and Aggression in Professional Sports." *Journal of Personality and Social Psychology* 54, no. 1 (1988): 74–85, doi:10.1037/0022-3514.54.1.74.

Garcia, Stephen M., Avishalom Tor, and Richard Gonzalez. "Ranks and Rivals: A Theory of Competition." *Personality & Social Psychology Bulletin* 32, no. 7 (2006): 970–82, doi:10.1177/0146167206287640.

Gentile, Douglas A., Craig A. Anderson, Shintaro Yukawa, Nobuko Ihori, Muniba Saleem, Lim Kam Ming, Akiko Shibuya, Albert K. Liau, Angeline Khoo, Brad J. Bushman, L. Rowell Huesmann, and Akira Sakamotoet. "The Effects of Prosocial Video Games on Prosocial Behaviors: International Evidence from Correlational, Longitudinal, and Experimental Studies." *Personality & Social Psychology Bulletin* 35, no. 6 (2009): 752–63, doi:10.1177/0146167209333045.

Gilbert, Daniel T., and Jane Ebert. "Decisions and Revisions: The Affective Forecasting of Changeable Outcomes." *Journal of Personality and Social Psychology* 82, no. 4 (2002): 503–14, doi: 10.1037/0022-3514.82.4.503.

Gino, Francesca, Shahar Ayal, and Dan Ariely. "Contagion and Differentiation in Unethical Behavior: The Effect of One Bad Apple on the Barrel." *Psychological Science* 20, no. 3 (2009): 393–98.

Gitter, Seth A., Patrick J. Ewell, Rosanna E. Guadagno, Tyler F. Stillman, and Roy F. Baumeister. "Virtually Justifiable Homicide: The Effects of Prosocial Contexts on the Link between Violent Video Games, Aggression, and Prosocial and Hostile Cognition." *Aggressive Behavior* 39, no. 5 (2013): 346–54, doi:10.1002/ab.21487.

Gladwell, Malcom. *David and Goliath: Underdogs, Misfits, and the Art of Battling Giants.* New York: Little, Brown, 2013.

Goethals, George, and John Darley. "Social Comparison Theory: An Attributional Approach." In *Social Comparison Processes: Theoretical and Empirical Perspectives*, edited by Jerry Suls and Richard Miller, 259–78. New York: John Wiley & Sons, 1977, doi: 10.4324/9781410615749.

Green, Shawn, and Daphne Bavelier. "Enumeration versus Multiple Object Tracking: The Case of Action Video Game Players." *Cognition* 101 no. 1 (2006): 217–45, doi:10.1016/j.cognition.2005.10.004.

———. "Action-Video-Game Experience Alters the Spatial Resolution of Vision." *Psychological Science* 18 no. 1 (2007): 88–94, doi:10.1111/j.1467-9280.2007.01853.x.

———. "Effect of Action Video Games on Spatial Distribution of Visuospatial Attention." *Journal of Experimental Psychology* 32 no. 6 (2006): 1465–78.

Green, Shawn, Alexandre Pouget, and Daphne Bavelier. "Improved Probabilistic Inference as a General Learning Mechanism with Action Video Games." *Current Biology* 20 no. 17 (2010): 1573–79, doi:10.1016/j.cub.2010.07.040.

Greene, Edith. "Whodunit? Memory for Evidence in Text." *American Journal of Psychology* 94, no. 3 (1981): 479–76, doi: 10.2307/1422258.

Greitemeyer, Tobias, and Silvia Osswald. "Effects of Prosocial Video Games on Prosocial Behavior." *Journal of Personality and Social Psychology* 98, no. 2 (2010): 211–21, doi:10.1037/a0016997.

Hepper, Erica G., Tim Wildschut, Constantine Sedikides, Timothy D. Ritchie, Yiu-Fai Yung, Nina Hansen, Georgios Abakoumkin, Gizem Arikan, Sylwia Z. Cisek, Didier B. Demassosso, Jochen E. Gebauer, J. P. Gerber, Roberto González, Takashi Kusumi, Girishwar Misra, Mihaela Rusu, Oisín Ryan, Elena Stephan, Ad Vingerhoets, Xinyue Zhou, "Pancultural Nostalgia: Prototypical Conceptions across Cultures." *Emotion* 14, no. 4 (2014): 733–47, doi:10.1037/a0036790.

Hirschman, Elizabeth C. "Differences in Consumer Purchase Behavior by Credit Card Payment System." *Journal of Consumer Research* 6 no. 1 (1979): 58–66, doi:10.1086/208748.

Hofer, Matthias, Werner Wirth, Rinaldo Kuehne, Holger Schramm, and Ana Sacau. "Structural Equation Modeling of Spatial Presence: The Influence of Cognitive Processes and Traits." *Media Psychology* 15, no. 4 (2012): 373–95, doi:10.1080/15213269.2012.723118.

Howes, Mary J., Jack E. Hokanson, and Daniel A. Loewenstein. "Induction of Depressive Affect after Prolonged Exposure to a Mildly Depressed Individual." *Journal of Personality and Social Psychology* 49, no. 4 (1985): 1110–13, doi:10.1037/0022-3514.49.4.1110.

Hsee, Christopher K. "Less Is Better: When Low-Value Options Are Valued More Highly Than High-Value Options." *Journal of Behavioral Decision Making* 11 (1998): 107–21, doi:10.1002/(SICI)1099-0771(199806)11:2 107::AID-BDM292 3.0.CO;2-Y.

Hyun, Gi Jung, Yong Wook Shin, Bung-Nyun Kim, Jae Hoon Cheong, Seong Nam Jin, and Doug Hyun Han. "Increased Cortical Thickness in Professional Online Gamers." *Psychiatry Investigation* 10 no. 4 (2013): 388–92, doi:10.4306/pi.2013.10.4.388.

Jin, Seung-A Annie. "Avatars Mirroring the Actual Self versus Projecting the Ideal Self: The Effects of Self-Priming on Interactivity and Immersion in an Exergame, Wii Fit." *Cyberpsychology & Behavior* 12, no. 6 (2009): 761–65, doi:10.1089/cpb.2009.0130.

———. "'I Feel Present. Therefore, I Experience Flow': A Structural Equation Modeling Approach to Flow and Presence in Video Games." *Journal of Broadcasting & Electronic Media* 55, no. 1 (2011): 114–36, doi:10.1080/08838151.2011.546248.

Johnson, E. J., and Daniel Goldstein. "Do Defaults Save Lives?" *Science* 302 (2003): 1338–39, doi:10.1126/science.1091721.

Johnson, Robert D., and Leslie L. Downing. "Deindividuation and Valence of Cues: Effects on Prosocial and Antisocial Behavior." *Journal of Personality and Social Psychology* 37, no. 9 (1979): 1532–38, doi: 10.1037/0022-3514.37.9.1532.

Kahneman, Daniel. *Thinking, Fast and Slow.* New York: Farrar, Straus and Giroux, 2011.

Kahneman, Daniel, Jack L. Knetsch, and Richard H. Thaler. "Experimental Tests of the Endowment Effect and the Coase Theorem." *Journal of Political Economy* 98, no. 6 (1990): 1325–48, doi: 10.1086/261737.

Kivetz, Ran, and Anat Keinan. "Repenting Hyperopia: An Analysis of Self-Control Regrets." *Journal of Consumer Research* 33 (2006): 273–82, doi:10.1086/506308.

Klein, Stefan. *The Science of Happiness: How Our Brains Make Us Happy—and What We Can Do to Get Happier.* New York: Marlowe & Company, 2006.

Klimmt, Christoph, Dorothée Hefner, Peter Vorderer, Christian Roth, and Christopher Blake. "Identification with Video Game Characters as Automatic Shift of Self-Perceptions." *Media Psychology* 13, no. 4 (2010): 323–38, doi:10.1080/15213269.2010.524911.

Knox, Robert E., and James A. Inkster. "Postdecision Dissonance at Post Time." *Journal of Personality and Social Psychology* 8, no. 4 (1968): 319–23, doi: 10.1037/h0025528.

Kowert, Rachel, Ruth Festl, and Thorsten Quandt. "Unpopular, Overweight, and Socially Inept: Reconsidering the Stereotype of Online Gamers." *Cyberpsychology, Behavior, and Social Networking* 17, no. 3 (2014): 141–46, doi:10.1089/cyber.2013.0118.

Kramer, Adam D., Jamie E. Guillory, and Jeffrey T. Hancock. "Experimental Evidence of Massive-Scale Emotional Contagion through Social Networks." *Proceedings of the National Academy of Sciences of the United States of America* 111, no. 24 (2014): 8788–90, doi:10.1073/pnas.1320040111.

Kridel, Donald J., Dale E. Lehman, and Dennis L. Weisman. "Option Value, Telecommunications Demand, and Policy." *Information Economics and Policy* 5, no. 2 (1993): 125–44, doi:10.1016/0167-6245(93)90018-C.

Kruger, Justin, and David Dunning. "Unskilled and Unaware of It: How Difficulties in Recognizing One's Own Incompetence Lead to Inflated Self-Assessments." *Journal of Personality and Social Psychology* 77, no. 6 (1999): 1121–34, doi:10.1037/0022-3514.77.6.1121.

Kutner, Lawrence, and Cheryl Olson. *Grand Theft Childhood: The Surprising Truth about Violent Video Games and What Parents Can Do*. New York: Simon & Schuster, 2008.

Kuznekoff, J. H., and L. M. Rose. "Communication in Multiplayer Gaming: Examining Player Responses to Gender Cues." *New Media & Society* 15 no. 4 (2012): 541–56, doi:10.1177/1461444812458271.

Lambrecht, Anja, and Bernd Skiera. 2006. "Paying Too Much and Being Happy about It: Existence, Causes, and Consequences of Tariff-Choice Biases." *Journal of Marketing Research* 43 (2006): 212–23, doi:10.1509/jmkr.43.2.212.

Leboe, Jason P., and Tamara L. Ansons. "On Misattributing Good Remembering to a Happy Past: An Investigation into the Cognitive Roots of Nostalgia." *Emotion* 6, no. 4 (2006): 596–610, doi: 10.1037/1528-3542.6.4.596.

Lefkowitz, Monroe, Robert R. Blake, and Jane Srygley Mouton. "Status Factors in Pedestrian Violation of Traffic Signals." *Journal of Abnormal and Social Psychology* 51, no. 3 (1955): 704–6, doi:10.1037/h0042000.

Lewis, Joshua M., Patrick Trinh, and David Kirsh. "A Corpus Analysis of Strategy Video Game Play in *StarCraft: Brood War*." In *Proceedings of the 33rd Annual Conference of the Cognitive Science Society* (2011): 687–92. http://mindmodeling.org/cogsci2011/papers/0138/paper0138.pdf.

Lin, Tao, Zhiming Wu, Ningjiu Tang, and Shaomei Wu. "Exploring the Effects of Display Characteristics on Presence and Emotional Responses of Game Players." *International Journal of Technology and Human Interaction* 9, no. 1 (2013): 50–63, doi:10.4018/jthi.2013010104.

Locke, Edwin A. "Motivation through Conscious Goal Setting." *Applied and Preventive Psychology* 5, no. 2 (1996): 117–24, doi:10.1016/S0962-1849(96)80005-9.

Loveland, Katherine E., Dirk Smeesters, and Naomi Mandel. "Still Preoccupied with 1995: The Need to Belong and Preference for Nostalgic Products." *Journal of Consumer Research* 37, no. 3 (2010): 393–408, doi: 10.1086/653043.

Madrian, Brigitte C., and Dennis F. Shea. "The Power of Suggestion: Inertia in 401(k) Participation and Savings Behavior." *Quarterly Journal of Economics* 2 116, no. 4 (2001): 1149–87, doi:10.1162/003355301753265543.

Maguire, Eleanor A., David G. Gadian, Ingrid S. Johnsrude, Catriona D. Good, John Ashburner, Richard S. Frackowiak, and Christopher D. Frith. "Navigation-Related Structural Change in the Hippocampi of Taxi Drivers." *Proceedings of the National Academy of Sciences of the United States of America* 97, no. 8 (2000): 4398–4403, doi:10.1073/pnas.070039597.

Marsh, Herbert W., and Kit-Tai Hau. "Big-Fish–Little-Pond Effect on Academic Self-Concept: A Cross-Cultural (26-Country) Test of the Negative Effects of Academically Selective Schools." *American Psychologist* 58, no. 5 (2003): 364–76, doi: 10.1037/0003-066X.58.5.364.

Martin, René, Jerry Suls, and Ladd Wheeler. "Ability Evaluation by Proxy: Role of Maximal Performance and Related Attributes in Social Comparison." *Journal of Personality and Social Psychology* 82, no. 5 (2002): 781–91, doi:10.1037//0022-3514.82.5.781.

Martins, Nicole, Andrew J. Weaver, Daphna Yeshua-Katz, Nicole H. Lewis, Nancy E. Tyree, and Jakob D. Jensen. "A Content Analysis of Print News Coverage of Media Violence and Aggression Research." *Journal of Communication* 63, no. 6 (2013): 1070–87, doi:10.1111/jcom.12052.

Mather, M., E. Shafir, and M. K. Johnson. "Misremembrance of Options Past: Source Monitoring and Choice." *Psychological Science* 11, no. 2 (2000): 132–38, doi: 10.1111/1467-9280.00228.

Mazar, Nina, On Amir, and Dan Ariely. "The Dishonesty of Honest People: A Theory of Self-Concept Maintenance." *Journal of Marketing Research* 45, no. 6 (2008): 633–44, doi: 10.1509/jmkr.45.6.633.

Mazis, Michael B. "Antipollution Measures and Psychological Reactance Theory: A Field Experiment." *Journal of Personality and Social Psychology* 31, no. 4 (1975): 654–60, doi:10.1037/h0077075.

McClure, Samuel M., Jian Li, Damon Tomlin, Kim S. Cypert, Latané M. Montague, and P.Read Montague. "Neural Correlates of Behavioral Preference for Culturally Familiar Drinks." *Neuron* 44, no. 2 (2004): 379–87, doi: 10.1016/j.neuron.2004.09.019.

McGregor, Ian, Reeshma Haji, and So-Jin Kang. "Can Ingroup Affirmation Relieve Outgroup Derogation?" *Journal of Experimental Social Psychology* 44 no. 5 (2008): 1395–1401, doi:10.1016/j.jesp.2008.06.001.

Medvec, Victoria Husted, Scott F. Madey, and Thomas Gilovich. "When Less Is More: Counterfactual Thinking and Satisfaction among Olympic Medalists." *Journal of Personality and Social Psychology1* 69, no. 4 (1995): 603–10, doi:10.1037/0022-3514.69.4.603.

Melby-Lervåg, Monica, and Charles Hulme. "Is Working Memory Training Effective? A Meta-Analytic Review." *Developmental Psychology* 49 no. 2 (2013): 270–91, doi:10.1037/a0028228.

Mowen, John C., and Nancy Spears. "Understanding Compulsive Buying among College Students: A Hierarchical Approach." *Journal of Consumer Psychology* 8 no. 4 (1999): 407–30, doi:10.1207/s15327663jcp0804_03.

Muraven, Mark, Dianne M. Tice, and Roy F. Baumeister. "Self-Control as a Limited Resource: Regulatory Depletion Patterns." *Journal of Personality and Social Psychology* 74 no. 3 (1998): 774–89, doi:10.1037//0022-3514.74.3.774.

Murray, Scott O., Huseyin Boyaci, and Daniel Kersten. "The Representation of Perceived Angular Size in Human Primary Visual Cortex." *Nature Neuroscience* 9, no. 3 (2006): 429–434, doi:10.1038/nn1641.

Nauroth, Peter, Mario Gollwitzer, Jens Bender, and Tobias Rothmund. "Gamers against Science: The Case of the Violent Video Games Debate." *European Journal of Social Psychology* 44, no. 2 (2014): 104–16, doi:10.1002/ejsp.1998.

Nunes, Joseph C. "The Endowed Progress Effect: How Artificial Advancement Increases Effort." *Journal of Consumer Research* 32 (March 2006): 504–12, doi:10.1086/500480.

Olds, James, and Peter Milner. "Positive Reinforcement Produced by Electrical Stimulation of Septal Area and Other Regions of Rat Brain." *Journal of Comparative and Physiological Psychology* 47, no. 6 (1954): 419–27, doi:10.1037/h0058775.

Pope, Devin G., and Maurice E. Schweitzer. "Is Tiger Woods Loss Averse? Persistent Bias in the Face of Experience, Competition, and High Stakes." *American Economic Review* 101, no. 1 (2011): 129–57, doi:10.1257/aer.101.1.129.

Postmes, Tom, and Russell Spears. "Deindividuation and Antinormative Behavior: A Meta-Analysis." *Psychological Bulletin* 123, no. 3 (1998): 238–59, doi: 10.1037/0033-2909.123.3.238.

Poundstone, William. *Prisoner's Dilemma*. New York: Random House, 1992.

———. *Priceless: The Myth of Fair Value (and How to Take Advantage of It)*. New York: Hill and Wang, 2010.

Prelec, Drazen, and George Lowenstein. "The Red and the Black: Mental Accounting of Savings and Debt." *Marketing Science* 17, no. 1 (1998): 4–28, doi:10.1287/mksc.17.1.4.

Prelec, Drazen, and Duncan Simester. "Always Leave Home without It : A Further Investigation of the Credit-Card Effect on Willingness to Pay." *Marketing Letters* 12, no. 1 (2001): 5–12, doi:10.1023/A:1008196717017.

Przybylski, Andrew K. "Who Believes Electronic Games Cause Real-World Aggression?" *Cyberpsychology, Behavior, and Social Networking* 17, no. 4 (2014): 228–34, doi:10.1089/cyber.2013.0245.

Przybylski, Andrew K., Edward L. Deci, Scott C. Rigby, and Richard M. Ryan. "Competence-Impeding Electronic Games and Players' Aggressive Feelings, Thoughts, and Behaviors." *Journal of Personality and Social Psychology* 106, no. 3 (2014): 441–57, doi:10.1037/a0034820.

Przybylski, Andrew K., Scott C. Rigby, and Richard M. Ryan. "A Motivational Model of Video Game Engagement." *Review of General Psychology* 14, no. 2 (2010): 154–66, doi:10.1037/a0019440.

Przybylski, Andrew K., Richard M. Ryan, and Scott C. Rigby. "The Motivating Role of Violence in Video Games." *Personality & Social Psychology Bulletin* 35, no. 2 (2009): 243–59, doi:10.1177/0146167208327216.

Raghubir, Priya, and Joydeep Srivastava. "Monopoly Money: The Effect of Payment Coupling and Form on Spending Behavior." *Journal of Experimental Psychology, Applied* 14 no. 3 (2008): 213–25, doi:10.1037/1076-898X.14.3.213.

Reid, Scott, and Michael Hogg. "Uncertainty Reduction, Self-Enhancement, and Ingroup Identification." *Personality and Social Psychology Bulletin* 31 no. 6 (2005): 804–17, doi:10.1177/0146167204271708.

Ridley, Matt. *The Origins of Virtue: Human Instincts and the Evolution of Cooperation*. New York: Viking Penguin, 1997.

Rigby, Scott C., and Richard M. Ryan. *Glued to Games: How Video Games Draw Us in and Hold Us Spellbound*. Santa Barbara, CA: Praeger, 2011.

Rosenberg, Robin S., Shawnee L. Baughman, and Jeremy N. Bailenson. "Virtual Superheroes: Using Superpowers in Virtual Reality to Encourage Prosocial Behavior." *PloS One* 8, no. 1 (2013), doi:10.1371/journal.pone.0055003.

Ryan, Richard M., and Edward L. Deci. "Self-Determination Theory and the Facilitation of Intrinsic Motivation, Social Development, and Well-Being." *American Psychologist* 55, no. 1 (2000): 68–78, doi:10.1037/0003-066X.55.1.68.

Ryan, Richard M., Scott C. Rigby, and Andrew K. Przybylski. "The Motivational Pull of Video Games: A Self-Determination Theory Approach." *Motivation and Emotion* 30, no. 4 (2006): 344–60, doi:10.1007/s11031-006-9051-8.

Salganik, Matthew J., Peter S. Dodds, and Duncan J. Watts. "Experimental Study of Inequality and Unpredictability in an Artificial Cultural Market." *Science* 311 (2006): 854–56, doi:10.1126/science.1121066.

Salovey, Peter, and Judith Rodin. "Some Antecedents and Consequences of Social-Comparison Jealousy." *Journal of Personality and Social Psychology* 47, no. 4 (1984): 780–92, doi:10.1037/0022-3514.47.4.780.

Schindler, Robert, and Morris Holbrook. "Nostalgia for Early Experience as a Determinant of Consumer Preferences." *Psychology and Marketing* 20, no. 4 (2003): 275–301, doi: 10.1002/mar.10074.

Shampanier, Kristina, Nina Mazar, and Dan Ariely. "Zero as a Special Price: The True Value of Free Products." *Marketing Science* 26, no. 6 (2007): 742–57, doi:10.1287/mksc.1060.0254.

Sherif, Muzafer. *Intergroup Conflict and Cooperation: The Robbers Cave Experiment*. Toronto: York University, 1961.

Shin, Jiwoong, and Dan Ariely. "Keeping Doors Open: The Effect of Unavailability on Incentives to Keep Options Viable." *Management Science* 50, no. 5 (2004): 575–86, doi:10.1287/mnsc.1030.0148.

Shiv, Baba, and Alexander Fedorikhin. "Heart and Mind in Conflict: The Interplay of Affect and Cognition in Consumer Decision Making." *Journal of Consumer Research* 26 (1999): 278–93, doi:10.1086/209563.

Shu, Lisa, Nina Mazar, Francesca Gino, Dan Ariely, and Max Bazerman. "Signing at the Beginning Makes Ethics Salient and Decreases Dishonest Self-Reports in Comparison to Signing at the End." *Proceedings of the National Academy of Sciences* 109, no. 38 (2012): 15197–200.

Skalski, P., R. Tamborini, A. Shelton, M. Buncher, and P. Lindmark. "Mapping the Road to Fun: Natural Video Game Controllers, Presence, and Game Enjoyment." *New Media & Society* 13, no. 2 (2010): 224–42, doi:10.1177/1461444810370949.

Smith, Glenn E., Patricia Housen, Kristine Yaffe, Ronald Ruff, Robert F. Kennison, Henry W. Mahncke, and Elizabeth M. Zelinski. "A Cognitive Training Program Based on Principles of Brain Plasticity: Results from the Improvement in Memory with Plasticity-Based

Adaptive Cognitive Training (IMPACT) Study." *Journal of the American Geriatrics Society* 57 no. 4 (2009): 594–603, doi:10.1111/j.1532-5415.2008.02167.x.

Soman, Dilip. "Effects of Payment Mechanism on Spending Behavior: The Role of Rehearsal and Immediacy of Payments." *Journal of Consumer Research* 27 (2001): 460–74, doi:10.1086/319621.

———. "The Effect of Payment Transparency on Consumption: Quasi-Experiments from the Field." *Marketing Letters* 14, no. 3 (2003): 173–83, doi:10.1023/A:1027444717586.

Spears, Dean. "Economic Decision-Making in Poverty Depletes Behavioral Control." *The BE Journal of Economic Analysis & Policy* no. 213 (2010), doi:10.2202/1935-1682.2973.

Strack, F., L. L. Martin, and S. Stepper. "Inhibiting and Facilitating Conditions of the Human Smile: A Nonobtrusive Test of the Facial Feedback Hypothesis." *Journal of Personality and Social Psychology* 54, no. 5 (1988): 768–77, doi:10.1037/0022-3514.54.5.768.

Tajfel, Henri. "Experiments in Intergroup Discrimination." *Scientific American* 223, no. 5 (1970): 96–102, doi: 10.1038/scientificamerican1170-96.

Tassi, Paul. *Fanboy Wars: The Fight for the Future of Video Games*. Forbes Media, 2014.

Terlecki, Melissa S., and Nora S. Newcombe. "How Important Is the Digital Divide? The Relation of Computer and Videogame Usage to Gender Differences in Mental Rotation Ability." *Sex Roles* 53, no 5 (2005): 433–41, doi:10.1007/s11199-005-6765-0.

Tversky, A., and D Kahneman. "Judgment under Uncertainty: Heuristics and Biases." *Science* 185, no. 4157 (1974): 1124–31, doi:10.1126/science.185.4157.1124.

———. "Advances in Prospect Theory: Cumulative Representation of Uncertainty." *Journal of Risk and Uncertainty* 5 no. 4 (1992): 297–323, doi:10.1007/BF00122574.

Valins, Stuart. "Emotionality and Information Concerning Internal Reactions." *Journal of Personality and Social Psychology* 6, no. 4 (1967): 458–63, doi:10.1037/h0024842.

Van de Ven, Niels, Marcel Zeelenberg, and Rik Pieters. "Leveling Up and Down: The Experiences of Benign and Malicious Envy." *Emotion* 9, no. 3 (2009): 419–29, doi:10.1037/a0015669.

———. "The Envy Premium in Product Evaluation." *Journal of Consumer Research* 37, no. 6 (2011): 984–98, doi:10.1086/657239.

———. "Why Envy Outperforms Admiration." *Personality & Social Psychology Bulletin* 37, no. 6 (2011): 784–95, doi:10.1177/0146167211400421.

Verplanken, Bas, and Astrid Herabadi. "Individual Differences in Impulse Buying Tendency: Feeling and No Thinking." *European Journal of Personality* 83, no. S1 (2001): 71–83.

Vohs, Kathleen D., Nicole L Mead, and Miranda R Goode. "The Psychological Consequences of Money." *Science* 314, no. 5802 (2006): 1154–56, doi: 10.1126/science.1132491.

Vohs, Kathleen D., Roy F. Baumeister, Brandon J. Schmeichel, Jean M. Twenge, Noelle M. Nelson, and Dianne M. Tice. "Making Choices Impairs Subsequent Self-Control: A Limited-Resource Account of Decision Making, Self-Regulation, and Active Initiative." *Journal of Personality and Social Psychology* 94, no. 5 (2008): 883–98. doi:10.1037/0022-3514.94.5.883.

Vohs, Kathleen D., Roy F. Baumeister, and Dianne Tice. "Self-Regulation: Goals, Consumption, Choices." In *Handbook of Consumer Psychology*, edited by P. Haugtvedt, P. M. Herr, and F. Kardes. New York: Lawrence Erlbaum, 2008.

Vohs, Kathleen, and Ronald Faber. "Spent Resources: Self-Regulatory Resource Availability Affects Impulse Buying." *Journal of Consumer Research* 33 no. 4 (2007): 537–47, doi:10.1086/510228.

Voyer, D., S. Voyer, and M. P. Bryden. "Magnitude of Sex Differences in Spatial Abilities: A Meta-Analysis and Consideration of Critical Variables." *Psychological Bulletin* 117, no. 2 (1995): 250–70.

Wheeler, Ladd. "Motivation as a Determinant of Upward Comparison." *Journal of Experimental Social Psychology* 1, no. 1 (1966): 27–31, doi:10.1016/0022-1031(66)90062-X.

Wheeler, Ladd, Richard Koestner, and Robert E. Driver. "Related Attributes in the Choice of Comparison Others: It's There, but It Isn't All There Is." *Journal of Experimental Social Psychology* 18, no. 6 (1982): 489–500, doi:10.1016/0022-1031(82)90068-3.

Wildschut, Tim, Constantine Sedikides, Jamie Arndt, and Clay Routledge. "Nostalgia: Content, Triggers, Functions." *Journal of Personality and Social Psychology* 91, no. 5 (2006): 975–93, doi:10.1037/0022-3514.91.5.975.

Williams, Alishia D., and Jessica R. Grisham. "Impulsivity, Emotion Regulation, and Mindful Attentional Focus in Compulsive Buying." *Cognitive Therapy & Research* 36 no. 5 (2012): 451–57, doi:10.1007/s10608-011-9384-9.

Wirth, Werner, Tilo Hartmann, Saskia Böcking, Peter Vorderer, Christoph Klimmt, Holger Schramm, Timo Saari, Jari Laarni, Niklas Ravaja, Feliz Ribeiro Gouveia, Frank Biocca, Ana Sacau, Lutz Jäncke, Thomas Baumgartner, and Petra Jäncke. "A Process Model of the Formation of Spatial Presence Experiences." *Media Psychology* 9, no. 3 (2007): 493–525, doi:10.1080/15213260701283079.

Wirth, Werner, Matthias Hofer, and Holger Schramm. "The Role of Emotional Involvement and Trait Absorption in the Formation of Spatial Presence." *Media Psychology* 15, no. 1 (2012): 19–43, doi:10.1080/15213269.2011.648536.

Wirth, Werner, Fabian Ryffel, Thilo von Pape, and Veronika Karnowski. "The Development of Video Game Enjoyment in a Role Playing Game." *Cyberpsychology, Behavior, and Social Networking* 16, no. 4 (2013): 260–64, doi:10.1089/cyber.2012.0159.

Worchel, Stephen, Jerry Lee, and Akanbi Adewole. "Effects of Supply and Demand on Ratings of Object Value." *Journal of Personality and Social Psychology* 32 no. 5 (1975): 906–14, doi:10.1037/0022-3514.32.5.906.

Yan, Ting, Frederick C. Conrad, Roger Tourangeau, and Mick P. Couper. "Should I Stay or Should I Go: The Effects of Progress Feedback, Promised Task Duration, and Length of Questionnaire on Completing Web Surveys." *International Journal of Public Opinion Research* 23, no. 2 (2010): 131–47, doi:10.1093/ijpor/edq046.

Yee, Nick. "Motivations for Play in Online Games." *Cyberpsychology & Behavior* 9, no. 6 (2006): 772–75, doi:10.1089/cpb.2006.9.772.

———. *The Proteus Paradox: How Online Games and Virtual Worlds Change Us—and How They Don't.* New Haven, CT: Yale University Press, 2013.

Yee, Nick, Jeremy Bailenson, and Nicolas Ducheneaut. "The Proteus Effect: Implications of Transformed Digital Self-Representation on Online and Offline Behavior." *Communication Research* 36, no. 2 (2009): 285–312, doi:10.1177/0093650208330254.

Yee, Nick, Nicolas Ducheneaut, and Les Nelson. "Online Gaming Motivations Scale: Development and Validation." In *Proceedings of the SIGCHI Conference on Human Factors in Computing Systems* 2803, no. 6 (2012), doi:10.1145/2207676.2208681.

Yperen, Nico W. Van, Melvyn R. W. Hamstra, and Marloes Van Der Klauw. "To Win, or Not to Lose, At Any Cost: The Impact of Achievement Goals on Cheating." *British Journal of Management* 22 (2011): S5–S15, doi: 10.1111/j.1467-8551.2010.00702.x.

Zeigarnik, Bulma. "On Finished and Unfinished Tasks." In *A Source Book of Gestalt Psychology*, edited by W. D. Ellis, 300–14. New York: Harcourt Brace, 1938.

Zell, Ethan, and Mark D. Alicke. "The Local Dominance Effect in Self-Evaluation: Evidence and Explanations." *Personality and Social Psychology Review* 14, no. 4 (2010): 368–84, doi:10.1177/1088868310366144.

Zimbardo, Philip. *The Lucifer Effect: Understanding How Good People Turn Evil.* New York: Random House, 2007.

INDEX